City of
Secrets

One Woman's True-life Journey
to the Heart of the Grail Legend

City of Secrets

One Woman's True-life Journey
to the Heart of the Grail Legend

Patrice Chaplin

QUEST

BOOKS

THEOSOPHICAL PUBLISHING HOUSE
Wheaton, Illinois * Chennai, India

First Quest edition 2008

First published in the UK by Constable, an imprint of Constable &
Robimson Ltd., 2007

Quest Books
Theosophical Publishing House
P.O. Box 270
Wheaton, IL 60189-0270

www.questbooks.net

Cover design by Kirsten Hansen Pott
Cover photo: ©iStockphoto.com / Ana Rodrigues

LIBRARY OF CONGRESS CATALOGING-IN-PUBLICATION DATA

Chaplin, Patrice.
City of secrets: one woman's true-life journey to the heart of the grail
legend / Patrice Chaplin. – 1ˢᵗ Quest ed.
    p.   cm.
ISBN 978-0-8356-0871-8
1. Chaplin, Patrice.   2. Spiritual biography.   3. Grail.   4. Gerona
(Spain) I. Title.
BL73.C375A3 2008
946'.73—dc22   2008003884

5   4   3   2   1   *   08   09   10   11   12

Printed in the United States of America

In memory of Alice Thomas Ellis

ACKNOWLEDGMENTS

With gratitude to Jesus Villalonga for the generous use of his painting, to Lidia Arias, and to Tove Frisvold for her tireless and invaluable participation during the months and years of research. And to the people of Girona.

DRAMATIS PERSONAE

While the events and conversations described in this book are true, the names of most individuals have been changed to protect their identities.

Emilio Aldecane, local football trainer
Carmen Aragó, member of the society
Dr Arbós, heart surgeon in Girona

Lauren Bacall, legendary movie actress who worked with
    Patrice on the (unfinished) film of *Harriet Hunter*
Dr Baró, psychiatrist
Antonio Barrés, Catalan film-maker
Abbé Bieil, director of the seminary of St Sulpice
Abbé Bigou, priest
Monseigneur Billard, Bishop of Carcassonne
Henri Buthion, owner of Saunière's properties

Emma Calvé, opera singer
Quim Carreras, priest
Dr Colomer, psychiatrist
Jean Cocteau, film director
Aaron Cohen, member of the Sephardic group in Los
    Angeles
Pep Colomer, artist
Noël Corbu, one of the subsequent owners of Saunière's
    properties

Pep Dalmàs, partner of Joan Puig
Marie Denarnaud, Saunière's maid at Rennes-le-Château

Umberto Eco, novelist
Salvador Espriu, writer
Eva, cleaning woman at the Residencia Internacional hotel

the Frenchwoman (Maria Tourdes; Mme Mathieu)

Monsieur García, a Parisian taxi driver; neighbour to PC
Geli, cathedral organist (José's cousin)
Zelman Goldstein, American associate of José's Cabbala Centre
Señora Guilini, member of the society

Ingrid, German citizen who lived in America; high initiate; Cabbala expert

José, custodian of the society
Juli, organist; canon (one of Jose's ancestors)
Señora Juncosa, friend of Maria Tourdes

Max Kander, journalist; broadcaster

Moshe Lazar, eminent Ladino scholar
Lluís, friend; bar owner
Josep Luna, ex-Churchman; accountant

Manolo, night concierge at the Residencia Internacional hotel
Clara Mascaró, local (Catalan) actress
Roger Mathieu, 'man of letters'; husband of Maria Tourdes

Paco, medical student

Joséphin Péladan, founder of l'Ordre de la Rose Croix Catholique et Esthétique, du Temple et du Graal

Josep Plà, Catalan writer

Rafel Pons, businessman

Joan Puig, partner of Pep Dalmàs

Rosa Quintana, proprietress of the Caldes spa

Gerard Ruiz, owner of the bookshop

Quico Sabater, Catalan resistance fighter; political activist

Julien Sacaze, French writer on the Rosicrucians in the 19th century

Abbé Saunière, priest

Alfred Saunière, Abbé Saunière's brother

Gérard de Sède, author

Lucia Stilman, heiress

Prologue

I took a room in the Hotel Centro, the last of the old places still left. It had housed my love for José, soothed my pain, given me hope. Since the last century little had changed. The spacious, old-fashioned bathrooms, the pedestal sinks decorated with china cupids, the huge lofty rooms, peeling paint, mosaic floors, had remained due to lack of money or a desire for an authentic time which had gone. My room, pale green with lace curtains, made the light soft. For a moment there was the thrilling damp atmosphere I remembered from the first winter when I was his fiancée.

He tapped on the door, punctual and polite, and suggested we eat locally in Girona. His embrace was as always, but fast, as though someone was waiting for him. We crossed the bridge to the square with the restaurants and he went automatically into the Casa Marieta, one of the family-run businesses where the three waitresses still wore yellow and were kind and motherly. Not surprisingly, the place was filled with regulars. The owner had married the fourth waitress, tiny, perfectly shaped, nicknamed 'Snow-White'. She had a wonderfully optimistic attitude that went no deeper than the pale perfection of her skin. I asked why we hadn't gone to Cal Ros or one of our other favourite places. 'They've all changed now,' he said.

It was 1972, and Girona had indeed changed. The chain shops from France and England had replaced many of the Catalan businesses. A local café had become an English pub. The clothes were the same as anywhere else, and the young were learning English. Something had gone out of José, a light, a flame. He'd been instrumental in getting the Fontana d'Or gallery established, and I was surprised to hear he was no longer there.

'They are short-sighted and have no vision,' José continued. I took it he meant the money people at the municipality. The new mayor and he did not get on.

While I'd been in Los Angeles and New York selling my books for films, writing scripts, making a documentary, he had lost the fight to keep his position and had even considered leaving the city. But he'd recently found something bigger and more glorious.

He seemed preoccupied and finished his food quickly. Then he asked about the boys. I didn't tell him much about my life except that I never stayed away in the US for more than three weeks at a time – whatever the deal – as I needed them to have security.

'The Jews were here in medieval times,' he said. 'They brought skill and brilliance to this city. They were the craftsmen, doctors, jewellers, lawyers, and teachers and brought wealth and quality of life to the whole province. It was known as the Golden Age. The Jewish mystics in the thirteenth and fourteenth centuries were born here.' He described them as the heart of Cabbala, the secret teaching involving Jewish mysticism and theosophy. 'I want to restore this, our heritage, and build a Jewish site, a centre of Cabbala.'

He took me back to the Roman stone wall opposite his mother's apartment on the carrer de la Força. All I could see was what had always been there, a high stone wall, part of this ancient narrow street continuing up the hill without a gap until out of sight there was a stairway leading to a drinking fountain with an animal's head. He tapped the wall. 'There is nothing behind here.'

I said I'd never thought about it one way or the other.

'No one has,' he said. 'It's never been questioned. Everyone thinks behind this wall is the next passageway and those buildings up there.' He pointed to some visible walls. 'They have no ability for mathematics in this town. And behind here …' he walked further up the carrer de la Força and slapped more stone. '… is an eighth-century street. And I will open it up.'

For once I had no questions. Except one: 'Do you still love me?'

He took me back down to the arch at the bottom of the street and we curved under it, through the tunnel, up the stairs around the crumbling wall as we had earlier that day. The entrance to the wasteland was through a broken piece of wall covered with high, tough weeds. The ground was full of rubbish, dirt, dust, and was used by tramps, the homeless, prostitutes, and ownerless dogs. The wall along the carrer de la Força kept it private. Who would want to be here anyway? He said occasionally there was the sound of digging in the night. 'They came here, an old man and his son, to dig for the treasure of the Jews.'

He pointed to a high stone building with an open terrace at the top, and above I could see a timber-beamed underside of the flat roof. 'That is one of the oldest and best houses in Girona. It belongs to Carmen Aragó, the most cultivated woman in the city.'

I thought 'best' was doubtful. The smell rising in the heat from the desolate area was terrible.

To one side, trees hid broken steps to a lower level of further desolation, paved with uneven stones. The rest of the surrounding stone buildings in disrepair seemed closed and dark, with an occasional shuttered window in a smashed façade beyond a wall.

'This was a flourishing area of twenty-four houses and a courtyard.'

What was left of them was hard to define. This wasteland had been the courtyard where the great Rabbinic scholar Nachmanides had, through Cabbala, pierced reality as we know it. José said the Jews were expelled in 1492 and the area had been closed by order of the Church ever since.

'How did you find it?'

He paused. 'I lived opposite as a child but did not know it was there. There were stories, more legends, passed down through generations.'

So I asked how he would restore it, and he said by raising money. And he mentioned a sum which I thought was high for the municipality.

'Oh, no, they're not having this. It will be privately owned.' He sat in the dust and held a piece of stone, rolling it around in his hand. 'This is what it is.'

'This?'

'What they're all looking for. The mystery. It's here.'

He seemed older in an obvious way, but there was something else as he looked at me. I thought it might be sorrow. He was still absolutely beautiful.

1

I first saw José years ago on the stairs of the old Residencia Internacional hotel. I looked at him, he at me, then we both carried on walking, he up to the bar and I to the main door. It didn't seem too much to me, but then I wasn't aware in those days just how important a look can be. I travelled further south for more adventures with my friend Beryl, and he did whatever he did, which I didn't find out until much later. Beryl and I were fifteen, it was May 1955, and we had all our lives ahead of us. We took the roads as they came, as long as things were new and different to where we'd been. That's all we asked.

Girona, a pre-Roman city about forty miles inland from the Costa Brava, had a vast old quarter with a much-visited cathedral, Arab baths, and monumental churches. Bells rang across this forest of stone every fifteen minutes, day and night. The cobbled alleys and crumbling stairways, the deep arches leading to unexpected courtyards, were all stone, medieval or pre-Roman. Parts of the original city wall still stood as clumps of stone covered with weeds, thousands of years old. The buildings, huge buttresses of Roman craft, leaned together across the strip of street leaving only a shine of brilliant sky. The stone made the town echo and enhanced all sound. Only the bells were free as they tolled high above the buildings. Girona holds on to its atmosphere and makes sure the past is there always, solid, unconquered by decay. It was said the stones had a magnetism that drew certain people back time and time again. I believe it. Carcassonne has the same legend and I've heard it's to do with the ley lines. At certain points across the earth the energy builds up and creates a pull, a pulse, and in these places unusual and mystical things can happen.

Beryl and I were Bohemians and wore rope Roman sandals you could buy in London's Charing Cross Road for three and sixpence, and very tight, black drainpipe trousers. Our black sleeveless tops were lopsided, hand-made, falling apart. Our nails were painted black and we wore beautifully applied white lipstick. We dressed the same as we did when dancing all night to trad jazz at Cy Laurie's club in Soho, or Sidney Bechet's in Paris. In Girona that first time, the Spanish had never seen anything like it. They hadn't seen many foreigners. Tourism hadn't even begun. The women threw round prickly things that stuck to our hair, the kids, stones, and the men, glances long and curious. They were more concerned with what was underneath our extraordinary clothes. Beryl wore gold hoop earrings, mine were dangling silvered chandeliers. We put on a huge amount of make-up – the longest task of the day was getting that on. Brigitte Bardot kiss-curls covered our ears, and our hair was streaked with gold dust that in certain climates turned green. In the evening we wore white fisherman's sweaters reaching our knees, also bought in Charing Cross Road. And the obligatory black duffel coats, the pockets filled with make-up and Coty perfume. Beryl was indeed beautiful, which made being her friend difficult. I didn't compete; even at fifteen I knew that was a mistake, but I certainly tried to be always at my best. I wanted to be a gypsy. My father didn't consider that a career, but I knew I'd travel. I had a great love of life in those days.

We came from Albany Park, in Kent. No description really fitted that place, so housing-estate will do. Most of it was pre-Second World War, a lot of bungalows, and there were no scandals except what Beryl and I provided with our appearance. I was dying for the fabulous, the superb.

Before long we hitched a lift to Barcelona and then south to Castelldefels, which consisted then of two hotels. We didn't eat much because we didn't have any money, but we were filled with a lovely shivery excitement. We danced as we breathed – if there weren't clubs and dancehalls, then in the streets. In Paris people had thrown us money, which was better than working in bars, modelling and sometimes begging. And we had the big one on our side – youth – but we didn't even consider that. Ageing, like death, was a process that didn't happen to us.

Over the next few months, I sometimes thought of Girona, its strong skyline with the cathedral and the church of St Felix, and oddly an ordinary house with a rather grand tower that stuck up incongruously amidst the ancient buildings. They said it belonged to a Frenchwoman.

When I set foot in Girona the second time I knew I was where I should be. It took the second arrival to capture me, and once that happened I had no desire to move again.

They were lighting fires at the edge of the old quarter, and the sky was violet and flashing with huge flat stars. The sun was up there too, setting behind the last bridge in a blaze of scarlet rage. The narrow streets were full of music, perfume, the smell of wood smoke. The church bells chimed as though for a celebration and all the lights of the city came on, hundreds of yellow eyes. It was a true welcome.

Beryl said we should work in a club. We'd say we were eighteen, so where was the problem? There was no language difficulty – pouring drinks. Our Spanish was limited. *Guapa* – beautiful, *dinero* – money, *rubia* – blonde, *morena* – dark. That way we missed a lot of indelicate talk.

Cal Ros, the smart restaurant excelling in regional delicacies, was already filling up. It was a clamorous night, everybody on the street, the bars full. There was a definite feeling of fiesta and yet it was just another evening for them.

We turned into the alley beside the Cal Ros restaurant and two men came towards us. One was Lluís, a cathedral guide I'd met the previous time, the other shorter one was his friend. We exchanged names, shook hands. The friend wore a blue shirt and dark patterned pullover. He had a persuasive voice and, even on such an insignificant occasion, his speech was salted with irony. He was alive in every part of him, the opposite of anything I'd encountered in Albany Park, and he wasn't afraid to show it. He said there was a film director in town and maybe Beryl and I should apply for roles. After all it was a coincidence. The director arrives, then we arrive. Coincidences should never be dismissed. The next week he'd be shooting a sequence up near the cathedral. The director's name was Jean Cocteau.

'He wants a ballet dancer.'

'That's me,' I said immediately.

'Yes, you look as though you should be a ballet dancer, but can you dance? Lluís for example is a born writer but has never written a word.' He clapped his hands, dismissing mere talent.

Lluís spoke fluent English, and his friend bits of every-thing. He laughed a lot, but it was attractive. When we said good-bye I knew where I'd seen him. He was the man on the stairs of the Residencia Internacional hotel.

Suddenly all the radios played the haunting Spanish song that we thought was a flamenco chart buster. It was in fact an advertising jingle. The music was full of the melancholy and desire that the south conjured up. I thought it announced the beginning of a huge and deathly passion. How right I was.

2

Before the Romans arrived, Girona was an Iberian trading centre. The first known inhabitants, at least 5000 years ago, were Iberians living in the Catalan country village of Ullastret. The Phoenicians settled in Girona province, leaving artefacts and sacrificial stones. The Greeks left a settlement along the Catalan coast named 'Empúries', a Spanish translation of the Greek name 'Emporion'. Then came the Romans, who built a large part of what is now the old quarter. Charlemagne marched into the city and left his influence, as did Napoleon III. Girona won the Moorish invasion, but lost against Franco in the Civil War.

They all left something.

Believed to have begun as a simple pagan temple for the Romans, the cathedral is now predominantly Gothic. Near the altar is Charlemagne's chair. A museum houses masterpieces from every century, including the much-visited 'Tapestry of the Creation'. With its disproportionately large nave, the fact the building stands up at all is a miracle.

And there were other settlements not yet rediscovered, but their presence added to the force of the atmosphere.

Perhaps because so many cults and religions have flourished there, no one of them is remembered exceptionally.

Historical finds occur frequently, giving evidence of much older civilizations. Girona celebrates its past with fiestas, legends, ritual, and theatre. The only sign of what has been so important there, and then completely forgotten, is the stones.

I think Beryl and I, as we walked on that magical evening through these unimaginable streets, sensed the imprint of some of this, although we knew nothing of its outer knowledgeable form and could not have put any of it into words.

They remembered us with pleasure at the Residencia Internacional hotel, which couldn't be said for a lot of places we revisited. Manolo, the night concierge, got out the drinks and Eva, the cleaning woman, ran down the stairs to welcome us as though it was an occasion. It was the first time I'd felt important anywhere.

'Who needs a St Christopher medal?' said Beryl. 'This place has all the luck we need.'

And then José was there and asked if we were runaways. He looked as though he could handle a drama. I explained our career was travelling, and that we were making our way to Bohemia in mid-Europe.

'Why?'

'Because we're Bohemians.'

'I'm sure Bohemians dance exquisitely. There's a fiesta tonight. I'll take you.'

Eva told me later that José thought I was twelve. He did ask how we had got our passports so young. I'd persuaded my father that Beryl and I were going to do a language course in Paris at a youth centre. It was the only way we could get passports under age. I was the one with the ideas, and Beryl went along with them and shared the consequences.

For the fiesta we wore skirts, but that didn't mean we were dressed right. The skirts were tight, with slits at the side. When the wolf whistles started, so did the insults. The women thought we were whores, the men hoped we were. All that quietened down when José caught up with us. He commanded respect.

The chirp of insects, the delicious breeze from the south, the distant music, the Mediterranean night, thrilled me to the bone. All the joyous things were there. Life promised me that night I'd be happy.

We learned to dance the *pasodoble* and the traditional *sardana* – both the 'long' and the 'short'. Lamb was the speciality of the region and we had cutlets, salad, and a caramel custard with a burnt sugar top. We ate plenty because we were never sure when we would eat again. Lluís was there and he gave me an old piece of sculpture he'd found in the garden behind the cathedral. It was flat, smooth, and brown with horns and was apparently an ancient animal head. José gave him a knife and he etched my name and the date on the stone. Lluís was well in with the cathedral and had asked permission to open one of its properties as a bar, selling postcards and reproductions of the cathedral's treasures. Then when he'd got enough money he'd write full-time. José wasn't exactly quiet, but I got no impression of what he did, who he was.

On the way back I saw the Catalan trees like up-flung umbrellas, blue grey in the night light. The road, a mere strip, was hard and warm, and Beryl and I walked without shoes. All of it was beautiful. I wasn't in love that night, I just felt part of life, flowing with it, full to the brim. The champagne helped, and José was no slouch at pouring a drink.

'If only it could stay like this,' said Lluís suddenly.

'If only,' said José.

We walked together, the four of us – harmonious, good friends now, at our best.

3

Beryl was already mad about José. I knew by nature she was not an optimist, but about José she was prepared to be happy. He watched her elaborate make-up ritual, played with her kiss curls, and even provided a lace mantilla to further decorate her hair. He gave her a hug and as far as I knew that was as far as intimacy went. After a week she was completely baffled. I thought he found her amusing, like a pampered pet. He was clearly fascinated by her but didn't behave like the boys we were used to in Albany Park.

He also had another quality she couldn't define – kindness. She normally only went for shits.

She had other admirers. The local football trainer, Emilio Aldecane, stayed in the Residencia. He liked good food, elegant clothes, his own way. And he liked Beryl. Hans stayed too as a permanent guest. He worked in his uncle's meat factory in the modern sector. He liked Beryl. So did the Italian writer Umberto, who Eva said would be famous one day. A hundred husbands in the street liked Beryl.

Lluís was with me, that was understood. I could see what he meant about changing his life. Who'd want to be a cathedral guide if you could be a novelist? He talked about politics, which at first meant little to me. With José he laughed cynically at the world and used irony to try and express everything. They'd gone to school together, then university, and were around twenty-five. Unlike Beryl and me they approved of where they lived, and would fight to keep its identity. I wouldn't lift a finger for Albany Park.

I suggested we should all go along the coast and into France, and that's when I heard about Franco, the Civil War in the thirties, and Franco's hatred and suppression of Catalonia.

'You're supposed to have a permit to leave here,' said Lluís.

'But you're free.' I couldn't see it otherwise.

'Oh, but we're not,' said José.

The hotel, cool and very clean, had a deliberate simplicity. The decoration gave it character and was in the regional Catalan style that could not be found elsewhere in Spain. I loved the lights gilded with angels and Madonnas, and the huge metal sun with long tapering rays, mathematically exact, on the wall in the *salon*. It was the best sun I had ever seen and it gave me great pleasure looking at it. It summed up health and well being. The balconies were filled with scarlet flowers and cages of singing birds. The mirrors were old with elaborate gold frames and, as Eva said, cost a lot. Wooden wheels on the walls were filled with wild flowers, the floors of original red stone oiled to a delicious shine. The hotel had a feeling of being cared for and shown to advantage. Its identity had been provided by José, but at the time I did not realize this. He brought out the essence of whatever place he was in. He collected old objects from the villages, which in those days was a rare practice. Abandoned clocks centuries old were cleaned up and brought back to life. The paintings and sculptures were by his friends, many of them Catalan artists he supported.

Guests stayed permanently on full *pension*; those in José's circle visited daily for lunch or artistic events, and it was cheerful with new things always happening. There were no televisions or refrigerators in those days. Radios, gramophones, jukeboxes, and live bands provided constant music; theatres and fiestas, the drama. Dances were held every Saturday in the ground-floor room with a piano and drums. If the nights were cool they burned logs in the huge fireplaces and heated the rooms in winter with stoves, their pipes curling up through the ceiling. The water was always cold.

We'd been given a room with two beds on the first floor overlooking an alley. The wide-open windows let in the cries and smells, and music. The atmosphere of the town was always present in the room.

Although the *pension completa* came to less than a pound a day, we had even less. We tried some begging but kept it to the new part of town. The kinds of work we'd done so far were not suitable for Girona, so I told José we would have to move to a big city.

'But you are going to meet Jean Cocteau.'

'But what about the bill?'

'I'll sort it out,' he said, kindly.

He didn't say what he did or refer to his connection with the Residencia and made no mention of being its decorator and, as it turned out, much more.

I didn't realize he lived there until the following Saturday night, when he carried a tray of drinks across to a group of locals and collected money for the dance just beginning downstairs.

'Do you sleep here?' I asked.

He pointed straight up.

'Heaven?' I asked.

16

He laughed. 'Depends on whom I'm with.'

He called me Patrice.

'It's Patricia.'

He still went on with Patrice. 'Of course you should have a French name.'

As he liked it I accepted it. Looking back it was a baptism.

I asked how he knew French.

'I've always known it.'

'How?'

'Because we're near the border and some French come here. And Paris. Well, that's the place to be, isn't it? If you're an artist.'

Was he? He said he wrote poetry, and Lluís said it was the real thing.

I wanted to ask Manolo, the night concierge, about José, but then Beryl would think I was after him. It seemed he had many attributes, but I couldn't pin him down. In the end I would say he was a man who loved his town.

The town was touched with enchantment and on certain days, depending on the wind, even the air was charged, producing an instant excitement.

Beryl said it was like being on morning glory seeds, which she'd been offered in the Pigalle district of Paris. The burning wood, competing perfumes, black tobacco, harsh coffee, the river smells and other unidentifiable odours that belong only to hot places blended into a heady blast, and you took a breath and were in another dimension. You were seduced and changed into a different person, into its lover, because that's what the town wanted in those days. You laid your heart on the narrow streets like a newborn child at a sacrifice. The town approved of offerings on a grand scale. You'd be half accepted. A stranger could never really belong. It was a question of the stones, not the inhabitants. The stones housed the power. It wasn't simply a magnetism, more a magic. It seemed the place itself decided what happened. The people had no more choice than I did.

The spirit of the town, that's what mattered. It had to approve of you. If you were opaque with self-satisfaction or too bourgeois you'd pass through that old quarter and it would show you nothing. I believe the spirit of Girona did approve of me as I was then. Of course, it wouldn't let me go. A town's love did not die. There was a lovely mid-fifties optimism, and no political regime could quite suppress that. The town was touched by dreams. Dreams from other centuries reappeared in the legends, the poetry, even the birds' cries, and were passed down in the local street stories. It was the best time.

4

One day, unannounced, José took me to the cathedral to meet Jean Cocteau. On the location many men spoke to me and, as I didn't know what they were saying, I didn't get a real idea of which one was the director. After they'd looked at my posture from different angles, a Catalan film-maker, Antonio Barrés, took me to a garden up behind the cathedral and photographed my face. This was my film test, and, throughout, organ music lifted loud and magnificent from the cathedral. 'That's Geli, José's cousin,' said Antonio. José was there, so was Beryl. Not being at the centre of attention was new for her, and she sat in the shade not speaking. She'd been my friend for most of my life and for a moment I almost said, 'Do you want to do it instead?'

Antonio had me walk up and down, and then came the subject of the dreaded dancing.

'She'd be better just running,' said José immediately. 'She symbolizes freedom. Ballet is so artificial. Let her run and lift her arms as though she's about to fly.' He'd already got an idea of my limitations.

They'd dressed me in a long, full, black crêpe skirt, a very tight belt, high-heeled shoes. The pale blue sweater had a difficult neckline that was supposed to stand out straight across the top of my shoulders. Long silver earrings tangled with my hair, and the make-up started to disintegrate in the heat. Then Jean Cocteau was there and wanted to know why I kept doing my hair. José assured him that Bohemians always did their hair. In spite of the dozens of men, José was all I saw. I noticed Cocteau was looking at him in the same way. He asked why I didn't speak French properly. I decided then I would speak it excellently. But he wasn't criticizing me. He just thought it would serve me well in my present way of life.

'A waif needs to be articulate,' he told José.

José laughed, not the usual free, falling forward, true mirth, but an attractive laugh with a lovely sound full of charm. And then I realized the Frenchman was entranced by José and he should be the star of the film, of every film this director ever made. His companion Jean Marais had also seen the look. Cocteau, still openly watching José, said, 'He looks like Modigliani. At his best.' And that explained everything.

Cocteau wanted to go further into the garden, around the back of the house, into the house, under it, up the tower. Surely José had a key. He brought forward his own cameraman and the crew for this operation. José said the owner was away. And there followed a fast conversation in French which I did not understand, and I could see the point in learning languages.

The garden was overgrown, full of deep holes and tricky weeds. The surrounding walls, some of them forming part of the city wall, were broken in places. Steps up inside this thick wall led to a walkway and narrow defensive slits through which arrows and later bullets would have been fired. A huge old royal palm tree filled the garden and gave wonderful deep shade, for which I was grateful. The tower was attached to the side, and this was what stuck up so incongruously on the medieval skyline.

20

Cocteau was in no doubt José would find a way of getting him inside. There was quite a discussion about that.

The shutters were partially closed and the brown paint peeling. It was all run-down and dusty, and looked as though it had been abandoned for years. Beryl didn't like the garden, said it made her depressed. There was a feeling there, she said, and she wasn't happy. She always picked up on atmospheres.

Antonio Barrés was kind and encouraging, photographing me by the palm tree, sitting on the broken wall, walking as though to enter the main door, which stood directly on the edge of the common footpath. He said he was shooting a short film the following week with a local boy, and wanted me for one scene. Suddenly I had a career.

There was a considerable amount of waiting around. Beryl was thirsty and hungry, and not a café or bar in sight. The house was the last one on this country path, which began behind the cathedral and continued upwards, forking at a hill where there was a broken, round, fat tower. I understood it was called Torre Gironella, and the subject of legends.

I asked about this run-down house and its overgrown garden.

'Oh, this used to be splendid,' said Antonio. 'This was a superb garden, the talk of Girona, in its time.'

'Whose was it?'

'They had money and the house was done in the Parisian style with exotic sculptures and ancient effigies and magnificent fabrics. Yes, there was a fountain and for a while a carriage. And they had musicians giving concerts. Debussy came here.'

'Were these people royalty?' Beryl asked.

'No. A woman lived here. A Frenchwoman.'

Antonio was full of disappointing news. No royalty, and the Frenchwoman was gone and probably dead.

Cocteau was busy arranging ladders to get inside the tower. I didn't think he really wanted to make a film. He wanted to be inside that house. He peered in at every window, tried to get the door open. During its long life it had had several new and ever stronger locks and bars. The cameraman was encouraged to intrude as much as he could and get every angle possible between these half-open splintered shutters. When I got used to the gloom inside I could see a torn panel of gold wallpaper patterned with elegant birds in silver and a wonderful white and pale blue that was the purest, most innocent, optimistic blue ever mixed. It came from the first dawn of colour. It was something I'd have expected in the Louvre. I called José.

'The gold. It's real.'

'Well, yes. It looks it. The house had marvellous decoration in its day.' And he would say no more.

'That wallpaper is Parisian,' said one of the French crew. 'From Duchesne. And does it cost! It was around in the last century. When was this house decorated?'

'José would know that,' said Cocteau.

'It belonged to the priests.' And José walked away, smacking his hands one on the other, to get rid of the dust. And the subject.

Antonio Barrés came with us to the Residencia. Emilio was calmly eating his three-course dinner, and asked about the filming. José had stayed behind in the garden with the French crew filming every particle of the ground, stones, holes, the doorway. When I'd left they were taking measurements of the tower.

'He wants to film the house, not me,' I admitted.

'You've not got your eyes shut.'

'What is there to see up there?'

'You don't want to get into that.' Emilio spoke excellent English, having been the trainer at a football club in the north of England.

'It's folly to let that house get so rundown,' said another diner. 'They should make it into an art centre or hotel for artists, or …'

'Never,' cut in Emilio. 'No one would go near the place.'

'Who owns it?'

'The last I heard a Frenchwoman, but it's not clear if she's alive.'

Beryl was in our room, winding a string of beads around her forehead. A black ribbon around her throat looked new. Then she pinned on an antique cameo brooch. A large cup of chocolate milk was half finished. Shopping had occurred. How?

'You're after him,' she accused me.

I knew who the 'him' referred to, but still asked which one of her admirers she had in mind.

'You always speak French to him.'

'I've just been accused of not speaking French by the director.'

'Well, Spanish then.'

I promised her I was a Bohemian to the bone. I vowed that I would travel on until I became a true gypsy and went through their initiation. No man could stop that or get in the way of my friendship with her. As I said it I thought, for José, I'd give up everything.

'We leave tomorrow,' she said. 'This town is getting hot in every way.'

There was filming tomorrow and I suggested the day after.

'Tomorrow.'

I didn't want to lose Beryl, but tomorrow was only hours away. She started chucking things in her rucksack.

'We'll go to the other side of Spain. Eva told me it's green and cooler. There's a place called La Coruña by the sea.'

And she described a pilgrim route and I started to like it. I asked how she'd got money for the beads.

'I got lucky,' she said, and did more packing.

I said it made sense to wait one more day; then we could travel on the money from the film. She reached into her duffel coat pocket and pulled out a small wad of paper money.

'A man gave it to me.'

She described a man with pale eyes and grey streaked hair with a north European accent. Tall, elegant. She'd seen him around. I hadn't. She said he was up near the house with the tower, and while they were taking my photograph he asked her to do something simple. The favour would be paid for in advance. All she had to do was tell him how many went to a meeting in the basement of the Residencia, and if there was a large stone there. The meeting would be after dark. He would contact her later and she would receive more money.

'He's a spy,' I said.

'He said he would do it himself but he'd been called to Barcelona.'

She had asked Manolo about the basement and he said it was never used.

'Did you ask about the meeting?'

'The one thing he said was to keep it quiet.'

Had she told José? She said she would, and then produced a map. There was a train leaving in the early morning before the heat got up, and we could take that to the frontier and hitch from there. She even had a route planned. 'If I don't get out now I never will,' she declared. And she put glistening dust on her fringe.

5

Beryl didn't mention La Coruña again, although her rucksack stayed half packed. She asked me to get a torch from Manolo so we could look at the basement. And she told José about the elegant man with money in his pockets. I asked her if José was alarmed.

'No, he just laughed. He said the guy was a commercial traveller. They were always looking for a gathering where they could do some business. Gatherings were rare in Catalonia, he said, because Franco didn't like them.'

'A commercial traveller in what?' Beryl had asked.

'Obviously stone-cutting equipment,' José had replied.

I got the torch and we found a door, hard to open, leading to the cellar. It was filled with spare chairs and cobwebs. The only stone was the floor.

When did I first hear about the Frenchwoman? It was watching José rushing to go out, changing his shirt, splashing water on his face, followed by the essential eau de Cologne. 'Where are you going?' I asked, suddenly afraid he was going to something glamorous and life-changing, which would take him away.

'I am going to a meeting.'

'Can I come?'

'No.' He rinsed his mouth.

'Why not?' Jealous now.

'It's political.'

Eva laughed outright. 'Political, and he cleans his teeth. He's going to meet a woman.'

José, amused, said, 'Perhaps you should come, Eva, and reinvent Catalonia for us. You're good at invention.' And he charmed her with a laugh as he took his jacket and silk scarf. He promised to take Beryl and me to the Savoy Bar at eleven that night, so that made everyone happy. I was to wait in the alley by Chez Béatrice, and then he was gone, singing and whistling and calling to the birds, his tread unique and unmistakable on the stairs.

'It would take a Frenchwoman to trap that one.'

'What woman?' I felt emotional.

'The Frenchwoman who lives up behind the cathedral. He goes to see her.'

'What is she like?'

Eva indicated curvaceous. And then she said other things, but I hadn't got far enough with the language barrier.

Then, suddenly, he was gone. Emilio said he'd left in someone's car early that morning.

'Where is he?'

'He's trying to get away from that French director and his obsession with that house and its tower.' Emilio knew everything.

'Is that true?' Beryl was shocked, her enviable pink cheeks too red.

'How do I know?' And Emilio carried on reading his newspaper. 'The man's a poet. Since when do they need truth? It's got a strong atmosphere, that house. Probably because it was once so special and now all that's over.'

'What is he talking about?' asked Beryl, irritated.

'The Frenchwoman,' said Emilio, lightly. 'She'd been happy there and then that time was over. It would be reflected in the atmosphere of the house.'

I remembered Jean Cocteau assuming José had the keys.

Emilio's eyes looked endlessly dark. I asked who owned it.

'They just call her the Frenchwoman.'

Because I was now a film star my photograph was in the newspapers. They even put me on the radio. The begging we'd been doing had to go underground. Then I did Antonio's short film, and then a small scene for a Spanish director. Again it was poetical, its theme unending love. Girona was certainly the place for that.

The press wrote that I was an existentialist, and made a lot of my being at Jean-Paul Sartre's café table in Paris. I understood he was one of a group of French intellectuals helping the Catalan activists against Franco's regime. An underground newspaper had been printed in Perpignan and distributed in Spain.

I said I'd pay Lluís for the language lessons he gave me every afternoon in Spanish and French, but so far the film money was not in sight.

6

The Frenchwoman's house intrigued me. It was the only domestic building in that whole quarter. Was it the glory that had been and was gone? And what about that panel of gold wallpaper more commanding than a painting? Why did the French film crew so want to get in, and why did José try to keep them out?

'Let's go there.'

Beryl wouldn't hear of it.

'We could dance up there in the garden. Lluís has a gramophone.'

She wasn't sure. So I said we could give a dancing performance and make money.

We went there as the day got cooler. At first I thought there was someone in the house because I heard steps.

'It's the shutters banging,' said Beryl. A wind had started up.

The garden was easy to enter and filled with rubbish. We climbed the wall and looked over the city, and I saw a long flight of small steps leading down to the shrivelled grass below. They wouldn't have been visible if the sun had not been in such a position.

We danced to Lluís's gramophone – trad jazz, jive, rock and roll, boogie. It felt as though we were being watched and I turned, expecting onlookers. Beryl said it was someone inside the house. Picking up the gramophone and records we started nervously towards the path. I gave the door a try. It was still bristling with locks.

And then I remembered the steps down the wall. Did they lead to another entrance?

'Why do this?' she said.

Why? Because if the worst came to the worst, as it had on some occasions, we could always stay up here. She wouldn't follow me down the flight of wall-hugging broken steps that hadn't been used for years and leaked sand and dust at every tread. A whole section of stone fell on my next step, and I clung to branches growing out of the wall and couldn't move. It was then I saw the door. It was above me and not properly closed. I was backing up now, not looking down, a slight vertigo beginning. Reaching the door was easier than climbing back into the garden.

Beryl was leaning over the wall giving advice. I pushed the door, trying to keep my balance, and it shoved forward grudgingly. Another step up and I got a better foothold and used more weight. It opened enough and I climbed up into the doorway. The ground, although cracking, was sturdy. I squeezed into the dark entrance. The door wouldn't open further. It was held partially shut by a stone. The floor was mosaic. There was a chandelier, half its bulbs broken. Against one wall stood an upright piano. I was drawn to the newspapers in a corner. They were French, yellowing and racing with ants, and dated from 1895 until 1917. There was a silent grandfather clock and an art-nouveau decorated mirror, and this was only the hallway. The chairs belonged in a palace.

The other room with the panel of gold wallpaper was spacious and grand. The table was long and polished in one part, thick with dust in another. The kitchen was from the thirties or older. The house didn't feel empty. Why weren't the rooms filled with stale air? And then I saw something that didn't make sense. On the draining board there were two big china cups, cracked, and they'd been recently rinsed and were still wet. I turned quickly, expecting someone, the worst figure my imagination could conjure up.

Beryl banged on the window. 'Now all you have to do is get yourself out.'

In the other room the floor in the middle was dug up. Earth and clay piled at the side of the deep hole were not dry. Tiles had been smashed in this unholy digging, which made the room smell rotten. What were they burying here? I hoped I didn't have to find out. The shutters were tightly closed. The fireplace was filled with half-burned papers. On a sideboard was a scattering of small photographs, old and tinted, and snapshots, trinkets, and quill pens. The ink bottle was dried out. I picked up a brooch, which looked antique and blackened. It had been scorched in a fire.

Beryl, or the wind, was thumping the kitchen shutters.

'Shall I get Lluís?' she shouted. She was as nervous outside as I was in.

'And leave me in here alone? I'll get out through a window.'

The windows had panels of stained glass and were too beautiful to destroy deliberately. I looked for an ugly one. Then I heard the creaking. It seemed to come from the floor above. It set off a cacophony of unexpected sounds. The house was not empty but filled by an unseen presence. Could I go down the broken outer steps of the wall? Nothing was faster than my feet kicking up dust and sand.

Sometime later I told José, and he laughed, a different laugh this time. 'The guttering is loose and rattles in the

31

wind, bangs against the stone. That's what you heard. You must not go up there again. It's not a playground.'

There had been something there, his laugh told me that. I didn't mention the recently washed cups.

A few days later a woman appeared on the stairs, then by the bar, behind the bar; she was everywhere. A cold cosmetic beauty, the epitome of the bourgeoisie, co-owner of the hotel – and José's mother. She had his eyes but without the glow. I asked where José had gone and she threw her hands about. '*Fuera de Girona.*' That meant he was out of town.

'Far?'

'Very far.'

So I used one of Lluís's instructions for questioning the future.

'Coming back? It will be long. Many days.' She swiped the bar with a dusting cloth as though killing a fly. 'You need to be with your mother,' she concluded. She wanted us out, and she was used to getting what she wanted.

'She says you've been prowling around that house,' Emilio warned.

So I asked what was wrong with it.

'It always belonged to the church and then something changed because a woman lived there on her own.' He rubbed his fingers together. 'Someone must have paid plenty. It can hardly be any worse in my view. A dubious woman.' He couldn't stand the church or be in the same room as a priest. 'They've held this country up for centuries. They've demanded everything, the land, the buildings, taxes, donations, and they've got fat. They knew everything about everybody. Now it's their turn to shiver.'

7

Then José was back. I recognized his footsteps on the stairs, light and quick. To him life was a dance, and he was filled with energy, laughter, music, and was always whistling and singing. He said he'd been staying in Tossa de Mar.

'So you've had a long journey.' It didn't occur to me his mother would not tell the truth.

'Of course not. It's just here on the coast.' He didn't say what he'd been doing.

Beryl lying motionless on her bed was another matter. Why wasn't she out dancing in the streets? She was missed. He brought her a bunch of wild flowers and some Torres chocolate bars. He was cheerful and saw the good side of everything, and finally made her laugh. He refused to be brought down. He was like an old-fashioned bird in a cage singing wonderful songs that had never been heard before. He was absolutely original in expression and thought. And he was kind. He took the wild flowers and adorned her, the whole of her head and body, lying there on the bed.

Then he was gone. It was always noticeable when he left.

'Well, he certainly likes you,' I said.

'No,' she said, quietly, 'it's you.'

Another lone tear splashed from her eyes, and I told her if she went on like that her mascara would be ruined.

Later I saw Beryl run to José. She put her arms around his neck and he tried to make light of it. She said something I couldn't hear and he replied gently, 'But you're a little girl.'

Head down she walked fast, as though stricken, towards our room. Then she stopped and turned, and looked at me. 'Well, you've got him.' And she went to our room. That was an exit.

I talked to José in my now halting French and Spanish about leaving for La Coruña, but he wasn't listening. He looked into my eyes, his heated up, and there was a stirring of recognition, of something familiar from some other time, a feeling I could not identify. It was too much for me, so I walked into the *salon* and leaned against the long gilt-rimmed table around which were placed a dozen grand chairs. José followed and put his hands on my shoulders. 'Such a little girl.' Then he took off his woollen sweater and wrapped it around me. 'I'll have to look after you.' He kissed my hair lightly and I felt I'd come home.

I felt so high that I ran down into the street and within minutes was in a part of town I'd not seen. I ran towards the cathedral but got lost, and the path was lightless yet I felt no fear. There was too much joy in me for that. I arrived at the house with the tower, and walked carefree along the wall.

I could hear a service in the cathedral, the voices lifting discordantly. I jumped and caught a branch of a tree, and swung until it drooped, and I with it, to the ground. The sound had a definite power because I was actually listening. It wasn't singing, but chanting – repetitive, hypnotic – and I realized it came from inside the house, behind the brown shutters, yet no light showed. The noise of the night wind covered my untidy journey to the window. I'd heard music in Lluís's studio called plainsong. Was it that?

The room, flickering with lights from an important looking ceremonial candleholder with six branches, was busy with shadows that sped and whirled onto every possible surface with a desperation not to be left out, like children playing a game of musical chairs. I could see only part of the long table and a few men around it, intoning phrases. They were the singers. Others were silent. The candles were tall, their light bending in the draughts. A man in black, his head shaven, held a scroll and put his hand on a substantial, engraved piece of stone in front of him. I thought he wore a headdress, but it was a shape behind his head like a star, which I found out later was a hexagram. The shutters kept from view other men, but the shadows dominated the room. These must be priests from the cathedral – yet why did people keep saying this house was never used? The sound became bigger as though forcing my head to expand, becoming unbearable, and I covered my ears.

There were many additions to this ceremonial scene that I noted but instantly forgot, because I'd been at the window too long and I was aware of eyes on mine and I ran for my life. The off-key chant expanded in my head, in my blood, and there seemed nothing I could do about it as I realized the priests were not clothed religiously but in ordinary suits.

Shoe broken, hair flying, gasping, sweating, I ran down the carrer de la Força. Lluís stepped out of a doorway and stopped me. 'Isn't it hot for running?'

I would have told him what I'd seen but I didn't feel sure of anything, because the eyes that had met mine at the ceremony were not those of a priest but the film-maker Jean Cocteau, and he'd recognized mine. He'd seen them enough.

They threw us out early the next morning. Beryl said it was 6 AM, and we didn't have time to put on make-up. The police escort took us by train to the frontier. There had been letters of complaint. The mayor wanted the police chief replaced. It was political, not really to do with us.

Once over the French side they dropped us without a word, a franc, or a peseta. Half our belongings were left behind. We hadn't said goodbye to anyone and we had no money, though we still had our visas back into Spain. They'd forgotten that.

Perpignan was a bad place, and we couldn't get a lift. The thrill of hitting the road was absent that day. I was seared with unhappiness. The early moon and the smell of the Mediterranean made it worse. Girona was just down the road, part of the smell, sharing that particular phase of the moon. The town had been the revelation of my life and yet I'd been put out like a disgraced dog. We had to sleep in the crowded Perpignan youth hostel and leave by the window the next morning.

'I know why they didn't take our visas,' I told her. 'They run out today.'

The wind and our luck changed, and the first car stopped and we started for Carcassonne. The pain started as well. I'd lost something for which my life would be always in mourning, the punishment for letting joy slip so easily away.

'Stop!' I must have said.

He thought I meant the car. I meant the world. I got out. Then Beryl got out. We weren't friends any more. It was terrible.

'You'll end up like those housewives in Albany Park,' she said.

She asked the driver to get my rucksack, and without another word got back into the car and sped off. I'd been her friend for years. It took José to break that. She went north and I south, and we never saw each other again.

8

I always knew when he was in the building. Sometimes when he'd sit writing on the balcony, the birds in their gilt cages would flutter gaily and the geraniums, catching all the light, would turn burning red until they became passionate, serious flowers to be offered as a pledge. José loved music, especially the French composers, and he'd sing in snatches to the gramophone record as he wrote on long sheets of white, lined paper, his handwriting fast and decorative. Each day was different and they were all good.

I refused to think about Beryl. I could cut anything out. It was the only way to survive, to go forward so only the present existed. I'd learned that young. I missed her terribly and had written a letter to see how she'd got back, and eventually I received a card of Soho and a cross showing Cy Laurie's jazz club, and on the back: 'Anticipation was the best'.

Lluís still gave me Spanish and French lessons twice a day, and I picked up some casual Catalan. He looked after the practical side of my life and helped me renew my visa. I organized the dances on Saturday nights, and taught jive and rock and roll. The press came around at the beginning, intrigued to find how I'd got back when I'd been put out so firmly.

Was I perhaps his '*novia*'? I didn't know what that was, so José said yes. I found out it meant fiancée.

'Am I?' I asked him.

'It's the only way you'll stay here, so you'll have to be.'

It was an odd betrothal.

Our doors were always open and I used to go freely to and from his room. His bed was narrow and hard, and the floor was patterned stone and cold. It was a heady, exotic room, but without comfort.

My own room was what would be expected of a fiancée with no money but some enemies, especially my future mother-in-law. It had been gone over with a policeman's eye by Eva, its contents listed and reported. Just wild flowers from my beloved, my language lesson exercises, and valuable editions of Spanish classics presented to José by his uncle, the city jeweller. Inside one of these unread books I found a curious paper. Dated 1950 and headed the World of Light, it gave notice of special lessons to prepare for the journey of light begun by Isaac el Cec.

El Mundo de la Luz

Solo podemos percibirlo con ojo espiritual.Se muestra a
acquel cuya co nciencia se ha transformado completamente.
Y ante ti abrira de parenar las puertas de sus recintas
secretos y pondira de manifesto ante sus ojos los tesoros
misma ocultos en las profundidades de su seno puro y
virginal.No contaminades por la mano de la materia solo
muestra sus tesora al ojo del Espiritu,ojo que jamas
se-cierra y para el cual no/hay velo alguno en todos
sus reinos.

Purifiez - vous.Vous etes le temple.

1,Ecoutez l:initiate le plus haut.Il sait comment travail
ler avec le son,al protection et rite coleur qui y
correspondent.
Il travailler avec la force de l:esprit du groupe.
2 Restraint.Utilisez la force,l:energie,d:une maniere
restrainte.C:est plein de force,pouvoir alors c:est dangeroux
dutiliser ces energies sans preparation suffisante.
Ce sont des forces divines.
3 Utilisez vos voix internes pour vous garder.

4   L:art

Translated in full on pages 322–23

9

One morning he was gone. It was a bright day in October and still warm. Eva didn't know where he was, but mentioned a dentist's wife. Then she had a better idea.

'Perhaps he's asleep. His nights are busier than most people's days.'

So I got the subject around to his love life. After all, I was the *novia*.

'I wouldn't think that one goes without. He's too beautiful. That'll be his downfall.' She poured me some coffee. 'They're all after him.'

'Is she beautiful, the dentist's wife?'

Eva indicated large breasts and provocatively moving hips. 'A proper Spanish woman. Made for love.'

She asked if I wanted omelette and bread. I did not. The 'made for love' speared my heart. It was the greatest possible accolade you could give any woman. 'Is she better than the lawyer's wife?'

'It doesn't matter because he won't go for a Spanish girl. She will always be French.'

I ran to Lluís's studio for the early language lesson. I didn't realize at fifteen that although perfect things happened, it was not a perfect world.

I told him Eva's prophecy about French women.

'The mother won't let him marry any woman, especially a foreigner. Especially one without an inheritance.'

That left me out.

'That's Catalan thinking. If he goes with you she'll cut him off. He'll lose everything. She's very possessive. She's already cut him down and gives five pesetas here, a "duro" there. She wants to starve you out.' His eyes moved behind the enlarging lenses of his glasses like fish in a tank.

Lluís thought perhaps he'd gone to Tossa de Mar. 'They have a large house and grounds there,' he explained.

'He keeps going off on his own, to meetings, he says. And he won't take me,' I complained.

'I did hear he goes to special instruction. I don't know what in. But it's not the Catholic religion. Has he mentioned a Frenchman, Julien Sacaze?'

I didn't think so.

'He must have changed his mind about Tossa de Mar.' Lluís pointed through his slit of a window and there was José walking swiftly through the dust of the old street towards the cathedral. There was a sense of purpose in his walk. No enjoying the gift of the hour. No poetical thoughts on this day. I didn't shout his name and join him, but followed along by the edge of the stone buttress, keeping to the shadow.

Behind the cathedral where the organ was playing, around the curve of the track, without hesitation he went to the brown, peeling door of the house with the tower. Two raps and the door opened. He slid in with no greeting, and the door shut, folding him into the secrecy of the house. So I went to the window I knew would be most suitable, with the shutters open but not too much. I could see him pacing to and fro, talking fast, clearing his throat nervously. No smiles, no laughter. So I took a chance of a better view and crossed into the garden and could see clearly from behind the palm tree. A stout woman sat at the table, her hair tied back in a bun. They spoke French and I understood a little. He wanted her to agree with something that should be done. At first I thought he was against her, but it seemed there was a third person, not present, who was the problem. She got up and her legs were puffy, and I thought she was in her late fifties, even older. Not the Frenchwoman, definitely. The cleaning woman, probably.

His eyes were not smiling, and they stayed fixed on her face. Then he took from some inner pocket a bunch of money that he placed on the table. For someone supposedly broke he wasn't doing badly. She was less impressed by the money than I was. He kept mentioning danger and she spoke in a calm monotone, quite attractive. He hadn't got his way because he slapped the table and notes flew around in the rising dust, dropping eventually to the dirt of the floor. Suddenly he grabbed her to him and kissed her face. I'd certainly never got so much passion. Then he shoved her so she tottered backwards to the wall and then he left, slamming the door. Was this the woman he was seeing who kept his nights busy? Surely not. He hurried down the path and, the next thing, she went after him in a pair of man's slippers, her ankles swollen.

She hadn't locked the door and I was in, up to the sideboard with all the trinkets and photographs. I took a handful of everything, then I was out and down the path as she was coming back.

She stopped and stared at me, her eyes small and almost lost in wrinkles. Dark, even black, eyes in a round, pale face. I wished I'd have stopped and spoken to her but I didn't have the courage, and I ran on as she said 'Bonjour'.

—⚬⚬⚬—

Should I tell José? She could not be the Frenchwoman, curvaceous, enticing, and yet he had kissed her and even shoved her, his eyes changed by a strange passion. Of course I'd not let it go but decided not to speak yet. The house was perfect for privacy. Hardly anyone passed along the track because there was nothing beyond except the countryside.

The next morning José said, 'Today we go to Barcelona.'

I told him I knew that city.

'You don't know the real Barcelona. It's my present to you. After all a fiancé must give something, no?'

He hadn't given me a ring, and I didn't ask for one.

That day was the stuff of his poems, full of gifts like a seasonal celebration. It was how Christmas should be. The light in the Gothic Quarter as though from another century flooded us with gold and then flickered, became insubstantial and presented figures made up of bits of light, dancing in and out of reality like characters in a fairground. We moved into the nostalgia and mystery of the old courtyards and streets, menacing with razor-sharp black shadows as though a crime was taking place. And then the doorway of the old palace, now converted into apartments, with music on every majestic staircase, and the higher I climbed the more joyful I became, part of his world now, and the day fitted him exactly, the outer expression of all he was.

Between us a fusion had taken place and it deepened until we were bound together. And he was father, lover, god to me and I felt so tight to the skin with him that I really was his, that he'd actually created me from some eruption not unlike the act of birth itself.

He had business to do in the town and left me in the Quatre Gats Café. There were two worlds. With him, without him. I wanted to marry him and have his child.

Then we ran out of money, so it was my turn to show him something from my life. I got us a free ride along the coast on the old line from Mataró to Girona, hanging on to the side of the train, and when we jumped down before the station he said for a while he'd felt perfect freedom, even from thought.

So I had to say, 'Do you make love to that French-woman?'

He looked suitably confused so I asked for money; a 500 peseta note would do. I needed things – shampoo, pearl nail polish, sanitary items, stamps.

He shook his head once. He had no money.

'Why?'

He didn't expect that. I said he had plenty of money for the Frenchwoman. Hadn't he smacked down several thousand pesetas on that dusty table?

He did pause, which was the only sign of acknowledgment. 'This is a hard country. You have no idea.'

And then I knew the danger. It was a change in the heartbeat, the temperature of my body. My legs got it too. Your body knew before you knew.

'Where did you get the money?' Not listening to the signs.

'A lottery,' he said, lightly. 'Where else?' Hadn't I heard of the Fat One, the lottery at Christmas?

So I said that was a lot of shit, and he looked at me and his eyes were not poetical but speculative.

'I think it's time you went to Paris,' he said.

10

The writer Salvador Espriu invited us to the fishing village of Arenys de Mar. Its yellow beach bleached by the sun, the extraordinary sky over-bright in its blueness, the shrieking white of the houses and the obedient palm trees so still in the midst of this assault of colour, were like a birth into a sphere of original brightness and light. The primal colours, all optimistic, reminded me of the pictures in a child's painting book. José for once did not see much that was special. Espriu said it wasn't a place but the antechamber of paradise, as he had written in his book of poetry, *Cementiri de Sinera*.

We had a drink in the Hotel Gaviota and walked directly out into the brightness of the beach. He asked José about someone called Maria Tourdes. Was the 'affaire Saunière' settled? José said his cousin Geli took care of things.

The women's long black dresses and shawls, their crabbed shadows against the blazing white walls, took my attention. They were too present, as though something divine had slipped into that moment. Was it only the amazing light?

'Who is Saunière?' I asked. And the breeze shook the palm trees, lifting the scent of the flowers, and the shadows continued along the wall like figures in a ceremony. And the church bell gonged the hour and the birds shrieked out to sea and it wasn't a fishing port but a temple.

They both answered differently.

Espriu said, 'A priest from France.'

José said, 'You really are a Sherlock Holmes.'

Further along the beach, before we took the bus, I made José stop and sit down. His visit to the Frenchwoman's house. Could he deny it? The name Maria Tourdes had set it off. Was this the Frenchwoman? I needed to resolve this. I had a *novia*'s rights. So he said the house was disused and I'd got the wrong place. So I pulled out the sample of letters and photographs from my duffel bag and assured him that as he'd come out of the door I'd gone in and here was the proof. Admittedly he wasn't in any photograph. The letters were in French and dated 1892, torn and dusty. Most of the photographs had the garden as background. A woman in a long skirt served wine to distinguished-looking guests. And by the palm tree stood a priest with a handsome, strong face, and he watched her with a certain admiration.

José took the letters and read part of one, and then stayed silent.

I knew from Lluís the letters were about practical matters, times of arrival and departure with an underlying familiarity hard to define. They were full of pretexts, these letters, Lluís had said. José considered whether or not to give them back and then he said, 'Did you take more?' I had not, and he put the letters back in my duffel bag.

'Who are these people?'

He shrugged. 'It's such a long time ago.' He looked quickly through the snapshots and other photographs.

'I'll give them back to her,' I said.

Finally, he slapped the photographs together. 'As long as there's not one of a pretty woman in a chocolate advertisement you'll be all right.' He laughed, and the disquieting moment had gone.

I asked what that had to do with anything.

'Only jealousy.' And he got up and wiped the sand from his hands.

I wasn't moving. 'I should give them back to the actual owner, the Frenchwoman, when I see her. I only saw the maid.'

He waited, not answering.

'Shouldn't I? Is the Frenchwoman in Paris?'

'It's all from another time. Not important to us.'

'Yet it affects you. That letter moved you.'

'Other people's love stories are moving.'

'What do you mean about a chocolate advertisement? Why wouldn't the Frenchwoman like that photograph?'

'Because she could not be her. You've heard of jealousy.' And he moved his hand nearer to me and I still didn't take it. He'd told me nothing.

A taxi waited to take José out of Girona – something to do with his mother. I asked if she was ill. At first he denied it.

'So why are you in such a rush?'

'All right. She's ill.'

I was used to sick mothers, but it didn't mean I could handle it. 'Have they got a doctor?'

'Oh,' he sighed. 'You don't understand.'

I waited in his room and looked at his books. Lluís said my Spanish was now adequate and better than my French. I found a folder of pages, handwritten in French, and amongst them a letter to Juli, one of José's ancestors, dated 1892. The pages were from a work entitled 'Writings on the Rose Cross,' by Julien Sacaze. Wasn't that the man Lluís had mentioned?

Later, when I asked José about him, he showed me more sheets: 'Inscriptions Antiques des Pyrénées'. He said Sacaze had died before the work was published in 1892, and his part of the book had been sent to José's great-grandfather.

'Why?'

'Because whoever sent it thought my great-grandfather would be interested. There is no mystery.'

Lluís said Juli had owned a bookshop specializing in ancient texts and rare books.

I was surprised to see the mother later that night standing, full of health, in the dairy.

The outer door opened, closed, and I hoped it was him returning, but the footsteps were too ordinary. The fat police chief appeared at the top of the stairs, and Emilio said the bar was closed.

Eva, finished for the night, ran down from the kitchen carrying large bags of laundry. The chief asked her a question and Emilio answered for her. Then she turned pale.

'So where is José?' The chief looked at me. I wished I knew.

Emilio said he was at a Saint's Day dinner for one of the family. So why wasn't I there? The police chief asked. Emilio said I wasn't one of the family.

'José wants to revive the heart of Catalonia.' He chose me for that one. 'Its heart belongs to Madrid. He'll lose his life if he keeps on with this heart business. He's against the law.'

I pretended I didn't understand. The police chief left.

Emilio and Eva waited for the outer door to close. He told her to leave by the Saturday-night dancers' door, but she poured a glass of something herbal and strong and drank it fast. Her crimson lipstick looked wrong and cheap, and made her lips thin and old.

'It's forbidden for more than twelve to be around a table together or the police think it's a conspiracy. It's forbidden to change a programme to a concert or theatre production. The programme has to be submitted in advance for approval by Madrid. They don't like Catalan being written or spoken, or the *sardanas* performed. And they've sent a lot of hostile and authoritative people from all parts of Spain into Catalonia. You wouldn't get a Catalan behaving like Fatty did just now.' Emilio couldn't sound sarcastic enough.

I asked if José was all right.

'Obviously, or Fatty wouldn't come calling. He'll be at a political meeting.'

So he did go to meetings. I was relieved. I asked where.

'Some of the priests are helpful, so perhaps up by the cathedral.'

I asked why the police chief was after him.

'Because he thinks not all our guests are on show. And the shy ones might talk a little more if they woke up in Madrid.'

'You don't like him, do you?'

'I come from the Basque country and we have our own problems.'

'So whose side are you on?'

'Well, not the police, sweetheart. I've seen too much of their work in the Civil War. Your fiancé hides people in here and gets them over to France to safety. Catalan nationalists who want to free this province. He fannies up to rich types for money and some people say he's a gigolo. He needs the money to finance an escape for these people before Franco kills them. He may end up a hero, or just end up. So don't get too chummy with Fatty.' And he gestured I keep my mouth shut.

José didn't come back. I waited on his bed because it was comforting. I resisted reading his letters, but I did look at the photographs. I was looking for foreign girlfriends. I saw a young, dark-haired girl but wearing clothes from the last century, and recognized her as the woman pouring wine in the garden with the priest. There were two others of her with a group of priests. Several recent photographs included groups of artists, and I recognized Jean Cocteau, Pep Colomer the painter, who would later become my friend, and Josep Plà, the most well known of Catalan writers.

The candle by the bed danced in the thousand draughts and produced a ballet of shadows across the walls. The cathedral clock chimed midnight, and then I saw the brooch from the Frenchwoman's house, the one burned by the fire. And I thought that whatever I'd believed was not the reality here. And my mind couldn't grasp it, not remotely. And it wasn't to do with hiding men on the run.

11

Some days later, a small, dusty car drew up alongside us as we walked towards the Residencia.

'It's Paco!' A delighted José gripped his hands. After a fast conversation the door opened and José squeezed me into the back. The car shot off with José in the front.

Paco was a medical student with curly auburn hair and a freckled friendly face.

'Paco's going to Arenys de Mar. So we'll have lunch at the port.'

He drove as though there was a medical emergency, and got the car there faster than a train.

It wasn't as impulsive as it seemed, this rush to the sea, because Espriu was waiting for José at the restaurant. He'd ordered the fish of the day fried, on a large platter with a garlic sauce and salad.

'The priest is still giving some surprises. Or, his property is,' said José, before we'd sat down. 'It's been opened as a hotel.'

Espriu looked surprised. 'By the same owner? The one who bought the villa?'

'Yes, the villa was on sale for almost thirty years and Mademoiselle Denarnaud, who hadn't accepted one offer, however generous or crazy in all that time, let Monsieur

Corbu in without a second thought. Well, one. She had to go on living there. In the presbytery.'

Espriu looked puzzled. 'But that was years ago.'

'In 1946. But my uncle never liked the sound of it. He thought the sale was dubious. Corbu explained that he liked the view.'

Espriu looked at his beloved beach. 'It could happen.'

'He's been talking about treasure and gold ingots and the secret of Saunière.'

Espriu, expecting the worst, would have to leave paradise and do something about the news. 'But Mademoiselle Denarnaud would never ever speak to anyone. That was understood.'

'She's dead. How do we know?'

Paco nudged José and looked at me.

'She doesn't understand much,' said my fiancé, revealing a foolishness I should note. I understood a little more than he thought. Lluís was a good teacher and I a quick learner.

'And he's opened the hotel and a restaurant below. Visitors find the tower interesting, and he's started to give talks.'

'Why?'

'To attract custom,' said Paco.

'It'll be the press next,' said José.

Espriu, cautious now, said, 'What does he say in his talks?'

'That the treasure belonged to Blanche of Castille.'

'Oh well, that's all right then.' Espriu rolled a cigarette.

'People have gone there and started digging,' said Paco. 'I was there this morning.'

'People?' asked Espriu.

'Treasure seekers,' said Paco.

'Well, that's all right then.'

Paco laughed.

We ate the crème caramel in a sudden silence. 'What about Maria Tourdes?' said Espriu, as though to himself. 'What does she say?'

'She doesn't say anything,' said José. 'And a North European type – that's how he was described – came with bribes to Patrice's friend. Wanted to know about meetings I held, how many came and if there was a stone present.'

Espriu sucked in his lips as though forbidding them speech. Paco was looking at me. I hoped I was looking at the sea.

'Corbu's new restaurant is called La Tour,' said Paco.

Espriu released his lips. 'I live in paradise and that's how I like it. Trouble doesn't come from here. The trouble is the outside.'

'Stop being selfish,' laughed Paco.

'What do you want me to do?' Espriu looked at José.

'Go up there. With Paco. *Do* something.' And José hit the table so the glasses shivered. 'See the mayor.'

Eva said the hotel restaurant was going to close for winter. Regulars such as Emilio, Hans, who worked in the meat factory, and the two schoolteachers would eat locally. I took it personally. As Lluís had said, the mother was starving me out.

'Is it normally shut in winter?'

Eva rubbed her fingers together, meaning money. 'What has normally got to do with it when you've got all that.'

And then José appeared wreathed in smiles, so everything was all right again. I made sure the morning walk took us up the carrer de la Força, up the cathedral steps and round to the narrow country path which led to the empty house. On the steps he hesitated. Perhaps he did not want to go near that place. I asked him about its legends that had so interested Jean Cocteau. A rush of priests came down towards us like blackbirds, and I thought he shivered.

The house looked closed, and I was far from sure how I should readdress the subject of the meeting in the kitchen. The woman with José had obviously been the cleaning woman or concierge. Where was the other? I hoped the house would provide the solution, a door opening, a name called, a moment of truth from my fiancé.

He passed the brown, shabby dwelling and continued, relating a story about the Napoleonic War in 1810 and how the city had finally got the French out. We could hear his cousin Geli playing the organ. 'Palestrini,' said José. 'My great-uncle was also the organist and one before him. They have all been organists and canons.'

'And lived in the house with the tower?'

He didn't answer, but I had seen the 'House of the Canons' over the garden entrance.

As we walked back the front door opened and two women stepped out, quite gaily and quite different from the usual people of the town. There was an extra quality even at that distance and I thought it could be drink. They stood talking on the path, and then they saw José and their eyes became still and curious like those of birds of prey. One was the overweight woman, her legs in medical stockings, and the other a quite rough looking, younger woman with a tough face, wearing a suit. We were still some way off and I knew, how I did, that if there were some other solution to passing them he would take it. He slowed down and they hovered in the doorway talking about us.

'Who are they?' I asked.

'Prostitutes,' he said. 'They use the house because it's abandoned. All sorts of people just go there.'

I'd already seen twenty around the table conducting a service.

'And the Frenchwoman?'

'Oh, she's gone,' he said.

And we drew level with the women, the one in the suit with eyes like a bird's, darting all over him, pecking him with her intrusive glances, and he smiled, suddenly warm as he greeted them. I thought the younger one had hit rough times.

We were around the corner now and the organ music pounding from stone wall to stone buttress trapped – unable to get out – cut off his words and he had to say them twice. 'They are not women you should know, so you're not to go back there.'

I could have brought up the subject of the burned brooch in his room but I didn't want any more Paris talk. His one suggestion after the day in Barcelona had sounded final. A one-way ticket for one. Instead I asked about the house.

'It used to be the priests' house,' and he turned and went back to the garden and pointed to the sign over the arch, written in Latin, that I already knew: 'House of the Canons'.

'It's been there for years. No one goes there.' He sounded over-adamant.

'Why not?'

'It's cursed.'

I would have gone with him to his room to straighten out what was becoming hostile and mysterious between us, but his mother was waiting by the bar. She wore a conservative outfit and her hair was dyed black and permed rigid.

Her mouth was grim as she flicked a tea-towel along the counter. You'd never get one over on her.

She clattered away in an angry monotone, then looked at me, one high-voltage jolt from those condemning eyes. Then she left.

It was some days before we were alone in his room. I held a letter from my father asking when I was coming back. The marvellous thing about my mother was that she had absolutely no conception of what my life was like. Her ignorance gave me the sweetest gift – freedom. I had told my father I was learning languages, so my dishonesty had turned into truth.

I wanted truth. I wanted to get behind José's charm and find the man the police came looking for and who visited a house dramatically, denied it, then said it was cursed.

He said, 'With me you'll flourish. You'll see.'

'When will we get married?'

'When the time is right.'

'Why do you say you don't go to the house with the tower?'

He tried to laugh. I picked up the brooch and showed it to him.

'It was on her table. And now it's on yours. Is it her brooch?'

'Brooch? But it's not a brooch, Sherlock. It's a priest's ring.' And he took it and looked at it as though for the first time.

'Who burned it?'

'The person who threw it in the fire.' And he put it in his pocket. I'd seen the initials.

'Who is BS?'

He didn't answer. Instead, he arranged to meet me at Chez Béatrice, one of our favourite restaurants, late that night.

12

I waited for him in the alley by an old French chocolate advertisement. The poster gleamed in the damp air and looked ancient, probably there since the forties. It had become stained into the wall. The cathedral bell chimed and clocks all over the town started up. I counted eleven and realized I was as starving as the cats that flicked along the alley.

Footsteps approaching disturbed the cats and they became part of the darkness, unmoving. A woman came to the entrance of the alley and hesitated, surprised to see me. She was wearing exquisite boots of tender pale leather or suede that laced up at the front, knee-high. The heels were delicate and made a musical noise. I had never seen anything as glamorous, even in films. And her coat was long to her calf and hanging open and the dress beneath, in spite of the chill, was silk and cut low on her generous breast. And she wore serious jewellery and her hair was up in a chignon and her face was superbly made up. Did she wear a hat? She was well made and she was old.

And then she was gone and I thought I'd seen a ghost and I couldn't hear her heels on the stone. She did touch the poster before she left with a gloved hand, soft kid gloves to the elbow.

I'd never seen anyone like her.

José said she didn't exist and laughed openly at my description. But his eyes weren't laughing. Lluís said it was one of the prostitutes from the Barrio Chino. But she wasn't from that world. And she'd worn a perfume and I was sure it was the one I loved, Je Reviens by Worth.

The next day I was standing with Eva in the butcher's shop and saw a basket being made up of different meats. The delivery boy was called in.

'It's for the Frenchwoman.'

So I asked where she lived. I was learning Spanish quickly and discovering Cocteau had been right. To survive you had to know the language.

The boy looked hesitantly at the butcher so I followed him outside. He pointed to the cathedral, and I understood him to say, 'Behind there.' He lowered his voice. 'She has a car.'

And yes, that was important to add. Cars were rare in those days.

I was walking along the narrow part of the wall, balancing as though on a tightrope, and the house looked empty as always and no car outside. I was practising this skilful walk because I had decided my future. I would get work in a circus. Pep Colomer wanted me to model for him, balancing on a ball. I'd take ballet lessons in Girona and find a trainer in acrobatics, create my own act.

The woman with swollen ankles came into the garden. She must have come through the back door that opened onto the steps. Where else? I greeted her formally and she replied in Spanish. 'You are José's friend?' And she sat on an iron chair and watched me. 'You are double-jointed,' she said. 'But you must look at one point, and keep your eyes focused.' She pointed, 'Focus on the mark on the tower.'

So I looked at the mark. She gave me more advice and then I jumped down and asked about the tower. It seemed very old.

'Oh, just a hundred years. It was built in 1851.'

She had something calm about her that was reassuring, and I told her my plans. She'd known all the circus companies in Paris.

'You can come and practise here. We'll put a rope between the trees.'

This was a marvellous idea. I always knew there was something good about that house. And then I considered 'cursed'. I asked where her mistress was and we got in a terrible muddle with the language and ended up laughing. She sat and laughed till her body wobbled and her face reddened. She wiped her eyes.

I apologized, and said I meant the Frenchwoman who owned the house and went to Paris.

'What do you want with her?'

Want with her? I wanted to know if José was having an affair, if she had been the love of his life. 'It's not important,' I replied.

'We could get you a rebounding net so you could turn somersaults.'

Then she asked me inside the house for tea, and 'cursed' re-surfaced. I hung back.

'Come on. You don't look shy.' And she walked with some difficulty to the door at the back, and it was all so simple because a wide wooden extension with a rail connected the garden with the hallway. It could be pulled up and let down, like a drawbridge.

She put a kettle on to boil and sat at the long table, with one foot up on a chair. In spite of being overweight, of being old, she had a gracefulness and must have been lovely in her youth. I made the tea, and as I did this small service I felt as though it was another time, a different era, a happy, light afternoon with music in the garden. 'There's music,' I said.

'But yes, Geli is playing the organ.'

I'd meant violin music.

So I asked how long she'd worked in the house, in Girona. What had she done before? She said she came from Quillan, just across the Pyrenees. I let her ask me about my journeys, my desire to be a gypsy, and how the circus fitted in with that, and I felt she listened with interest, even gratitude. And then she asked if I went to church. I didn't. Did I believe in God? I was sure I did. I told her how I'd seen a group of men in this room engaged in some ritual. She knew nothing about it. I mentioned Cocteau.

'That explains it. It must have been a scene for a film. Why else would he be here?'

That felt right. I told her about José and how I'd felt from the first that I'd known him before and how he made me complete, but he was always involved with other secret interests and I did not see him enough.

'Then value the time you do have with him. You won't stop him doing what he wants. Accept it and love him.'

This felt more than foreign to me, and gave him too much licence. I asked outright if he had loved the Frenchwoman and had she loved him. I understood her to say the woman had loved someone but he was dead. A long time ago.

13

I told Lluís about meeting the Frenchwoman, and he said he'd never seen her. She wasn't part of Girona. She kept herself to herself. Then I said I should get José away from his mother. He said that José was part of Girona and what would he do elsewhere?

'We'll just travel,' I said. 'Keep moving.' Mistakes occurred when I stayed still.

'It might be a good time for him to see the world. He always talked about Istanbul.'

'I'd better hold on to that stone you gave me, the animal head, for luck.'

He laughed and showed a lot of big teeth, and the laughter had a touch of malice, a caustic undertone, and was unlike any other. It gave rise to his nickname, 'The Wolf'.

'I don't know if it's lucky exactly. José and I were up there by the tower one day, wondering if it could be a bar. We'd have writers present their work, and musical evenings, and then we found several things lying around just under the dirt.'

'Who is she?'

'She came and then she left. I'd be surprised if it's her up there now. I have it on good authority that the animal head comes from ancient Egypt, long before the Romans.

And it was with a piece of a rattle belonging to a goddess, worshipped at that time. And it was up there lying by the broken wall. It was originally used in burials of powerful and evolved people.'

'Does José mention her?'

'Not at all.'

'And yet he knows her.'

And then Lluís lowered his voice, although we were alone. 'Have you seen Sabater?'

I didn't think so. 'What does he look like?'

'Disguised.'

So I asked why he was important. Quico Sabater was a local hero and had fought exceptionally in the war against Franco, and from his hiding places in the Pyrenees continued it against the Guardia Civil, the uniformed local police. Most of the political activists were now imprisoned or in exile in France or South America. The Catalans were not militant, not like the Basques. They expressed their desire for freedom through art, writing, theatre. It didn't mean they didn't get imprisoned or killed.

So Sabater, supported mainly by the workers, was stirring up the move for independence but a new epoch was beginning: tourism. Foreigners brought money. They'd make Catalonia rich. Soon there would be no time for fighting in the streets.

'Don't go near Sabater. He's large with a big laugh and you'd get put in jail just laughing with him. Men are taken off into the night and shot. We always know when the dangerous ones, the grey police, are coming for someone, because their cars never have lights. We call them blind cars.'

—⁓—

José's mother wasn't really part of the Residencia, its atmosphere, its people. Yet when I was there she was constantly on the premises, looking out of place, as she tried to find something to do, running a hand over an immaculate surface, checking for dust.

Then she came into my room and spoke in a continuous monotone with no pause for breath or emphasis. I understood she was attacking me, and these thin official lips moving on all this hate belonged in a horror film. The mother did not wish me well – not with my health, future, career, even my offspring. I'd be damned in life and the hereafter for taking her son.

And then José was in the doorway and she begged him to leave me. I could hear the word for 'pure' and could make no sense of it. His eyes filled with tears and he took her into the passage and embraced her, and I'd never seen anyone hold a person as lovingly as she held her son.

When she'd gone I said, 'She cursed me.'

He didn't deny it.

'Why does she keep saying "Be pure"?' And then I had a good idea. 'Does she want you to be a priest?'

'Yes, that's it.' He seemed relieved.

If that was all it was. I said, 'Istanbul, José. I think it's time to go to another town.'

'Maybe, but I'll never leave this one.'

We were on one peseta's worth of white beans and one egg cooked on the stove late in the evening. I had the impression he ate something more substantial at his mother's home.

Perhaps it was the lack of food, but I suddenly felt transparent, as though the outside and the inside were curiously intermingled. I wanted something to hang onto. Some people had a crucifix or magic money, or a phone number. The inside of me wasn't strong enough to go up against another street, another dark alley, another mother. He took me out for a hot drink and it was then the quarrel started. I didn't know the Spanish for 'let me down' but he knew what I meant.

'I should never trust foreign girls. My mother is right.' And he left the bar.

I ran after him, screaming abuse in any language, every language. He shook me by the throat.

'Don't you dare make a scene! Don't you dare draw attention! This place is full of secret police. D'you under-stand?' He made a cut-throat gesture.

We were beside the chocolate poster again, in the dark alley. The cats were seething with starving howls, their eyes more brilliant than the street lamps.

'That's the way to get people killed in this town.' And he pulled me down a flight of steps towards the Residencia.

'So what's the gripe, José? What do you do except sleep? And placate your mother. Do they kill you for that?'

'Tomorrow you go home, English girl.'

I ran through the dusk to the Frenchwoman's house and rapped on the door. Without doubt she peered through the shutters of the nearest window before letting me in. Her stuff was in boxes on the floor: books, shoes, statues, photographs, papers.

I could smell Je Reviens and it almost covered the smell of thick, old earth exposed by more recent digging in the other room. And then I saw the boots.

'They want me to leave. I did leave after the war, the Second World War, and never thought I'd come back.'

So I asked why she did.

'I have things to sort through.'

'Who wants you to leave?' The way it was going I'd be leaving with her.

'It's all changed here. It's not the way it was. And I know too much.' She sighed, tired.

So I asked how long she'd been in the house.

'If I told you I'd sound so old it would frighten you.'

In one of the boxes I saw a French train timetable from Cuixà to Perpignan. It was very old. I asked if I could look at it. She nodded. It was dated 1899, and Cuixà was underlined. There was an illustration on the front and the area looked agricultural with a high hill.

'Did you go on this journey?' I asked.

'No. Someone else did.'

I asked how long it took in those days.

'The Spanish trains were the problem. So slow. As now.'

I wondered if she would tell me the 'too much' she knew and, if not, could I ask her? She asked about the circus plans and I told her my life with José was a circus itself.

'Oh, being in love is a terrible business. It changes the whole thing. You should always keep your style. Be loyal to what you are.'

I had so many questions for her I couldn't ask one. She filled a kettle and placed some dry, delicious cake on the table. 'Have you been to the Savoy Bar?'

I said I particularly liked its style – the glass-topped tables and identical delicate designs in the middle of each, and the leather banquettes and walls covered with mirrors. I loved its thick, heady smell, and the seriousness of a place that was established and had built up its atmosphere for years.

It was her favourite, especially during the Second World War, when a group had met there regularly to help the

Free French, and she found photographs and showed me one of herself surrounded by men.

'I let them stay here.'

It reminded me of José. I asked how well she knew him.

'José? Very well.'

I asked her name. I wasn't really surprised to hear Maria Tourdes. I wondered how old she was. I wondered a lot of things. Was she one of the rich ones he tried to get money from for the escaping activists? I didn't think so. I asked where she was going on the night she was dressed up and unrecognizable. She said friends sometimes came from France and then they would eat in the Cal Ros. She made it sound so easy. Came from France? No suggestion here of any visa.

I told her about my problem with José's jealous mother, and I knew this was probably not a good idea. I had no idea of the lie of the land between Maria Tourdes and the Catalans. I did know it caused tension and words like 'cursed'.

'The mother is fearful for his life,' she said.

That led to another question from me. 'What does he do that is so dangerous?'

'It's not what he does but who he is.' I didn't understand and she changed tack. 'Because he's doing underground work against Franco. He's not just a too-beautiful boy getting up late and writing poems. He's deeply political.'

I could see it wasn't the very best time to be in love.

'Franco personally hates certain Catalans and dislikes the rest in general. He blames the Freemasons for the decline of values. He wants them put to death. If he can find them.'

I asked if it was the Freemasons who had held the ceremony in her house.

'Freemasonry is strong here in Catalonia. They have their meeting places and those are secret.'

After a pause she said, 'Does José talk about me?'

I shook my head and she laughed. 'What does he say?'

'That there's a lot of mystery about this house and you know it and it's connected to a priest. And some chocolate advertisement. Did you want to do it? Be the star?'

She laughed long, and her jewellery jumped and rattled, a cheerful sound. 'No, that's Emma Calvé, the opera singer. She advertised chocolate. Her face was everywhere. Have you heard of her?'

I hadn't.

'She was well known in those days, at the end of the last century. She knew the priest.' It was said dryly. 'It was a French company. First class. I'll try and find a picture of it.'

There was a tap like a code at the door. She said quickly, 'I'll go to Paris. I have an apartment.' And she said the address.

'Can I write it down? I'll never remember.'

She shook her head. There was definitely no writing things down in here, and she opened the door.

A priest greeted her in Catalan and I was introduced. It was José's cousin Geli, the organist. He was older than José, different in every way. She asked me to come again and showed me out.

So I left the house and the sense of mystery returned, thick and impenetrable. It wasn't to do with underground politics. She would either tell José of my visit or she wouldn't, and he'd see how I'd gone against his wishes. It wasn't a good day for *novias*.

14

Emilio warmed his hands at the stove. 'You'll need some clothes,' he said. 'Winter comes suddenly.'

Two spinster women who lived on the first floor joined us and read newspapers. The clocks were noisy and the stove hissed and smoked. I was hungry to the point of going to Chez Béatrice and asking for soup on credit.

'Have you seen José?'

Emilio shrugged.

I was so empty, I'd be thinking like Emilio next. All I needed was José to come up the stairs with the two eggs and packet of beans and cook them on the stove with a hunk of bread from Eva – all I needed was his steps musically on the stairs and everything would be as it should be.

'Why do you live like this? You could do so much. That violent scene in the street with him is no life for you.'

The clocks chimed and the spinster women wrapped their shawls around themselves and went to bed.

And then he was there, the fat police chief with a new haircut and a new mood. 'Passport,' and he stuck his hand out. A swarm surrounded him and searched the corridors and *salons*. They were not in uniform, which made them the grey ones you had to watch.

I had to go to my room to get my duffel bag, and Emilio told the chief to let me go alone. I was only a kid.

I did notice, as I got my passport, that the letters and photographs I'd taken from the Frenchwoman were gone. José's door opened and Eva was standing there, pale-faced and grim. A large man with a beard lay on José's bed. He looked earthy and strong and his eyes were superbly alive. 'They're after José,' I said.

The man laughed loudly. 'It'll come to nothing. No one gets anything on José. He could fall in a barrel of shit and come up smelling of perfume.'

That made him Quico Sabater.

The police chief looked at my passport as though it interested him. Outside I could hear the running of extremely fast feet, men shouting, sirens. My legs were shaking, but the chief wasn't done.

'Check out Goldilocks,' he said to one of the men.

Emilio stood in front of me. 'She's a child and a foreigner. She doesn't even speak the language.' And he took the passport from the chief and walked me to the top of the stairs. 'Chez Béatrice is a good place to find a fiancé.' And he nodded and put plenty into it.

José was in the alley by the poster. Footsteps closed up and José pulled me against the wall and held me. Two men passed. José kissed my neck and fumbled inside his jacket. He slipped something bulky and cold under my sweater.

'Lottery win. Give it to Eva. Make her lucky.'

And the men turned and came back and gave José a cuff that sent him spinning along the poster, tearing it.

'Who's the blonde?'

'A pick-up,' said José.

'So you like to pick up girls?'

'Who doesn't?'

'Makes a change from rich grandmothers.'

The alley was a dead end. The bulky object was giving my breasts a peculiar shape and slipping and sliding in the sweat of my fear. The other thug was peering at me. 'It's that English one – Goldilocks.'

José's assailant hit him a blow, which flung him round so his stomach was against the wall. And then I ran for it, past them, into Chez Béatrice, and told the woman to get the police.

She looked through the window. 'But they are the police.'

They were searching José, had his trousers down around his ankles. 'You travel light, poet.' And then to the other, 'Get Goldilocks. She's in with Béatrice.'

Béatrice swung open her back door and indicated I should climb the wall.

Eva was still in José's room, but the man was gone. I gave her the package, which contained either money or documents.

'They're beating him up.' And I ran back to the alley, but it was empty even of cats.

He tried to say the assailants were jealous, out-of-work gypsies from the south. He spat out a tooth and Eva gave him brandy.

I said we should go to the Frenchwoman's house. She would look after us. I told him I'd been there that evening – it seemed a lifetime ago. And that seemed to worry him more than anything else. In spite of his injuries he managed to frown.

'You've been with her?' He was silent. Then he said, 'Can it get worse?'

'Let's leave, José.'

'Exactly.'

For a moment I dared to be happy. 'Paris?'

'Go and pack,' he said.

Even by Beryl's standards it was spontaneous.

The next morning, a friend of José's from Barcelona came to visit, so we missed the day train. A student of law, he lived a lot of the year in Paris and was the son of a textile manufacturer, which made him rich. He sat on José's bed talking to him in soft, fast Catalan and did not like the familiar way I walked to and from the room. I did not like the way he held José's attention. Eva gave me compresses to place on José's various swellings and lacerations, and broth and yoghurt in case there was internal damage.

The next visitor was a young man from Girona about to enter the church. He was under the care of José's great-uncle Francesc and spoke about his studies, at least when I was present. I had a distinct feeling the conversation changed as soon as I left the room. I remembered his name, Quim Carreras.

I brought them tea, and he mentioned an organ concert José's cousin Geli was giving that night, so I said they should hold it in the garden of the Frenchwoman. Before the sentence was even finished, José looked at me hard. One shake of his head, just one, stopped me, so I talked about the circus. Quim Carreras nodded and prepared to leave.

'Take it seriously,' insisted José. 'She has gypsy magic. She was born with amulets, which means she travels through dangerous places where others would not dare.'

After he left I told José we should get the night train.

'There's no money for trains.'

'We'll hitch a ride.' I told him the marvels of hitching, the freedom, the excitement, and left out the unmarvellous stuff. At last I'd get him away. I'd have him.

Of course, the bad news hadn't yet been spoken. He did some more tea stirring, then let me have it.

'You go first, then I'll join you in a day or so. I'll get some money.'

I didn't like this idea.

'But we must have money.'

I promised that this was no problem. I knew how to work Paris. He took off his cross and chain and put it around my neck.

'I have to cross into France through the mountains. I am Catalan and have no papers or permission to be anywhere except Catalonia.'

He shaved and washed the blood off his hair, and looked all right again. He walked with me to the main road for France; we held hands and I believed everything he said. He'd come to Paris the day after tomorrow and I should wait for him at the Gare d'Austerlitz at 8.12 in the morning. He gave me a handful of coins and a hundred peseta note and stopped the first vehicle, a lorry.

He lifted his hand as I was driven away. I'd been thrown out of paradise and I didn't even know it.

15

I next saw José three years later, in 1958. My life was very different, and I certainly wasn't in the circus. When I thought of the Residencia Internacional days I knew they were tinged with decadence, mystery, and deceit, but it had been heaven on earth. Of course some of it was too painful. I cut a lot out.

I'd been accepted at the Royal Academy of Dramatic Art in London and was about to start a two-year acting course. I'd been lucky getting work – modelling jobs, fashion and photographic, chorus line – and I'd just finished a season in repertory theatre. I lived in Chelsea in an artistic house owned by a mathematician, Dr Cooke. It had once been the house of the painter Alma Tadema. After his pianist wife died, Dr Cooke wanted the right sort of company, and let out rooms for five shillings a week to young women of quality who had something to do with the arts. He wanted good conversation, chaste behaviour, a pleasing atmosphere. This community became a hive of obsession for male artists at that time, such as Lucien Freud, and many of the girls met their future husbands, and/or fathers of their children, outside the Gunter Grove premises. Dr Cooke kept a decorous house and did not want the intrusion of these virile interlopers. He liked to have six girls renting at a time. The one obligation was for each girl to spend an evening a week with him at one of his favourite pubs or restaurants. Choosing the right girls who would get on with him and also each other was a concern.

I was the wrong choice, and going out with a Sicilian doctor who worked most of the time in Rome. It was very alive and authentic in Chelsea in those days just before the shallow, gilded revolution of the sixties.

I got a small part in a production in Sloane Square. One day after rehearsals I did not meet Dr Cooke for the required outing to Salamis in the Fulham Road, nor did I phone the doctor in Rome. I veered off to Victoria Station and took the boat train to Paris. I always carried my passport, which had become a joke for those around me, including the doctor, although it was not so funny for him afterwards.

For my eighteenth birthday he'd given me £100, a fortune in those days, and at first I was delighted. I bought everything I thought I wanted and then those things that might change my life. I spent the lot. I'd never felt so empty. I didn't realize you could feel empty just buying things. Was it this that set me off on the old tracks? I wasn't even thinking about Girona, but the wanderlust was still inside me, if subdued, because of what I'd experienced in 1955. And it was very different without Beryl.

I decided to stay in Paris but it was no longer a fresh experience. The memories were waiting like creditors before I'd even got into the station. I realized that places kept the consequences of what had happened, so it wasn't about new territory, a high aliveness, any more. I'd had a too terrible time that last run through Paris, after José never showed at the Gare d'Austerlitz. I walked away fast from that memory, and eventually crossed over to the Left

Bank. Instead of going into the unknown I was re-meeting myself on every corner.

I sat on the terrace of the Café de Flore, and had to remind myself I could afford to eat and drink these days. Refusing to be more depressed, I ordered a life-lover's meal. Then I looked across at the Hotel Tarrane, and was sure I could see the Frenchwoman from Girona standing in the doorway. When I crossed the street she'd gone. I even went into the brasserie opposite to see if she'd gone in there.

It was probably that which made me take the night train south. I'd had some good things happen since I'd returned to London, a lot of luck, but nothing touched the joyousness of those early days in Girona. I'd realized that when I was spending the £100, and it had put me on the train to the past.

I arrived at the Residencia in the late afternoon and couldn't go in. I was scared to see him changed or with someone else. He could have slipped out of his exquisite skin and become ordinary. He could be not there. Then Manolo came out of the dairy, carrying plastic bottles of Leche Ram milk and glass ones of chocolate milk. He was eight sizes thinner and an immeasurable amount older. As he said, Spanish prisons were no health cures. They'd got him for attending a political meeting on the night the police chief came looking for José. He kept saying how pretty I looked, much more beautiful than before. All I wanted was the answer to my question to be positive.

'But he's here. Where else would he be? He can't leave Girona either.' And we climbed the well-remembered stairs together.

The door of the official *salon* opened and José stood against the wall like part of a dream, the perfect tin sun behind him. Then his eyes lit up and he came towards me with a soft tread. It was as though we'd never been apart. The time in between did not exist. He said he wasn't surprised.

'I've often thought you'd come back.'

'You never contacted me.' How could he? I'd never sent a message or an address.

'Oh, but I did,' he said warmly. Then he touched my head. 'By thought.' He clapped his hands. 'Come on, Manolo. Where are the drinks? She's back.'

We had dinner at the Cal Ros, which had become even smarter, and soon all the friends knew I was back and gathered around the table. José had a fatal charm. Given what would happen to some of the people involved with him, the adjective is not overdone. There was no sign of a girlfriend.

Then the young man who was preparing to be a priest sat next to me and reminded me of his name, Quim Carreras. He looked at my throat. 'The last time I saw you before you left Girona you wore a gold cross and chain.'

It was José's and had been sold off long ago. Pep Colomer gave me his chain with a stone, put it around my neck, and spoke kindly. 'You don't need adornments. But this belonged to my mother and holds a lot of love. I want you to have it.'

I thought he was also trying to draw attention away from what was missing. I could see Quim's eyes on me, grey, assessing, as though he was going to go on about the cross and chain again.

I told them some of what I was doing and the good news about drama school, but my language was unpractised and difficult. I breathed the air of another world that they for now had no hope of entering, and I supposed my freedom must have been attractive. I noticed at another table a grey-haired elegant man with blue eyes, not Catalan, probably from Northern Europe. I'd seen him before but always in the background. And I remembered Beryl and wondered if this was the man who'd given her the money.

After a walk through the old part we went to Lluís's bar near the cathedral. It was small, simple, with good jazz on a modern system. He'd opened the previous year and, once he'd got it under way, would start writing. He put logs on the fire and cooked sausages.

Quim Carreras asked how things had been in Paris, how long had I been there. It was all about Paris and whom I'd met. He was joined by an older man, scholarly and cold, not one of the old crowd. He seemed to be listening to my answers.

'What kind of people did you see? French? Did you know them? From here?' He meant when I'd left in 1955.

I thought the other one said, 'Ask her about Cocteau.'

'Why are you so curious?' I asked.

'Because it's interesting how you get by. Most people need contacts and support.'

After the recent unexpected assault of memory on every Parisian street, I thought I might be one of his 'most people' after all. It seemed every painful moment had left an imprint.

'I thought I saw the Frenchwoman,' I told José. He looked at me, eyes piercing into mine. I had nothing more to say on that subject.

'Have some more coffee, some cake.' He could have added, 'Keep eating and shut up.'

Quim Carreras, always within earshot, asked, 'What did she say to you?'

'Nothing,' said José, 'she's not in Paris.'

'Oh, but she is,' Quim Carreras deftly responded. And to me, 'What did she say, by the way?'

José, alert now, tapped my leg.

'She said how much she liked you.' And I gave him the wide model smile, filled with emptiness. 'She said it's a pity he's a priest.'

The scholar got a good laugh out of that. They all did. Although they seemed occupied, the whole bar was listening to this interrogation. José soothed it down. 'Patrice has never seen the Frenchwoman.'

There was a lot of talk and laughter that night, but I only really saw and heard José.

16

He left the bar eventually and I could see he still loved the atmosphere of a group, whereas all I wanted was to be alone with him. He gave me his sweater and held me, and I wondered if this was the moment to introduce the Parisian betrayal. He would expect it, but I felt this moment was leading to better, happier moments, perhaps the closeness I'd always wanted. We walked back through the starving-cat alley and the old poster was more worn, parts of it not even visible. I felt marvellous again. I belonged to him. A simple walk with him in a squalid alley could do it. He could make anything magical. The high moments were touched with something from the past, a past I was not sure belonged to this century at all. It hinted at other, more sensuous times. He said we'd known each other before. The supernatural was a dimension of life not even to be questioned.

So I questioned it. How did he know?

'Oh, I have proof,' he said, lightly. 'Life gives it to me.'

He said he was trying to free Catalonia in a different way by encouraging artists and writers to fight through their work for their identity. He was organizing fiestas, exhibitions, theatre. Soon there would be money around. Tourism was beginning. He showed me a large empty building. 'This will be the biggest gallery in the province and will show Catalan work. It's my idea and I will run it. The Fontana d'Or. Do you like the name? The Golden Fountain.'

I was suddenly desperately tired.

'Let's have a drink,' and he crossed the road to a workman's bar. Openly he touched my hand. I'd come back. So the past was now in place. So was the warmth. Another brandy got the rest of the night fuelled up and my questions were greedy. I wanted to take in as much of him as I could. The fabulous smile was there in spite of the missing tooth. Was he with someone? It was easily done. Hadn't I done it?

He laughed, cynically. 'I saved that for you.'

'So we can be together?'

'Of course.'

I was happy until he said, 'When the time is right.'

I had my old room in the Residencia, opposite his. He kissed me briefly and prepared to leave, but I held on to him, wanting him to stay.

He moved to the door. 'I have only two minutes, I regret. There is somewhere I have to be.'

'Isn't there always?' I replied, sharply.

He swept his hands up through his hair. 'You have come here at the very worst time. I cannot get involved with a woman. I am sorry.'

I'd have challenged him about Paris, but he'd got the door open.

'My life is not something you want to get involved in. I'm not good for a woman.'

'But of course not. Perhaps you like men.'

'No, I'll leave those to you.' He pointed at the Sicilian's gold bangle and was gone. No one got the better of him on an exit.

I sat in the dark listening to the cathedral bells dividing up the last of the night. I couldn't rest, so went to find Manolo. As I turned out of the passage I saw José and a soldier go into one of the bedrooms and close the door. The stealth, the intimacy of it made me blaze with jealousy. But there was nothing I could do except spend the rest of the night in torment. In the morning I was going to leave and then realized there was something familiar about the soldier. It was Quico Sabater without the beard.

Of course I didn't see things the way they were. The town had been in trouble; men had been jailed or taken off in the night and shot. When people said 'Madrid,' they spat. But I saw the town through José's eyes.

Some of the old places were gone and I had to crisscross the bridges and the Rambla to find one favourite, the Café l'Antiga, opposite the town hall. I sat at the marble-topped table and took care of my exhaustion with nourishing home-cooked food. Espriu, the poet, was standing at the counter. I only noticed him when he was leaving. I asked him to join me but he had to get a train for Arenys de Mar. I asked if he'd sorted out the business of the hotel he and José had talked about in Arenys.

'That's been closed two years.'

'What happened to the owner?' He didn't seem to have lasted long.

'He left. But ...' Then he wondered if he should be talking at all. So I gave him a little help and mentioned Maria Tourdes and her swollen legs.

'But the press got it. He went to them with a treasure story and the too-rich priest.'

'Why?'

'To get clients for his hotel, I suppose. But it brought hordes of treasure seekers. The mayor stopped it. It's quiet now. The only way it can be …' And he was gone.

The light in the old quarter was off-key and melancholy. It was tinged with sadness.

I walked to the top of Girona and, below, the new part glowed extraordinary and sinister. The countryside began immediately on the other side of the broken wall, said to be at least 3,000 years old. The neighbourhoods on the plain where the poor lived were drawn up by the force of the light as though by binoculars, every tawdry, sad detail visible. Beside me, a crowded cemetery. I seemed to be in a place where life and death met and agreed what should remain. The wall was certainly one survivor. Even I could see the neighbourhoods looked precarious.

I heard a knocking of metal on stone and moved into the trees. This put the house with the tower on view and Quim Carreras with several men removing part of the wall by the brown, cracked door. Was she there? I recalled his interest in the cross and chain I'd hocked and how I was wearing it, he'd insisted, the last time he saw me. That was impossible. José put the cross around my neck as the decision was made for me to go on ahead to Paris. Paris – it did not wish me well. The bad times – they made you strong.

Pep Colomer left the group of men and came towards me. He led me down a narrow track, so I did not pass the house. I asked why he'd given me the stone belonging to his mother. I suggested it was to divert the interest of the novice priest Carreras.

'Stay out of it,' Pep warned. 'Especially the business of the cross and chain. They want to know what you did with it. Don't tell them anything.'

'Them?'

'Just give them a story.'

'I'll go and see the Frenchwoman.'

'She's not there. She can't help you.'

José was waiting in the hotel and said we should eat at Chez Béatrice. I told him about the extraordinary melancholy light in the streets, and how it brought back a sense of the past that was gone yet too strong to just be extinguished.

'But of course. Powerful events took place here.'

'Wars?' It didn't feel like that.

'Spiritual travel through time and place, so that Girona is forever connected to these other realms.'

'Who did this travel?' Perhaps my journeys should no longer be geographical.

'The mystics in the Middle Ages and before. This place has witnessed extraordinary events that are beyond human expectation. And less than a hundred years ago certain mystically inclined individuals came here and repeated these ceremonies – for their own grandiosity perhaps. And, in their pursuit of "direct knowing" of the divine, they let slip the earthly love, which was a gift beyond anything and that caused such tumult and such pain. Even death couldn't end it.'

Was he talking about himself? Had he been the victim of a grandiose mystic? And then I said laughing, 'It sounds like you and me.'

'Yes.' He wasn't laughing. 'What we share sometimes echoes what happened then. Of that I am sure. And we can never talk about it because what happened is cursed.'

I asked if he had known the people concerned.

'I knew the woman.'

I waited for him to say more. He didn't, so I asked who she was.

'It's not something anyone should talk about. I will answer one question and it will only lead to another.'

I knew it was the Frenchwoman.

'I have to protect my cousin, Geli.' He patted my arm and that was the end of it. For him.

I told him that Quim Carreras could not have seen me wearing the cross and chain. So why did he ask about it? He didn't expect that question.

'It was valuable.'

Where had he got it?

'Got it? It's mine. It belonged to a ...' He paused. 'A family, and it was blessed. It went through a certain ceremony, which makes it special. It brings protection to the wearer, and good luck. So, of course, I gave it to you.'

'How did he know I had it? How did he know you weren't wearing it?'

'He must have noticed it wasn't around my neck and assumed I'd given it to you.'

'So he sees you naked. I thought he was a priest. Oh, but of course that fits.'

For a moment I knew he was going to slap me. He had a choice. He laughed instead, and the moment was over.

'You must have been through some hard times to get that bangle.' He pointed at my arm.

'No. The man who gave it to me is hard.'

And sometimes that hardness healed my spirit. It was a cool medicinal compress over too much emotion I didn't know what to do with.

I was glad when Quim Carreras came into Chez Béatrice with his friends, because I wanted my turn with the questions. He spoke English, so I could keep it away from José.

'Why did you think the cross and chain you mentioned was around my throat?'

'Because José gave it to you.'

'You said you saw it.'

'José had it, and then he didn't have it. It coincided with your leaving Girona.'

I thought priests weren't supposed to lie. I sensed he was a formidable opponent. I'd stick with what I safely knew. 'Do you check his body for lost jewels?'

Carreras laughed. 'I was told by someone who would know that he no longer wore the cross.'

'Someone who would know.' It allowed a host of jealous possibilities to present themselves. Stay away from that, said my wise mind.

'Did you give him the cross? Should I pay you something for it?'

'You couldn't.' And I think he tried to hide the anger. 'It is beyond price.'

I tried to remember what it looked like. A light, bright chain and a heavy cross, not plain. I was sure it had some decoration. It didn't have gems. I'd have remembered those.

And then I had a better idea. 'Is it because of who it belonged to? Does that make it valuable?'

'Exactly. Where is it?'

I'd given it to a man in Montparnasse for the price of a meal. He said, give me something, and it was all I had. José hadn't made me aware of any special value.

I remembered Pep Colomer's advice: Give them a story.

'I never had it.'

This seemed to distract him, so I asked if he knew the Frenchwoman well.

'All my life.'

I asked what she was like.

'But you knew her,' he replied, eventually. 'You met her twice.'

'Why were you taking her wall apart? I saw you today.'

'To see if it's hollow,' he said. 'Parts of the house have hollow walls and let the water in. She's away, so I look after it.'

I didn't believe him. His words sounded more hollow than any wall.

'What do you know about Maria?' he asked, softly.

I didn't answer.

By now Carreras, a companion of his, and I were walking into Lluís's bar and José was talking to the group at the back. Carreras and his friend had me to themselves.

'What did she tell you?' Carreras pressed on.

'Why did she have to leave?' I asked.

His turn to be silent. His companion was busy giving him advice.

'She seemed alone,' I said.

He agreed with that. 'It must be hard after the life she knew. She had a real love affair. It makes contemporary ones seem so threadbare.'

At that moment a striking woman, dressed completely in gold – shoes, dress, earrings, bag – walked into the bar. She was wonderfully made-up and a little liquor high, which made her eyes sparkle. Her name was Lucia Stilman. Was she the girlfriend?

I could only watch as José moved up to her, not even thinking to disguise his pleasure.

Lucia was vibrant and rich like a gold bar, gold of high quality that you couldn't afford and could only covet from a distance. She was out of the range of most people. Even her make-up was gold, and her shoes with their skyscraper heels like gold ingots. She reminded me of a mythical city of gold from ancient times. Even the tone of her voice was rich, yes golden, and her laughter full of coins. She spent time on José, couldn't be bothered with the others. We were introduced and I kept my gold bangle, a mere beggar in this company, out of sight. She seemed impatient and then she hit the bar, got settled on a barstool, and Lluís put a serious drink in front of her and she was at ease. I watched her glass full of chinking ice constantly refilled, and she became luminous, exuberant, and we were all part of the next round. She'd accept anything by this point and then the next drink took her over the top and she shrank into herself, voice slurred. The gold still gleamed nobly and was loyal.

'She is a barfly,' said Quim Carreras.

I knew he'd be the one to make that remark.

Lluís talked to her ironically about Spanish politics and made her laugh.

'She is marvellous,' said José.

And I knew she wasn't the girlfriend.

'She is as fragile as a golden butterfly,' said Umberto, the Italian writer. He was not too sober either. Nobody was sober.

'Is the Frenchwoman coming back to Girona?' I asked Carreras.

'José would know that. I'm sure she writes to him.'

'Did she sleep with him?'

Carreras's companion laughed and suddenly discovered he could speak English. 'If she paid enough. It is for the freedom of Catalonia, so I hear, so I'm sure he gives a bit extra.' He thought he'd shocked me and waited for a reaction.

'Why did she go?' I tried to sound calm.

'Ask Miss Midas,' he said. 'She has all the answers. I think Maria wanted a bigger life. This is so provincial.

There are people of her quality in Paris.' He was doing all the talking.

'Why did she live here?'

Lluís answered that one. 'Because she couldn't leave.'

'Oh, we don't talk about that here,' said Lucia, raising her glass. 'Why do you think I'm covered in gold? This is the place for it.' And her laughter was playful again and full of coins.

I looked at the objects in his room, picked them up, held them as though they'd give me the answers, supply what I needed to know and calm my torn heart. One of them was a document with strange symbols and writing on it. It seemed to be another instruction to do with the journey of light.

'Your friend Lucia has a problem with drink.' I didn't like the way he'd let her kiss him goodbye.

'Not at all,' he said. 'She just likes it.' He was lying on his bed, hands behind his head, covered with money that I'd thrown at him.

'Carreras tells me you screw women for money.'

'Surely not, if I'm homosexual?'

'What do you actually do?'

'You might say I restore the past. Madrid is always trying to tear down a medieval building to put up a tourist cafeteria. If I can keep one thing still standing I'm lucky.'

'Do you have sex with women?'

How he wanted to deny it. He didn't know how much I knew. Who'd been saying what in that smoky, drunken bar.

'Not in a way that means anything.'

Furious, jealous, I told him he'd fucked up my life. And once again I'd lose out. I was thinking of the Sicilian lover.

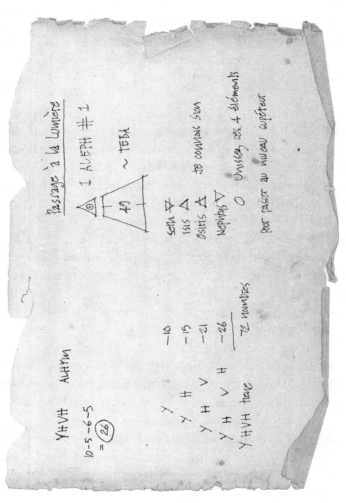

Document found in José's room

'And what do you think you do to mine? You put me into shit up to here!' He gestured at his throat. 'You bring me …' He couldn't think of a word bad enough and had to rely on a Spanish one I didn't know. 'Because I was with you, my mother cut me out of her will. I've lost my share of this hotel because I would not give you up. I could have been married perhaps.'

'The "perhaps" is the significant word in that sentence. Still, I didn't make you sleep with guys. I saw the soldier chum last night. I would say that was your main problem, not shares in a hotel and a bourgeois wife.'

He denied it, so I described the soldier in some detail. José bit his lip. So many lies must have come to mind he didn't know which one to use. 'So what. He had nowhere to sleep, so I let him have somewhere free.'

'And you had to sleep with him. Is that part of the "free"?'

He was off the bed, slapping the table so all the objects, letters, and photographs that were in disarray slid into a kind of frightened tidiness. I saw a letter signed 'your friend Maria'. The brooch, or priest's ring, was no longer there.

'Keep your voice down. We don't have the luxury of free speech in this place. Go back to your glamorous life.'

'Maybe it wasn't a soldier last night but Sabater, dressed up as one. He's great at disguises, and you're good with the women, so I hear. As long as they pay.'

He tried to slap me, and the row really began.

17

José's bed had not been slept in and on the coverlet I found a crumpled paper, which I picked up eagerly, thinking it was a note to me. What had he decided at some point in that hostile night and then reconsidered in the sweet freshness of the earliest morning? It wasn't his writing. It seemed to be part of a letter in French on old, coloured, and expensive paper:

Sometimes in the evening I sit on the wall of the garden and look over the town to Canigou and remember all that was in this garden, the richness, the joy. It seems from another world, and me, that person then, I can hardly reach now. It only makes me sad if I do. To think I had so much and now it is only reached by memory which is uncertain. Was he wrong or right?

Not written to José, not a love letter. The handwriting was choppy and its content echoed exactly everything I felt. The joy of those original days in Girona, followed by the writer's final question that so fitted mine about José. Except that for 'right' or 'wrong' I'd put 'good' or 'bad'. I wasn't sure it was from Maria Tourdes.

Manolo was playing cards in the bar opposite and said José was at a reunion. Political? That word got him up from the table and over to the doorway. What sort of reunion? He didn't know. Social? He shook his head. How long would it take? His arms opened generously. Any time. In the privacy of the street, he said, 'There were people from France and rich ones from the province, and professional ones from this town. The top drawer.' He added it had happened before. 'A ceremony.'

'In the Residencia?' I remembered the basement.

'Oh no. A private house. It used to be part of a palace.'

In the late afternoon, I saw José crossing the square with the cafés and restaurants, by the river. I was beside myself with rage. And then I saw his face. He was, for him, pale. It was the first time I'd seen him shaky. He breathed unevenly and kept clearing his throat.

'I'm sorry,' he said.

Anger all gone, I was only concerned for him. A drink? Sit on a bench? A hospital? He took my arm and held onto it and we got as far as the Devesa. Then he gripped his head. 'The sound. It keeps on.' He walked a few more steps as though trying to hurry away from what was inside him. Then he fell forward, face down onto the ground. Before I could even realize my full fright he was up again, on his feet, as though taking part in a slapstick comedy. Into the Rosaleda restaurant. A quick drink. Another. All strong.

'What happened?'

'A loss of consciousness. I don't know.' His colour was back. He seemed all right.

'Has it happened before?'

Another cognac pushed more colour into his face.

'What is the noise in your head? Is it from the ceremony?'

He wouldn't sit down. I asked what sort of noise.

'I can't describe it. It's not like anything I know.'

'Has it been like this at other ceremonies?'

'No.' And then he said something I never thought I'd hear. 'I'm in trouble.'

'I'll help you.' Help him? I'd die for him. I was going to suggest leaving Girona, but we'd tried that one.

As though knowing my thoughts, he said, 'I can't leave.'

'I will help you.'

'I wish.' And he tossed back a last drink, walked out, didn't even pay, and Lucia Stilman was suddenly beside him. I was sure she told him not to say anything in front of me.

She was dressed in pale daytime gold, which had cost more than a year of my life. On top, a wisp of yellow fishnet with long voluminous sleeves and a hood hanging down at the back, lined with silk. The effect was ethereal. Make-up did all it was meant to do and the hairdresser had done the rest. She looked as though she was *en route* between the last hangover and the next high.

'I should not do this,' he said. 'You have to be strong and on a certain level to be there at all.'

'What level?' I got that in fast before she started covering it all up.

'Evolved.'

He didn't seem drunk, but she held his arm as many had hers, and we walked back towards the Residencia. She assured me he was all right, just tired.

I asked what the ceremony was, exactly.

'It's not good,' he said. 'It must be stopped.' And he stopped. 'People get too greedy. They want to go too far, be too empowered. With power they should not have.'

Lucia said, 'All they think about is money and the look of the thing.'

I thought she was one to talk.

'But I have it. The secret.'

'Yes, José.' She tried to get him walking.

'It's in these walls. Hidden behind a wall.'

She thought, not unwisely, that he was drunk and should be home.

We crossed a bridge, untidily, and reached the Rambla.

'He's had a shock,' she explained.

I asked if we should get a doctor.

She became agitated. 'Not any doctor. Good God, I'll get Dr Baró.'

José didn't want doctors, suitable or not. He'd go and sit by himself in the Frenchwoman's garden. And suddenly he went ahead of us, fast up the carrer de la Força.

'Now, perhaps they'll stop this.' She wasn't listening to me. I tried to ask about the sound, the one that filled his head unbearably. She was puzzled. 'Sound? What sound?'

I tried to describe it.

'Speak English. I've lived in New York.'

Then Umberto and his friends greeted her and invited us for a drink. She couldn't wait to get away to that barstool.

Emilio was sitting in the Savoy Bar, drinking a mixed-fruit drink with hot water. His hair was streaked with grey and he was well toned, thin, with a beautiful posture. He trained some top Barcelona players now and rarely came to Girona. When he did, he still stayed at the Residencia.

The conversation turned to the usual subject.

'So you've come back for José. You'll have to get him away from that mother.'

I asked about girlfriends.

'Not if the mother can help it. She wants him pure.'

'What about Lucia Stilman?'

He didn't know much about her, except her bank balance. She had an enviable inheritance and was married to the owner of one of the big drinks companies in Italy.

'José's mother wants him to join a religious order. It's not one I've heard of. José's family is rich. They're all involved in the church. His uncle owns jewellery shops, another is a lawyer. They did well at university and mix with the right people. They've always had a connection with France. There are stories about that family. Secret practices. I don't believe it, so I won't go into it. All I'll say is, José isn't what he seems and the camouflage is wearing thin.'

I asked Emilio if he knew Sabater.

'Of course not. He hides out in France.'

So they'd been under the same roof and Emilio hadn't known it.

I went back to the Residencia and José was in his room sorting through papers. I told him something of my conversation with Emilio. He didn't much like it.

'Emilio is jealous. Always has been. Why would you go to him for explanations about something as precious as the past?'

'So the past is precious all of a sudden?'

'Infinitely more than the present.' And he really looked at me then, his eyes passing through my clothes, skin, all the frivolous things that would change until he located what had first attracted him, a feeling of joy that was not unfamiliar. Then he said we'd known each other before, had met up again for better or for worse.

'Do you remember taking a cart full of ice to Tossa de Mar?'

I could still see the chunks of ice gleaming in the sun. I didn't want to be an extraordinary actress or live in Hollywood. I wanted the past back. The cart had been drawn by a slow, brown horse. José had worn a dark blue shirt, and I remembered that around his neck hung the gold cross and chain. I asked who it had belonged to. 'My great-uncle gave it to me.' He did some throat-clearing. 'It came into our family.'

'Was it the Frenchwoman's?'

'You don't want to get into that. Quim Carreras is right.'

'Why did you make the Frenchwoman leave?' I remembered the pile of money on the table.

'Because I was worried for my cousin Geli. I had to protect him.'

'Why? Was he in love with her? It runs in the family. Impossible love affairs.'

Full of charm, he agreed.

I noticed a pile of documents in the corner. They looked legal.

'Why were you worried for your cousin?'

'Because of a story. It's a long time ago.'

He didn't stop me as I looked at letters from Maria Tourdes, and asked why she wrote to him. He came up with a reason, something about keeping contact with Girona. It had meant a lot to her. I knew what he was saying was not even meant to fob me off. He no longer cared what I believed.

In one letter Maria Tourdes wrote that 'if the truth ever got out it would be unholy and we were accursed.' And she only knew a portion of all that had gone on. She used 'unholy' again and the blackness it would bring to the world. And I realized we weren't looking at protecting cousins here but something that was bigger than us, for which the word 'accursed' was not overdone.

Under the letter was a design like a pyramid with names I could not know rising up from the bottom. And there were numbers and equations. The top word was Jov.

He almost grabbed the paper and placed it on the pile of legal documents and covered it with a heavy book.

'What language is it?' I asked.

'Egyptian, or ancient Hebrew.'

There was another, dated 1910, with the same design but Maria's name on it. It said, 'I guard the secret and I ask of God exclusively.'

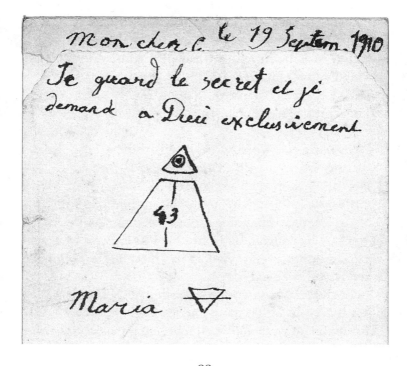

And I recognized on the pile of old, stained books the train timetable from Maria Tourdes's dining room. He said he was looking after her things for now. I asked about the priest's ring.

'Oh, I expect it will go in a museum.' And he signed whatever he was writing.

I asked for her address so I could visit her in Paris. I'd already seen it on the letterhead.

'She's not there,' he said, automatically. 'She goes to Belgium. She travels.'

He came with me to the station and we had a drink in the buffet. They were building a large new station further down the line to deal with the expected tourist trade. A lot of the old places would go. Chez Béatrice would be a hamburger café. And I saw the elegant grey-haired man pass through the station and asked José who he was. José turned slightly, said he hadn't seen him.

I changed the subject. 'Your mother did a good job. She doesn't want anyone having you.'

'No, that's not right.' I'd not seen him so forthright. 'I have responsibilities and I should take care of them. That concerns her. You've become hard. It must be your environment.' Eyes on the bangle again. 'It's taken you over.'

'We had no money,' he added.

'You could have used some of the pile I carried for Sabater.'

'That money is not for me. I would never touch one peseta. It keeps alive the ones who can really do something.'

'So you'll spend it on Sabater but not on me.'

I didn't hear what he replied. As I got onto the train I believed he'd have sold me into hell for his province. He kissed me warmly. 'We are on some magnetic path so we will be together. I am absolutely sure.'

For a moment the sun was behind his head and it glowed around him like a halo, which he certainly didn't deserve. I didn't think Lucifer had a spit big enough to put him on.

'Don't judge me,' he said. 'I don't judge you.'

'Are you good or bad? I must know, José.'

But the train pulled out and I talked to my aching heart like a baby. 'I'll never see him again. That's for sure,' I promised.

But I'd already sacrificed my heart by laying it out on Girona's narrow streets. By rights he should have been mine.

18

When I married, in 1961, I remembered saying not exactly a prayer, more a message of gratitude to God and the universe that at last I knew happiness with someone I loved and I would protect it with my life. Being with him was like stepping inside to a calm place, out of the storm.

After having my first child, I was ill and it was decided that when I'd recovered I should go for a holiday. My friend Stewart, an actor from Manchester, was about to start a job as a travel rep for a package firm on the Costa Brava, so I went with him. I tried to reach José, contacting everyone I knew in Girona. Most of them now had telephones. He was gone. No one had seen him for months, maybe two years. 'The bird has flown,' Lluís laughed.

Stewart and I stayed in a traditional hotel with good food on the shore near Cadaqués, and he made me laugh from the first moment of the morning. These new tourists who were opening up the Costa Brava, wanting only fish and chips, made his job laughable. Girona was no longer part of my memory, let alone my life.

At some point Stewart had to go to Barcelona, and at the last minute I went with him. It was agreed with the taxi driver that the sea route was the most pleasant, although longer. Passing through a resort, Calella, the taxi started to bump disagreeably. A petrol leak? The driver brought us to a halt and got out.

'It's the wheel,' and Stewart opened his door.

A black stone had pierced the tyre and was stuck. The wheel would have to be changed. I asked what Calella was like. Not worth looking at. Idly, I crossed the dusty road to stand in some shade. There was no one about, not even a cat, and it was too silent. I turned into a side street. A man was leaning sensuously against the wall. He was looking right at me. The man was José.

He said he was waiting for a man from Barcelona to take him to a sanctuary in Ripoll. That's what it sounded like. He hadn't been in Girona much, staying near the Pyrenees. He'd had a book of poems published and the exhibition centre, the Fontana d'Or, was under construction. Lluís's bar was doing well, so now he was too rich to write his novel. I didn't say I was happy. I didn't even tell him about the baby.

I got back into the taxi. He didn't let go of the door. 'Why don't you stay? Barcelona will be too hot for you. Your friend can pick you up on the way back.'

We were now into dangerous talk.

'Don't you want to see Girona?'

All I could see were my husband's eyes, beautiful and glittering like diamonds. They could be as hard.

When José and I got to Girona, a letter from the French-woman Maria Tourdes changed his plans. She'd asked him to visit urgently and he asked if I'd take the night train to Paris with him. While he made the arrangements I waited in a local bar where old men watched the over-loud television and played cards. I recognized Manolo, his face over-bright in some places and too dark in others like a Hallowe'en lantern. He was old when José and I first met.

'Ah, the English girl!' He admired my clothes, which still gave me a certain Bohemian style.

He said he hadn't seen José much lately, but couldn't be sure where he'd been. 'The mother wanted him to go into a seminary. But not an ordinary one, you understand.'

'Where?'

'Up beyond Ripoll in the Pyrenees. And have instruction from a master. Not a priest as such. Certainly not the Roman Catholic Church. That has to be unusual; they're in business, José's family.'

'Did he go?'

'He doesn't say, but he's been out of Girona months at a time.'

Manolo limped into the street behind me as I left the bar, and said something as though answering a question. 'I don't think his way of life is suitable for a woman. He hasn't the time to be domestic.'

I was glad I'd seen Manolo, because I had a child and a husband and I needed to be domestic.

In Paris I noticed he'd brought a folder of documents and letters, and a bag of photographs jumbled together. He also had papers for Maria to sign and said they had to do with the house. The mayor wanted it sold.

'She says she's without money, so this is not such a bad idea. She always says she has nothing.'

A woman in Girona had been looking after Maria's business affairs on and off in the last years. It seemed she had not gone back since I saw her preparing to leave in 1955.

He asked me to wait in the Café de Flore while he met Jean Cocteau, saying he'd only be a few minutes. Over an hour later I left the café and started towards the taxi rank by the Brasserie LIPP. He caught up with me as I queued for a taxi.

'For a Spaniard, a few minutes can mean anything. You should know that.' He said he'd had private business with the French director, and that we would have dinner with him that night.

As far as I was concerned, that night did not come into it. I was on my way home to London from Spain. I'd just decided to go via Paris at the last minute.

Maria Tourdes's apartment was on the other bank, and José didn't leave me in a café this time. Although she was ill the reception room was filled with people smoking and talking, intellectuals mostly. It was a substantial flat, ageing gracefully, in a state of slight disrepair with beautiful things. There were gaps of placid whiteness on the walls where photographs had been taken down. I recognized the dark, rough-looking woman from Girona. She said she was a friend of Lucia Stilman, who had called to see Maria earlier that day. I was introduced to a French writer, much younger than the other guests, and he kept talking about a Madame Mathieu. I didn't know who he meant. It seemed also he was preparing a thesis on one distant aspect of Maria's life and had been worried her protective friends would put a stop to it. Now there seemed to be an even worse adversary – death. He asked how long José would be. Judging by my earlier wait in the café, any time at all.

The bedroom door opened and José waved for me to go in. Maria was sitting up in bed, but exhausted. The shutters were partially closed but I could see old age had arrived and, although roughly covered with make-up, could not but be acknowledged. It was a shock, which I hoped I kept to myself.

She remembered me but didn't speak. José did the talking and she watched him as though wanting to take in, absorb, his life-love. Just some of it. She told him how much she had wanted to see him before things got worse. It was her first wish. She sounded as clear and calm as ever.

'Worse?' He wasn't having that. She'd had flu and was tired. It was natural. He was with her and nothing bad would happen.

On the floor were framed photographs, most of them facing the wall. I supposed they were the ones that had been taken down from the room next door.

He helped her sign two serious documents and, as her hand took the pen, a ring she had been holding fell and rolled down the bedcover. I saw the burned metal and the initials BS.

I was sure Maria Tourdes had given José some rights. I kept seeing his hand holding hers so the pen stayed on the paper. I thought at first it might be her property in Girona, but then assumed that would require a lawyer's presence.

José asked what she planned to say to the keen young writer.

'My life – why not. Someone will get it sometime.'

He didn't like that reply.

'No one gets anything, Maria. We both know biographies are novels in disguise.' He said the party in the next room should continue elsewhere and he would send them all away.

'Just leave the priest,' she said.

Outside, and the sun was still there. José was too attractive, and I watched as his hand just did not touch mine. His eyes matched mine, the intensity unsuitable, this look

I'd wanted since the day I was born. And I turned and walked fast, faster, remember this is Paris, it does not wish you well, it will strip you of everything. And I did not look back.

Back in my life in London, I believed I had the safety to evaluate the chance meeting in Calella. Yet I did not feel safe. I'd always believed fate was kind. I thought it came along with God and the inevitable. It was bigger than I so it had to be on my side. I didn't know that in some cases it should be fought to the death. José came along, one of fate's little gifts, and for years it pleased me to say 'Well, he was fated'. There was nothing I could do about it. Meeting him because a black stone damaged the taxi wheel – yes, fate could be said to have had a hand in it. Seeing him on that side street was not altogether a surprise. I felt the life which had gone before was merely a waiting time for that moment.

In Girona, the light of the street had put on all its best colours. That kind of light got me into trouble. José loved his town more than he could ever love a woman or himself. He would protect it from the rape of Madrid with his life if necessary. Catalan history was spotted with charismatic figures who, bearing the secret of the stones, cherished and defended it. They were a product of the soil and the wind. After all, myths and religions had flourished there.

19

When the reality of Girona became memory, it seemed even more vibrant. Perhaps that was how legends were started. José had always been out of reach. I had never possessed him except perhaps in those moments when he came suddenly into my mind. Then I'd find him very near, as though he was all around me. Good things happened in the mid-sixties and I had my share of celebration, but somehow the top note of high happiness was missing. José was the one to open the champagne with. He would come to me, almost visible, his presence in a rain-soaked summer London street. The smell of wet June leaves would bring him instantly – so did the occasional smell of wood smoke, and then I'd promise I'd find a way to go back there. Just once. I had a good marriage, and the longing passed. I had another son in 1966. I'd started writing and that took over from acting, and I sold first a short story to the *London Magazine* and then a novel in the US and England. And then José came to London.

His visit had to do with some cup or artefact being put up for sale at an auction, and he was instructed to get it back. He played it down. Some precious ornament from his family. A mistake had been made. I never saw it, but I knew he'd paid a lot of money for it.

He was 37, unmarried, still staying mostly with his mother. His father had died and the days of the Residencia were over. It was now in the hands of his sister's husband and had nothing to do with artists or writers, and would not last. I asked what he was doing and he mentioned the Fontana d'Or and writers from the old days such as Umberto Eco, who was writing a novel about monks to be entitled *The Name of the Rose*.

He was happy, he said, that my life was as I wanted it to be. He got on well with my friends, especially Richard Cobb, the historian, and his wife Margaret. Richard thought a lot of José, and they sat up many nights drinking and talking. José had an originality that Richard approved of, and he suggested a position at Oxford on Catalan poetry.

Before José left London, he said, 'You can't lose what really belongs to you. Even if you throw it away.'

I'd always known José wasn't just a love affair. He was a gift, and an extraordinary delight in a life which had been quite often low on delights. Now I'd seen him again I knew nothing else would work for me. Yet I couldn't just leave my husband. It took months, and was the hardest thing I ever did.

In 1968 José, the boys, and I moved into a rented fisherman's cottage, next to the butcher's shop in Puerta de la Selva, just across the border from France. The living-room was small with a low raftered ceiling, and held the air and the smell of another century. It had bottle-green doors with panelled glass windows in the top half, and against these hung white pieces of silk stitched with *broderie anglaise*. Hanging over the table a lamp, consisting of three bulbs like bulging pears, could be brought low by pulling a weighted chain. José said it was over a hundred years old.

'It's still in the last century, this house. It has no need to change. Don't you love it?'

As long as he was in it.

The wife of the butcher looked after the children for three hours a day, and José employed a girl from the village to clean the house and wash the clothes. The gas for the cooking stove was supplied by gas butane canisters, which also heated the water. We had lunch with the children at a small *typique* restaurant, and José cooked dinner. In the morning I wrote, in the afternoon we walked along the beach to the next village. There was a powerful, lovely smell of flowers which grew at the edge of the sand. He carried the baby on his back, and my other son ran along the beach in and out of the shallow waves. José taught him Spanish words, read him Spanish stories, and sang him songs. Often the children stayed behind at the small playground on the beach with the fishmonger's daughter.

José pointed to the small town with the railway station, beginning across the bay. 'That's Llançà. She used to stay there, Maria Tourdes.'

Our village was stacked against the mountain like playing cards, brilliant white with coloured shutters and doors. The fishing boats were lolling on the small tide waiting for the night. Umbrellas over the beach café tables, flung up by the wind, looked like tulips. An act of love had put our bodies so much together. I felt complete, as I should be, rich in myself. I heard the butcher rattle up the slope on his motorbike and open the shop.

The sky was angry, speckled, and there was rain over the mountains. The kitchen was full of stillness. 'Good people have lived in this house,' José said. Like a hand, the stillness folded over the words and snuffed them out. I was without shoes, wearing only a silk dress, tousled, bruised, used and wonderfully heavy in my whole being. I belonged to the earth, the hour, all that was. We sat together peeling potatoes, and the kitchen soothed all need for spoken words and held back the future. I felt then as I had when I'd first met him, in the days when I did something I wasn't afraid to call living.

I saw the car below the windows with foreign number-plates and the driver standing with the door open looking up at the kitchen, and as I looked down our eyes met, and his had a blue intent unnecessary for such a casual glance. I didn't say anything to José.

At night José would light the log fire and read his poetry, always about a time that was gone and the transformation of the dark forces into joyousness. And a black priest like a black bird fondling the head of the devil.

I did ask why he hadn't made love to me before, why wait till I had married?

He said he had his mother, there was no money. That I was a little girl and he had the grey police after him. And much worse: a Society of Rosicrucians. Which really meant trouble. And then there was the Vatican.

20

Outside Lluís's bar I saw someone I thought I recognized and almost greeted him. He was dressed in quiet colours with elegantly cut grey hair and expensive soft leather shoes. I asked Lluís to come and look, but the man was walking fast and Lluís didn't know him. Later I remembered he was the North European type with pale eyes who'd paid Beryl.

I walked along the path behind the cathedral, and at first I didn't notice the house was gone. I turned back and still couldn't see the space where it had been. It was as though I had lost it.

The town hall was in the process of restoration work, so the walls destroyed by old wars were being rebuilt and the pathways laid out with new stones. As far as it went, this renovating the old was not bad, but it wasn't the simple dusty track full of atmosphere that I remembered. The money came from tourism. Its coastline made Catalonia rich.

José wanted to visit his cousin Geli. At the cathedral, he disappeared into a fluttering black bunch of priests and I was left staring at Charlemagne's chair, which had the position of honour near the altar. And I thought there was so much history here, in such abundance, that things and events could get so easily lost and hidden.

We walked as far as the Torre Gironella because José wanted to show me the levels of rebuilding and the planting of trees, which went down in terraces from the usual path to areas I had never been aware of. The levels were reached by many flights of stairs, and pieces of sculpture were positioned on mounds of grass, yellowing through heat and lack of rain. He stopped in grief at the space where the Frenchwoman's house and tower had been.

'Why did they pull them down?'

'One day they were just gone. Even the royal palm tree was cut down, its huge root lying there as though wounded, gaping to the sky. Why did they have to do that? The whole town was outraged. Obviously they were looking for something, lifting stone by stone.'

'They?'

'Even under the tree.'

'How did they get away with it?' I asked.

'Paid off the municipality. There was some fairy tale about making room for the renovation. I don't see any.' He walked back quickly along the path. 'Do you?'

They'd left the garden intact, and left the arch with the 'House of the Canons' inscription.

'My cousin Geli tried to stop it. This is an unholy act. Anyway I am going to do something for her, for the Frenchwoman.'

He stood by the angry hole the tree had left. 'I will look after this garden. They will not touch it again.'

'But why did they do it?'

'To mend that!' He pointed to the broken, crumbling wall. 'I don't see too much mended. They've certainly searched deep into it!' He kicked at loose stones.

'So the politicians did it.'

'Never. They didn't have the power. Someone has been paid handsomely so they could take every stone apart.'

'But who are "they"?'

'A society that wants what is here!' He chose the words carefully. 'Too late. Poor thieves in the night; the treasure was already gone. Long ago.'

I tried to ask who exactly the society was, but he stared at me as though making a discovery. 'You have always been highly sensitive. You can feel things extremely.'

I had no argument with that.

'The Frenchwoman said you were intuitive at the very least.' He handed me a piece of stone. 'What do you see?'

I held the stone. 'Nothing.'

Then José said, 'It broke her heart to lose this house. She knew they'd tear it down. But she couldn't live here.'

'Why not?'

'Too many memories. What had been so glorious now was gone, caused such pain.'

I understood that.

'And she was frightened. She died in Paris. She was much older than she looked. Anyway, I am going to Quillan. That's where she comes from. I'll make sure there is nothing else for anyone to get.'

He said it was just over the border and we could go by car, with his old friend Dr Arbós. He spoke as though making a vow.

Dr Arbós took the panoramic route to Quillan, avoiding Perpignan and going inland. He spun through great sculpted traps of rock, whole bunches of it going sheer downwards to the ravine where thinner, sharper rock jagged upwards like a hundred open sharks' mouths. The road became too narrow, with torturous turns, but Arbós avoided all oncoming cars with a magnificent arrogance. He handled hairpin bends and any other surprises with the finesse of a heart surgeon, which it turned out he was. He had the radar of a bat. He had to be back at the Girona hospital before dark.

The rocks in all their dramatic configurations pleased Arbós. 'They're ancient, the oldest known thing in the region. This was the area of the Visigoths. A whole empire lived up on that hill – Rennes-le-Château.'

'Why?'

'Because it's very high, so strategic. They say treasure is still in Rennes-le-Château.' He swept a hand off the wheel to wave at the rocks. 'That's the treasure ...'

José nudged him in some way because a new sentence was left unfinished. We travelled for some moments through a tunnel of rock.

'This route was carved out of the rocks by a priest in the eighteenth century. It linked up these dying villages with the main roads to the south. The inhabitants could get in to the area and out. Priests in this area seem to be remarkable.' Arbós turned to José. 'What was his name?'

'It was Armand. They call this route "Le Trou du Curé", the Priest's Pass.'

José pointed at the sign for Perpignan station. 'The French priest must have that sign inside his head, wherever he is, even in hell.'

Arbós tried to calm the subject, saying I understood Catalan. José ignored him. 'He spent enough time at that station. Frightened time. He never knew if he'd get away with it and trains were always late in those days. They ought to name a seat after him. He was always delayed getting back for the Sunday service. One day he had to

'Le Trou du Curé'

have a coach and horses to get him back from the border. My uncle told me. Later he hired a car and chauffeur.'

'He didn't have to worry about money,' said Arbós.

'But he had to worry.'

A sign told us we were now in Cathar country. Arbós overtook the car ahead as though it was a rock on the roadside, and the one in front of that. I remembered Paco at the wheel on the way to Arenys de Mar. These journeys about this business in France were always in the hands of speeding doctors. I was glad the children were being looked after in Girona by Eva.

We had lunch in Quillan, a huge hefty sustaining meal of cabbage, sausage, potatoes, and meat. Dr Arbós was middle-aged but youthful, and was one of the few people not influenced by José's charisma. He paid the bill and wanted the search carried out within the hour.

First we had to visit the man who looked after the house. He was eager to talk, to reminisce, about the young Maria Tourdes, but Arbós said he needed to get a move on because he had to be back at the hospital. He took the key deftly from the old man's hand, as though he was removing something distressing medically. Then, with José beside him, he hurried ahead.

I thought it polite to stay with the old man, and as we walked slowly he described the old Café Rouzaud and how it was famous for staging operettas before the First World War. Maria loved all the gaiety. I asked what she was like then.

'Pretty enough, but her older sister Annie was the looker.'

The men were out of sight and he tried to speed up. 'It's been empty for years, so whatever they're after won't run away.'

He said he was over eighty and used to work in the hat industry, big in that area. Every man with a sense of class wore a hat from Quillan.

He pointed to an empty building across the main road. 'That was the Grand Hotel des Pyrénées and they hired out the transport in those days. A coach and horses – a *calèche* it was called – with a driver, and sometimes a *diligence* – a bigger coach which took luggage, packages, and many people. And Abbé Saunière thought nobody knew how often he hired one to take him to the station and sometimes to Perpignan. Where did he go from there? You tell me, Madame. The driver had to wait on the hill at Rennes-le-Château but outside of the parish so the villagers didn't see anything, or know how often he travelled. But they knew. I heard so many things I never knew what to make of it all. A sermon into the unknown. It will never be understood.'

Although only two rooms contained scattered abandoned objects – furnishings – they searched, methodically, the whole house, lifting floor coverings in the vacant rooms, opening every cupboard. I found train timetables to Perpignan from different decades, and a Parisian hotel bill for 33 francs. José had found a notebook with names and addresses in a young person's writing, and one letter which both men read and José slowly folded into his shirt pocket.

'At least she's safe,' and José held open the front door. I understood the letter was not of importance. Everything

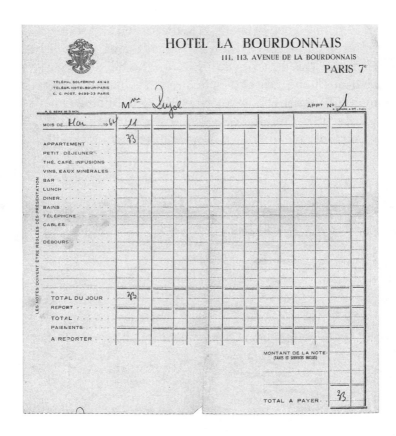

had been stirred up again since the decimation of the palm tree back in Girona. The urgency of the visit to the house was to make sure there were no effects for others to find there, either.

Dr Arbós looked up at the sky. 'The church – while the light's good? As we're here.'

José was suddenly unsure, but he still got into the car.

'You never know.' And Arbós sped circling around the high hill, the summit still not in sight. 'Saunière used to walk up and down in those days to the village.' He

118

pointed. 'Couiza.' The car shook to a stop and the view was awesome. 'You could almost see into Spain,' said Arbós. The houses seemed to wait in the light syrupy sun while a cool breeze sent a tree rustling, swell and fall of summer sound across this strange territory. Everything was in various stages of decline.

José and Arbós went straight into the church at Rennes-le-Château, and told me to follow. And there over the curve of the land a tower poked up and I knew I'd seen it before.

'Come on!' Arbós's tone allowed no negotiation. He told José he didn't want people knowing visitors were about. Over the church doorway was a message that I assumed I'd read wrongly: 'This is a terrible place'.

The inside of the small wooden church was startling in its clear, bright colours and imagery; the wide use of sky blue was almost hypnotic. St Germaine held a luxuriantly embroidered cloth, with fluffy creatures I took to be lambs jumping at her legs. It looked energetic for the depiction of a saint. I asked who had decorated it.

'He did. The priest. Over sixty years ago.'

The priest had been definite about colour. The decorative journey to the Cross was unlike anything I'd seen in a church. A devil crouched in the doorway, with an unforgettable face.

'Asmodeus,' said Arbós. 'The guardian of the temple of Jerusalem.' He pointed to a pink pentagram on the wall. 'You won't see that in Catholic churches.'

'What is it?'

'Rosicrucian, I should think.' José nudged him again. 'Or it's a Jewish symbol, and …'

And then, on the base of the holy water stoup, I saw the initials BS and that made me suddenly cold. I'd last seen them on the scorched ring Maria was holding in Paris. Above the red circled initials was the message: *Par ce signe tu le vancras* – by this sign you shall conquer him.

'Why did he leave this? It isn't a Bible quote, is it?'

They were looking above the dark wooden confessional and in the small room by the altar. The atmosphere worried José, and he kept sighing. They worked fast, even flicking through a torn prayer book.

I sensed that it was a treacherous yet beautiful church, somehow on the edge of something that was not safe or even divine.

And then I saw it, the thing that could not be here, not even in a nightmare, not even in the last, mad, hellish thought. In front of the Stations of the Cross was a dark, hunched being in priest's robes. His eyes like swords swung into mine, jet black, filled with power built up from hundreds of years of unimaginable existence. And behind him, coming out of the dust and dark, was a picture. And for a moment, it looked exactly like the old poster in the alley.

In a rich and deep tone, he had spoken the words: 'Only from a gold cup.'

It must have been the way the light fell and the shadows lengthened. Or I was tired and stressed and deeply anxious on a level I couldn't even locate. Was the figure a ghost? It had been more real than Arbós. It did not wish me well. I was there, seeing too much, without understanding anything and shouldn't be involved at all in this conspiracy of darkness. If I told José he'd deny it. Everyone would. I did. I made excuses for what had been there. Why wasn't it a hallucination? Because I'd never had one, so why now? Would I know one if I had it? In his hands there had been two swords crossing over his chest.

As I ran wildly from that place, circling down the road back to civilization, I decided never to talk about what I'd seen. I'd believed this world was basically a good place, and complied to a reality that was understood early on. Yet I was sure it was beyond human power to give me an explanation. If I spoke, it would make it more power-ful, and perhaps attract more visitations of the same sort. Arbós was talking to me professionally, and José folded me in his arms, tight against him. It's all right. We're all alive. I kept saying this inside myself to stop going mad.

What had I seen?

Of course they asked me that and, of course, I didn't tell them. I wouldn't tell anyone. I'd witnessed something that was real that had no place in reality. It would take almost another twenty years, when the Grail books and Rennes-le-Château phenomenon began, before I would even begin to understand the significance of that place and what I'd seen.

Back in the Hotel Centro José kept saying, 'But you must talk to Arbós. He's a doctor.'

I said I was all right. I never said that unless I was really in trouble.

The images were all too big in my mind – the tower, the initials, the devil crouching ugly by the church door. 'Who was the priest?' I managed to say.

José waved dismissively as he wrapped an object in towels. I asked what it was. He said it was just an old thing he'd found in the French garden. It looked like the object someone had tried to sell in London and he'd rescued. It was time to talk. During the ritual that had made him collapse a few years ago, what was the sound that was so unbear-able? What was the process that he and Lucia Stilman said should be stopped? Who were the Rosicrucians? Who was the priest? Why was the Frenchwoman so important? Why had he gone on a retreat for months in the mountains?

His answer was to unwrap the object from the borrowed towels. It was small and dirty and looked very old. A cup. A drinking vessel. Archaic.

He gestured towards it as though concluding a conjuring trick that had worked.

'It's all about this.'

'But who was he?' I insisted, with lips that were still shaky. 'The priest?'

José dismissed him again.

My next question, 'Are there tranquillizers in this town?' got Arbós in the door. I got the pills and he got his turn with the questions. I understood he didn't want me going off with startling news that would bring undesirable attention. After all, whatever it was had had me fleeing half crazed, shouting in perfect French. Describe the figure I'd seen? He allowed me a pause. Was it then an object? Did I experience a chilling of the atmosphere? Had I sensed a figure was about to appear? A sound perhaps? He did not like being fobbed off with talk of shadows. He saw it as an attempt to shut him up and get him out of the room. He put a hand on my forehead, held my wrist. The shock was over, from a medical point of view. José stayed with me that night, and the windows were open onto the lovely and unknown Hotel Centro garden.

The priest was of no importance. José even asked me: which priest? What about the old cup from yesterday? It certainly wasn't in the room now. 'You came to London to get it back. Someone had put it up for sale. That cup.'

122

He hesitated.

'A cup the size of a small vase. You wrapped it in towels.'

'Ah, the goblet!'

'Where is it now?'

A careless shrug took care of that.

'It's not mine,' he said.

'So, who does have it?' I was sure Lucia Stilman fitted that role.

'It doesn't belong here.' And the conversation was over. For him. He was going to take the children to the hotel garden. I wouldn't let go of the subject. I was tired of being on the outside of these objects, these appearances which were of no importance when I was interested, but of deep and obvious concern when I was not. Was it metal, or stone? It could have been either or both. It was a dirty and ignored dark thing. Yesterday he'd described it as the cause of everything. Today, other than saying it was made of the oldest materials existing on the planet and had always been used with discretion, there was no more he could tell me.

'What about the letter you found in Quillan?'

Almost eagerly he took the paper from his shirt pocket, unfolded it, and placed it on my lap.

'Was this what you looked for?'

'No.'

The letter, its style formal, written to Maria by a man, asking about measurements of a building, made no sense, and I gave it back.

'What are you really doing?'

'She was a good friend. I wanted to make sure there was nothing of hers just lying around for people to get hold of. I wouldn't want her good name to be tarnished.'

Tarnished? Too near gold. I finished the coffee he'd brought me while he described how she must be virtuous, how that was the most important consideration above every other.

'Why?'

'Because otherwise they'd think she was a woman of easy virtue.'

I cut through all that. 'What about the address book you took?'

'She was an elegant woman. Unique in her way. Of course I will protect her. She was a close friend of my uncle and my cousin.'

I remembered her large china cup, cracked, and decorated with bright flowers. And the scorched ring. I asked what the initials BS stood for. He said he didn't know.

I hadn't missed any of the earlier mention of the Rosicrucians and the Vatican. Now might be the time to find out what he'd meant. Not so cautious now, he simply said there was still an abundance of priests about in the fifties, even in his family. And there was bound to be some intrigue when a woman lived near them alone.

21

I sat in the garden of the Frenchwoman and the wind through the trees gave the same silvery sound as in Puerta de la Selva. It was as though the trees had a message for me and it would be a lovely one.

I had not been satisfied with the folded letter in the shirt pocket and had looked in his jacket. Folded into the address book was a hotel bill from Paris for a single room without *'petit dejeuner'* for a Monsieur Pons, dated 1947, and a bill for a consignment of goods by *'diligence'* to Perpignan in 1891.

José came up the steps through the arch which still bore the inscription 'House of the Canons' and he, too, listened to the trees, nice enough but not grand like the murdered royal palm.

'There were fruit trees, when I was a boy. I just remembered. The priest had brought them originally and my uncle helped plant them. They came from France and bore very good fruit. Soft and …'

The organ started up, its sound swelling through the garden.

'Where are the fruit trees now?'

'Perhaps they weren't meant to last. He was fond of exotic plants and had them sent from various countries.'

He'd given too much away. There was no point in denying the priest's existence.

'What was his name?'

'I forget. But he was French.'

When I came back with the boys after lunch, José and two other men were digging in the garden. The stone they'd uncovered was immense, and at first I couldn't see its full size. It was down in the hole made by the removal of the palm tree, and I was surprised to see tunnels leading off through the exposed earth, large enough for a man to crawl through. The three of them were standing in the holes and I recognized the medical student Paco with his red curly hair, who'd once driven us to Arenys de Mar. He explained that in times past a network of tunnels was necessary during the wars and also during the time of the Jews. The tunnels led beyond the city walls, down the bank to the valley and the village of Sant Daniel.

I wasn't aware of a Jewish presence in Girona.

'Well, you wouldn't be,' said Paco. 'There isn't one. Not since the Expulsion of the Jews in 1492.' He pointed across to the hill opposite. 'Montjuïc. That's a Jewish enough name. There are signs of their history every-where. The legends say the gold of the Jews is buried in Montjuïc.' He pointed to the stone they were still trying to free, and wiped off the dust so that carved markings were visible. 'That's not Jewish. It's one of the oldest stones recorded.'

I asked why it was so important.

'It's a ritual stone,' said Paco. 'If it's the one in the docu-ments it is very important.'

'It was used by an ancient civilization,' said the third man, whom I did not know.

I asked why that made it important. I was really longing for José to leave this digging, which could surely be done another day, and come back to the coast.

'It would have certain powers,' said the man.

'How will you know if it is?'

'It would have to be verified.'

Paco stopped digging, sweat dripping from his face. 'I don't know about that.'

José laughed. 'Who could that be? The one who verifies this particular stone? I've yet to meet him.'

A cloud moved and the sun shone directly onto the stone's surface, and I could see lettering carved along the side.

'It could be a sun stone. That's my feeling,' said Paco. 'The cult of the Mithras. The Romans were here. Didn't the soldiers worship the sun god?'

'Oh no,' said José. 'This is much more wonderful than that.'

I asked what it was doing here.

'It's part of things left in the house.' Paco tried to speed up the work.

'It will take four or five men to lift it,' and José put down his shovel. Then he turned to me and asked if I'd go to Lluís's bar and get some bottles of water. He searched in his pockets for money.

Paco and the third man discussed the stone's security. Paco wanted it moved now and was prepared to hire a van. José preferred it to remain in the garden. 'It's been here for hundreds of years, and they, the fools who dug up the tree, couldn't even find it.'

So I asked why not.

'Because it was covered with other stones. Only the patient get anywhere with this recovery. If this is what it's supposed to be, they've been searching for it for years.'

'Hundreds of years,' said the third man.

'Forget the water. Make it champagne!' And Paco gave me the money for Freixenet.

When I got back, Dr Arbós had arrived and there was a new discussion. Where should the stone be kept? Paco's garden? His garage? Arbós's patio? His cellar? They put forward several suggestions, including taking it to France, but José dismissed each one. I could see he had the power. Quite simply, he said, 'We leave it as it is. Who would think of looking for it here?' And they listened to him.

'Did the maid say anything?' asked Paco suddenly.

After a pause, José said, 'The maid?'

'The priest's maid. Did she say anything to Corbu – the man who set up the hotel in Rennes-le-Château – before she died?'

'He said not,' said José.

Paco put down the shovel. 'She died in 1953. We should ask him.'

'Difficult,' said José. 'He's dead.'

Paco raised his eyebrows but made no further comment.

'A lot of people get dead in this story,' said the third man.

I sat under the trees, feeding the children, and the baby loved the sound of the leaves and pointed up at them laughing. And in amongst that silvery sound I believed I could hear a voice, but I knew it was from memory. 'You have to stay focused. Keep your eye on the mark on the tower.' Yes, the Frenchwoman's voice was in my head, but it did feel for a moment as though the trees themselves were sending me a message.

'The Frenchwoman couldn't see much from here,' I said. The view from the garden was restricted because of the bulk of the back of the cathedral. You had to climb onto the city wall, but only then could you see across part of the city and river to the Pyrenees.

'She could see Mount Canigou. The sacred mountain,' said the third man, as though that was all she needed to see.

'She saw the mountain better from the tower,' said José. 'She could see right into France on a clear day. Madame Mathieu liked looking at France.'

'Why do you say Mathieu?' I asked.

'That's her married name. We, her friends, usually called her by the given name of Tourdes but others only knew her as Mathieu.'

'So, she was married?'

He paused. 'She must have been.' Pause. 'At one time.'

We were invited to Pep Colomer's dinner. 'He's giving a fiesta in the country to celebrate the death of the old and the coming forth of the new. We always have a bonfire on this day. The boys will love it.'

Too many people in Girona were after José, and I couldn't wait to get back to Puerta de la Selva. Sitting in Arbós's car waiting to go to the fiesta I could hear – how could I not? – a considerable quarrel start up inside the Residencia Internacional. I recognized José's voice, his mother's, and a young woman's. Lucia Stilman approached, walking a little unsteadily on extraordinarily high-heeled sandals. Seeing the children, she was delighted.

'They are the toast of Girona. They've taken over from me.' Her dress was of gold net, covered with a paler gold silk raincoat. A blast of perfume almost masked the smell of alcohol as she leaned into the car.

'You always wear gold,' I said. It was too obvious for comment.

'At least it's not hidden gold.' She laughed. 'That's the thing these days. I do my best *not* to keep in fashion.' She rattled her jewellery and turned to Arbós. He nodded, unsmiling. He disliked her. She disturbed many heavy bracelets as she pushed forward her arm to stroke my son's curls.

'Get José to bring you to my house at S'Agaró on the coast. I've got a pool and the children will love it.' She almost walked on, then turned to me. 'It might be good to have a talk.'

José rushed onto the pavement, his eyes wild, and Arbós opened a door for him.

'Families,' Arbós laughed. 'Thank God I'm an orphan.' He turned to me. 'I quote Dorothy Parker. Badly.'

José was a million miles from laughing. I doubted even Dorothy Parker could do anything about that. Then he saw Lucia Stilman and jumped out of the car. They embraced and he took her arm, walking purposefully away from us.

'Is this going to be long?' I asked Arbós, as though he'd know.

'Nothing lasts long with Lucia.'

22

Leaving for Puerta de la Selva, José told the taxi driver to keep going up into the hills. When we reached the top all the lights had come on in distant Girona, a cluster of sparkling colour, a superb necklace, a collar resplendent with gems. As if some unaccepted lover had adorned the nakedness of the city, celebrating its power.

José laughed. 'Of course there are those who leave gifts there. And secrets. It's the right place for it. Always has been.'

I, too, would have to make an offering in the end. I'd not get away untouched.

And then he had to say 'Something always interrupts what I want.'

'Don't let it,' I said, knowing his mother was pressurizing him. 'How old are you? Too old for possessive mothers.'

But it wasn't his mother's need of him this time. 'I have to take over a society which protects the old customs.'

'Why you?'

'Why me? Because I am the right person. Especially now. So much is changing.'

What did this mean for us?

He said he would spend two days each week in Girona and I should stay in the fisherman's house until winter, and then we would move somewhere warmer.

'Are they paying you?' I knew they weren't. 'You're always used. Sabater used you.'

'Why not? I was his front. A very good front. A decadent poet. You can't get better than that.'

'Why do all that for him?'

'He did what I could not. Fought for the ideals.'

'My husband, I'm sure you remember him, would not leave me destitute in Paris or risk my life carrying money.'

'It always comes back to money. I have never ever used one peseta belonging to Sabater, or – 'he paused, '– the other business. I will come to you at weekends.'

'How?'

'By bus.'

I wasn't accepting it.

'You can write in peace. The butcher's wife will look after the children.'

'And you run around with Lucia and her gold while your mother watches like an old spider.'

'Lucia is the one person who is probably on your side.'

I found that an odd thing to say. I was usually good at recognizing enemies.

I asked why everyone, apart from Lucia, was against me.

'Because you take me away from what I should do. What I am chosen to do.'

So I asked about 'the other business'. Was that the rituals, the meetings? And what else? The priest? I could see he chose a safe answer.

'Girona is a special place in that it is on a meridian, a ley line, and at this point there are pulses, energies, where things can happen that cannot happen elsewhere.'

I asked what that had to do with his exemplary behaviour with money.

He did not understand 'exemplary'. He said it was his to hold but not to use, and then muttered something about dark retribution.

I knew it was to do with the society. I wanted to know what had happened to whomever was in charge before.

I thought he said, 'She's dead.' Did he mean the Frenchwoman?

He was talking about people trusting her, absolutely.

'And before her?' I asked.

Always his family, he said, and at one point a lawyer was in charge.

My broken marriage? This society? Not much balance there. I said it was too high a price to pay and the argument that followed had to be concluded outside.

For some days we lived peacefully in the village, and then between one hour and the next the anxiety started. He blamed it on the *tramontana*, the mountain wind. He tried to calm me, said it made people mad. Without doubt it was a response to my broken marriage. It coincided with a phone call for him at the butcher's shop. The foreign car was back. I saw it park further along because there was no space by the shop. I recognized the Belgian number plates. The call was from his mother and I could see him making another conciliatory trip to Girona.

I found the letter amongst his writings. If trouble was coming I wanted at least to meet it halfway. It appeared to be from a woman and referred to a secret – 'one of the greatest secrets of our time, of all time, and I am intent on burying it.' In the letter she asked for documents to be passed to an FD. The Vatican had always been aware of 'its' existence. Geli, José's cousin, was mentioned. She wanted to 'let someone else find it' and expected a scandal if the thing got out. So I told José I'd looked amongst the things on his desk and didn't expect him to be pleased. Attached to the letter was a note from Lucia. 'José, do something about this.'

I asked him what the secret was that everyone was trying to find.

'Not find. Cover up.' He was clear on that.

'What is Lucia Stilman exactly?'

'Controversial.'

'But she's not Catalan.'

'Not exactly.'

'I understood you either were or were not Catalan.'

'Her spirit is Catalan.'

I suggested she didn't look like a resident of Girona.

'She was born in Girona. Her mother is French, her father South American, I believe. She's been brought up in many places, especially Paris. I went to secondary school with Lucia. We don't have a university here, so I went to Barcelona.' He spoke warmly. 'She thinks we belong together. You and me, she means.'

A dog started barking, as though in warning. We both felt it – and he said no more.

Hôtel
EDEN-LAC
Montreux

Le lundi soir.

Cher Amics

Depuis la mort de ma grand-mère,
j'ai décidé que la solution la plus sage
était de transmettre les matériaux à FD.

Je comprends bien que ce n'est peut-
être pas ce qu'elle aurait voulu, mais dans
le monde d'aujourd'hui cela ne peut guère
entrer en considération.

GT m'assure que le Vatican a toujours été
au courant de son existence. "Les amis" d'ici
ainsi qu'à Gérone ont avancé la thèse qu'il
s'agissait là d'une des plus grands secrets de
notre temps, de tous les temps et je suis

CH - 1820 Montreux/Suisse   Téléphone 021-963 55 51   Télex 453 151   Téléfax 021-963 18 13

CARLO DE MERCURIO ccm HÔTELS & RESTAURANTS

Translated in full on page 323

résolu à l'enterrer. Ma foi, que quelqu'un d'autre le trouve. De plus, ils défient mes droits.

↳ En conséquence, pourriez vous faire en sorte que les instructions et les documents s'y rattachant soient acheminés à la personne nommée ci-dessus

Votre ami CCC

et Marie Correse

PS Le scandale qui pourrait ~~attacher~~ éclater ne serait bon pour personne.

He closed the shutters because the wind was blowing up and lay beside me. I heard him say, 'It's old-fashioned here, but some things cannot be improved upon.'

And I was back in the alley where no light could reach and even the old-fashioned lanterns clanking in the mountain wind did not infiltrate this blackness seething with starving cats. A new moon was trapped at the end of this alleyway, without direction in the blind sky, its silver light shining on the eyes of these creatures giving away their secrecy, and they started to yowl and screech, obedient to this lunar influence. I seemed to be standing against the old stone wall, on it a poster from the early forties, peeling and torn. And I was back here where I used to meet him. A wind full of ice screamed down from Mount Canigou and I could hear the door of Chez Béatrice bump shut as a customer set out into the night, his shoes clattering on the broken cobbled street. And he was made up of a patchwork of darkness, even if he was wearing the most colourful clothes. Only black and silver existed here and no colour got through. And the cathedral bell chimed midnight sonorously and was echoed by lesser clocks across this beloved city, and I knew he would come and I knew this was the only place in existence that he could come. And then I smelt the eau de Cologne he wore in his hair and felt his hands reach out for me and I ached for the touch that would follow. No, for him, for this man who had even now all the memories of our lives, and his lips were against my ear and of course I could never see him.

'I had that dream again.' I was sitting up and José was holding me. And he must not speak and this time I must

137

remember. 'And I waited for him by an alley next to Chez Béatrice.'

'But that's been closed for years.' Not José's voice. Part of the dream then.

'And it's him and yet it's you. And the poster is there from the forties and yet it's older than that.'

And José comforted me and I was back in the present. But that black-and-white place with its lunar light was still there.

The first thing I saw in the morning was the Belgian car directly below my windows. I decided the driver was staying in the hotel facing the harbour. Sometimes he washed the car, polished it, even mended it, but his eyes were always on us.

'He's watching me,' I said. 'He's from my husband and the family.'

'No, it's for me,' said José simply.

He was right about that.

But there was a detective, too, and the deal was clear. If I didn't go back I might lose my children.

It came down to survival. I would never lose my children. I went back to London, to divorce.

23

I hadn't expected to come to Girona. I had been on my way to meet a director in Barcelona, who planned to make a movie of my first book. I was travelling by train because I'd dropped the boys off with their father. It was 1972, and I hadn't seen José for about four years. While I'd been in Los Angeles and New York selling my books for films, he had lost his position at the Fontana d'Or gallery but found something bigger and more glorious – his project to build a centre of Cabbala.

The ground was full of rubbish, dirt, dust, weeds and was used by tramps, the homeless, prostitutes, and ownerless dogs. The wall along the carrer de la Força kept it private.

He picked up a stone and rolled it to and fro in his fingers. He was good with stones.

'This is the *call*, the Jewish quarter, the heart of this city.'

He had to go to a meeting with associates, so I went to Lluís's bar. He was doing good business, but the bar retained enough of its original atmosphere. The fireplace had survived, as had the jazz, the low roof, and a few of the original clients in this safe, comforting cave. Lluís was still going to write a book, if a little different in content. He was married with two children.

Lluís was surprised about the Jewish plan. He understood the project was a '*typique Catalan cafeteria*' to open on a disused site. 'But José is more prudent these days.'

'The mayor doesn't like him,' said the man on the next stool whom I almost recognized.

'After the business of the Fontana d'Or,' said Lluís, softly. 'Of course it was José's idea and his work, but the municipality has other ideas. They think José and his group belong to a time that is gone, and that we are elitist and not representative of the new Catalonia. They want this city open for everyone. Myself, I worry about José because people are jealous of him.'

'He should have been the mayor,' said the man I now recognized as Jordí Soler, a journalist I'd acted with in a short film in 1955.

Lluís shook his head, a small shake but enough. 'José has other things to do.'

He put on a Miles Davis track of the Spanish concerto I loved and said I'd done the right thing. I'd followed my desire to write, to travel, to meet exceptional people, to go towards success and recognition.

'You couldn't have got that here.'

On the way back I noticed not only the chocolate poster was gone, but part of the alley had been torn down. I couldn't even find where Chez Béatrice used to be.

Later, I went with José to the lawyer's office to get the rights to the wasteland. I met his probable partner in the business, a young Catalan, Rafel Pons, who had recently inherited family money. I didn't hear talk of Jews and Cabbala but a cafeteria. The cost was equal to a quarter of a million US dollars, and even the lawyer looked surprised.

'We do things properly or we don't do them.' José cleared his throat and said he wanted the rights for free, as the venture would benefit the neglected area and those in the vicinity.

A quarter of a million dollars didn't seem to be present in that room, so José took the next best option. He rented two buildings around the wasteland and Pons produced the cheque.

I asked him why he'd been telling everyone he was opening a cafeteria.

'Let them go on thinking that. At least they'll get real traditional food. You have a job finding that in the rush to be modern in this town.'

He sat on my bed and just gave up. 'I often dream of Puerta de la Selva. I search along the beach but whatever I'm looking for isn't there. In and out of the cafés, swiftly through the fish market, up the steps to the fisherman's cottage. Into the living-room ...'

I hoped he was going to say he searched for me. He said, 'But I can smell the perfume. It's what she used to wear.'

'The Frenchwoman? That was Je Reviens.' I knew it was her he dreamed of.

He pulled me beside him. The truth was that the minute I heard his voice I felt all right, as I should be, connected to a seam of richness and gold I had not found elsewhere for all the travel and 'exceptional' meetings. The feeling of the afternoon in the room reminded me of another room, years before in the Residencia Internacional hotel, when he would come in with our two eggs and three pesetas' worth of white beans. He also came in with love and optimism.

Afterwards he said he had done a deal with Lucia and sold the battered dirty goblet. She wanted this accessory.

It was her family's right. Why should José have it? Because he was the one chosen as the custodian, a position he did not want then.

'Custodian?'

'Of certain matters relating to Girona. Lucia was confrontational with her ostentatious use of gold. She was showing us up, the private group, drawing attention to what we took care of. She wanted it known on an open level and to be understood as part of the spiritual life of everyone. To inspire that life, to better mankind. But that cannot be. People cannot receive it. You have to be in a super-conscious state …' He tried to find words I might understand.

'High on drugs,' I suggested.

'It is much higher than that. Substances like drugs only go so far. This super-conscious state cannot be reached by something as gross as drugs or drink. Please do not talk to Lucia about this if you should see her.' Then he stopped talking.

The cathedral clock chimed an hour he did not like. 'My God, I have to be at the town hall.' He was off the bed, running a hand through his hair. Then he saw my reaction. 'I'll come for you at nine.' I can't have looked much better because he said I was sad, due to Girona changing. 'We knew the good times.' He splashed water on his face.

I was sad because he was changed. 'The chocolate poster is gone. The one in the alley, by Chez Béatrice.'

He hadn't noticed.

And then I remembered the strange church on the hill in France, and the stranger things inside it. I asked if he remembered that journey. I was trying to stop him from leaving.

'I remember you were upset. What did you see? You never told me.'

He sat on the bed, so I told him.

'Perhaps it was the local priest, angry because we'd disturbed his church?' he suggested.

'And the voice?' I didn't think so.

'Maybe you tune into what cannot be seen in the normal way? You can reach a more acute sensitive level. I always said you have the amulets of protection, given to you from birth.'

He got up to leave, then said, 'I never forget you. There's never been anyone like you.'

At the end of dinner at Cal Ros, José described the Golden Age of Cabbala, and how the mystics were born in Girona and carried out experiments in the courtyard which was now a wasteland used by the unfortunates of the city. 'The mystical practice of Cabbala is handed on to a chosen few. In Nachmanides's lifetime it reached heights of excellence never since matched. We have to bring it back,' he concluded.

Some of the old group had joined us at the table. I understood this was the first they had heard of the Golden Age, and of the plans José was forming for its restoration. I expected Lucia would be the real source of the funding he'd mentioned.

'What will you call the centre?' she said.

'Isaac the Blind,' said José. 'He was a Cabbalist.'

I noticed she discreetly gave him money to pay for the dinner. On the way up to Lluís's bar I asked her about the restoration.

'I'll have nothing to do with it.'

So I asked about the ritual, the one she'd attended with José some years ago. What exactly was it?

I could see it was not to be discussed. She said, 'It's not transferable.'

'But he heard a sound. It drove him mad.'

'It's in people's heads, not in the room. I didn't hear it. I was there.'

'Do they still have these ... meetings?'

'No.' She was quite cut and dried.

We were at the door of the bar, the shutters open and festooned with advertisements for cultural events. I felt she was the one person who could give me some answers and tried to keep her back.

'Has he got a girlfriend?' I asked, bluntly.

'There are those who would like to be. The best would be to get him away from Girona.'

'How?' I almost held on to her silk chiffon dress.

They were calling to her from the bar.

'But he can't leave,' she said, quickly. 'Not now. When you were in Puerta de la Selva there was a huge fall-out with the mother.'

'Because of me?' Obviously. Waste of time, that question.

'Because he hocked the artefact to get money for you to live there.'

'To Arbós?' I tried to be discreet.

'To me. Watch the mother. She is powerful. And he has to walk a straight path.'

'Where is it now? The artefact?'

'Out of the way. I do it their way for now.' As we stepped into the bar she pressed my arm. 'Be careful.'

—⁓—

The next day I walked without direction through the old quarter, up stairways, courtyards, across bridges. José had told me he'd gone to Tarragona, and I'd discovered he had a small house, known as the *barraca*, which consisted of one room like something from a fairytale and stood in several acres of countryside. He'd planted a garden, made a pond. Lights hung from the trees. One day when he finally had money the *barraca* would be enlarged and become his home. Reached by the path behind the cathedral, passing the Frenchwoman's garden and the broken Torre Gironella beyond, the *barraca* had been inherited from his uncle.

He was coming towards me as I paused in memory by the Frenchwoman's garden. 'How was Tarragona?'

He hesitated. 'Tarragona?' his voice ghostly. He'd forgotten the lie of yesterday.

'You know Tarragona. The place you were supposed to be visiting.'

'It has stood for thousands of years. Why should a visit of mine bring any change?'

And then I saw a girl in the distance, in the *barraca* garden.

The truth, of course, was that we were changed people. I was no longer the fifteen-year-old travelling girl on the steps of the Residencia Internacional, ready for any experience, full of life-love, and he wasn't the divine poet who brightened lives and would give his own to free his town. He was 42 years old and his life was not as he'd anticipated. His role in the town was superfluous. There was nothing to fight any more. Lluís had said he was out of date. He had no wife, children, money, position, and he still lived with his mother. I was in my early thirties. The trouble was, when I was away from José I remembered him as he'd once been and that memory would not let me go. It had been a gift from God.

I lay on the noisy bed waiting, and the wind from the mountains started up. The used double-bed that had witnessed everything advised me like a wise friend, 'Don't lose all you've worked for.'

In a hired car, the director waited for me by the hotel entrance. 'Let's go and make this movie.' As though by chance, José arrived at the same time and stayed on the other side of the road. The director laughed and opened the car door. 'Come on, I'm your future. He's your past.'

As we drove to the coast I realized I hadn't asked about the girl in the garden.

24

During the Middle Ages, in a closed quarter off to one side of the carrer de la Força, the Jewish mystics, while in trance, could receive a vision of God. Cabbala practices were highly complex and secret and, I imagined, something like acid trips but with greater clarity and direction. The practices were handed on only to those evolved enough to use them with safety and respect.

Jews had been present in Girona during the Roman occupation, but they were believed to have arrived much earlier. In the fourth century it is thought they were banished from the city and moved to the nearby villages of Besalú, Montjuïc, Ullastret, Vila-sacra, and Vilajuïga. When José began his excavations he found remains of their ritual baths and synagogues, especially in Besalú.

In the ninth century they were invited back to Girona by the ruling counts, who found them more entertaining and cultured than local residents. They were allowed to buy twenty-four houses surrounding a communal courtyard in the shadow of the cathedral. After the Expulsion in 1492, the area was closed by order of the Church, and the rumour that the wasteland was cursed and that the mystical practices had left influences was passed down to the present day. It was believed that as the town had turned on the mystics, so the results could turn on them. The suffering of the Expulsion undeniably left a sombre resonance.

Instead of going home from Barcelona I returned to Girona. I first saw the French girl close up in the doorway of the Residencia Internacional hotel, just before it shut down. She was standing very near to José, as near as she could as the daughter of a respectable French Catholic family. The toes of her schoolgirl shoes almost touched his, the jut of her heavy breasts nuzzling his shirt like two unloved beasts straining over a hedge for attention. Her eyes stayed fixed on his, their breath mingled as they spoke. She was young, greedy, sexually untouched. The only thing about the sight of them together that reassured me was the fact that she could not possibly be his type.

We were introduced, and she spoke perfect Spanish with a hoarse voice. She was years younger than he, with an air of being well brought-up. She lived with her parents and was studying something in the arts. The way she offered him the gift of her body, her youth, in that shabby doorway was familiar. Years before I'd done the same. He very quickly explained her presence to me as a young girl needing the inspiration of Girona. She was a talented French artist and he was simply showing her the province to add something to her work.

He couldn't have been sure of her, of what he intended, because he'd asked me back. He'd said, 'I need you to help me.'

We sat in the dust of the wasteland, which now had an official door painted blue, and looked around at the mysterious shapes of the disused buildings that were beginning to take form, coming forward from the shrouds of time and from an enforced Papal silence. A loud bird with a jeering laugh brushed through the greasy, languid leaves of a stout tree, and José dropped the stone he'd been holding and took my hand.

'What do you think? Should I do it?' he said. 'Bring back this area into existence?'

I asked what the alternative was.

He let go of my hand. 'We could just go and live on the Atlantic coast as we always planned to do.' He mentioned the *rías* – inland waterway – below Santiago de Compostela. He had never ever before asked for my opinion.

I sat in silence. After a while the old lamps came on, cautiously, amongst the trees.

'We got them working. They're oil lamps.' He stood up. 'I want to show you this,' and he reached out his hand to pull me up. 'I found it when they were digging, this afternoon.'

Narrow, crooked steps had been partially uncovered, leading underground. 'Down here would be the mortuary.' I wasn't keen on following him. At the bottom he bent down and lifted a flat stone. Things crawled and scurried away in the near darkness and when the earth was still I saw a small mound of loose metal bits gleaming in the dirt.

'Coins,' he said, and picked them up with a familiarity I thought was either brave or foolhardy. The unknown disquieting presence of the place discouraged me. I wanted to leave. He let the coins drop. Was he disappointed with my lack of enthusiasm? 'They're only Roman coins.'

I went too quickly up the insufficient steps and slipped. My hand grabbed the wall of earth, which crumbled away to nothing, and there in the half-light was a container secured with small stones. He brushed them away as I regained some balance.

'I think it's an oven in here. A Jewish oven.' He reached down inside, and I dreaded what he'd touch and said to leave it. Out came his hand and he put the small dry object on mine. 'I think it's bread,' he said. For a moment his hand cupped mine as though holding an escaping moth. And as we looked at it, it expired in the air. Vanished. It had been sealed in all those years and couldn't survive the contact with freedom. 'It's nearly 500 years old.' He sounded over-awed. 'They were baking that and then had to escape. It was the last thing they did ...' Dark now, oil lamps flick-ering. 'If they left a piece of bread it meant one day they would return.' He spoke quietly, reverently. 'So it is here. The Jewish *call*.' He looked around, and the Atlantic coast and the *rias* suddenly seemed further away.

I said, 'I'll have to bring the children.' For a moment he wondered what I meant. 'With us.'

'But of course.' And he was looking at my palm where the bread had rested. Together we'd held in our hands a piece of history. I could only see it as an omen. He was meant to be here. I must have sounded hard, disappoint-ment making me unusually realistic as I said, 'You have to get the excavation carried out properly. Obviously these things can't just come out into the light of day.'

The piece of bread, or whatever it was, had been there. And then it was nothing.

When I arrived the next morning the French girl was deep in the hole, digging like a man. She didn't mind getting dirty, finding skulls, confronting rodents. She was in love. José was pleased with her and said so. Paco and Lluís, also visiting, looked to see how I was taking it.

'She works with stained glass. You wouldn't think these delicate hands could make something solid, would you?

But these hands are strong.' He lifted them up and was familiar with them. The hand-praising speech suggested he was more than her tour guide of Girona. 'We will restore this Jewish heart. It is a thing of destiny.'

She nodded fierce agreement to everything he said. I couldn't look at her. She was there at the corner of my eye, her fingers kept creeping over him, his thighs, his arm. In the end he brushed them off like an annoying insect – they had the same insistence, reappearing at his neck, his ear, like an outbreak of young flies. Her eyes were all over him, forever searching his. She loved him the way I did. She was the cashier counting every exchange he made with me, every compliment, even a smile. I understood her jealousy.

I couldn't stand any more and asked him to come with me to meet Lucia. She turned a shellfish pink and said she'd come too. I told her it was private business and looked at him for support. He swept away another set of fingers, and climbed out of the hole. I asked her where she came from.

'Paris.'

That figured. All the worst times were in Paris.

I rushed ahead of him along the Rambla, fury making me speed through the heat.

'You slept with her.'

'Of course not. She is …' He said a word like 'intact'.

'So how do you know?' I was prepared to run and he grabbed me.

'I have nothing to give her, or anyone.'

'So now I'm anyone!'

'Spain is hard. I get less money than you spend in bars. Or on this.' He pointed brutally at my dress. An unwise choice. It was already spotted with mud, soggy with sweat. 'I work like a dog for this city and don't have enough to keep my mother. And now the municipality is trying to take away

151

even that. They pay me only when I'm actually hanging up the lights for the fiestas. What about the weeks of preparation? I should do the concerts, the exhibitions …' He counted on his fingers savagely. 'For nothing.' His eyes glared, a hostile yellow. 'They're short-sighted fools who only care for tourist menus and high-rise hotels that ruin our coast. I rescue the past, so I'm a lunatic. If it wasn't for me Madrid would have turned this place into a hamburger stand.'

'What about that society you run?' 'Something about protecting the old customs …'

'Why do you ask about that?' Change of tune now, suspicious.

'Does that pay?'

'It does not. Carmen Aragó is the president these days. She was the cultivated woman with the best house in Girona. 'I'm simply the custodian again, now.'

'What about your partner? Rafel Pons – the one with the money.'

'Rafel Pons's money is secure in land and property. He'd have squandered it by now, trying to take a girl out. He's shy and he needs a lot of drinks to speak to girls.'

'So now you're the custodian of other people's fortunes?'

'Hopefully.' And he laughed and waited for me to laugh. It was going to be hard to dismantle our love affair, even for him. 'I am simply arranging an exhibition of her stained glass. Nothing more.'

'Together we held something valuable yesterday. It was there. And then it was not there. Be careful.'

I left him in the street and went towards Lluís's bar. I thought of Eva during that first winter, watching him get ready to go out for the night. What had Eva said? 'It would take a Frenchwoman to get that one.' Surely not her. It can't be her.

Lucia was standing by a car opposite the Town Hall. It was official-looking, with a uniformed driver.

'I am going to see my husband. Don't let anyone say I neglect my duty.' She was fatter, slacker, eyes a little unsteady in their sockets. The alcohol had had to go somewhere. It chose to become kilos of waterlogged fat. It wasn't my business, but I felt sad. We talked immediately about José. I asked what he was really doing.

'Getting into trouble. There are people closing around him. He should be careful.'

I asked what she meant.

'He's arrogant. I know he's had a disgraceful rejection from this city, after all he's done. But I'm talking closer to home. Men around him are becoming disappointed. José loses things. Or doesn't look after them properly. The cross and chain. D'you remember?'

I didn't at first.

'They took that seriously because I saw an ad for it in Paris. A reward offered for its return.'

'When?'

'Recently. They want it back.'

'They?'

She almost answered, then looked at me. 'Your life is elsewhere. You don't need trouble.'

The eighth-century street had been opened the previous week and was little more than a dust-filled gap with steep broken steps. Workmen were clearing rubbish. The entrance was halfway up, through a narrow arch. I asked a workman for José. He didn't understand my pronunciation and shouted a name and an official from the municipality appeared, then José's mother, two journalists, and finally the mayor. When I was surrounded by all the factions José would most want to keep in ignorance of our liaison, he appeared. He sounded formal as he introduced me, which made everyone immediately suspicious.

'This is the Cabbala Centre, "Isaac the Blind," in honour of a renowned Jewish mystic. We are excavating this ground.'

'Simply to build a cafeteria?' the official asked. The men laughed.

'Not at all.'

Then Rafel Pons was present and behind him the French girl.

'It began as a restaurant but then my good friend Rafel Pons and I made unimaginable discoveries. We have uncovered the Golden Age of the Jews.'

I think it was the first Rafel Pons had heard about it. But he had to look proud as co-owner for the photographs, and then he began to be excited by the immensity of the project. Workmen were laying a Star of David in marble on the courtyard.

'Isn't it marvellous?' José continued. 'Jews and Arabs produce the most horrible wars, yet here in Girona it is the Arabs who create for the Jews their symbol. In Girona we are at peace.' He indicated the two doves by the archway. 'Perhaps here is the promised land? The lamb lies down with the ...'

'Lion?' I suggested.

Surrounded by the financial and political establishment that had fired him from the Fontana d'Or, he said, 'Snake.'

The French girl was nodding vehemently at whatever he said. She couldn't nod enough. I think it was that which made me ask the unaskable in this company. 'Do you think Jews will be welcome here?'

'Of course. We in Catalonia welcome all religions, all customs, however extreme.'

The mayor looked as though he deeply regretted removing José from the safety of the art centre. The reporters scribbled things on their pads, the municipality official looked unconvinced. So José reclaimed control. He brought forward the award-winning designer of the Star of David, who worked in Toledo. This man explained the use of marble and gave them something concrete to think about. I didn't think José would get a municipal subsidy.

An electrician and his staff brought in dozens of different-sized light bulbs. At night the courtyard would blaze with a glory only José could provide.

The owner of the Hotel Centro called to me from the doorway. She had a letter from Lucia:

I have been thinking about what I said. It's not only José in trouble, but you. 'Trouble' is too slight for this. Of course he doesn't see it. You have to remember he and Lluís, Jordí Soler and Carlos and some of the others have hardly left Girona. You and I have seen it differently. I pray that you leave. I brought some letters to you from those in the past who are responsible for all this. As you have left the hotel I have given them to José.

Lucia.

It wasn't Lucia's concern that made me leave. José was hosing the *barraca* and I waited for him to finish. He was stripped to the waist and his skin was olive silk, every movement supple and exact. I asked how Rafel Pons had taken the change in his investment plan.

'He's very lucky. Instead of a bar casino he's got a revelation. It started as an ordinary commercial venture and

155

now he has something that will recover history and go down in history. His father can't believe it.'

This was no time for laughter but a little shaky one escaped, and he watched me with eyes that did not move. He had changed. Was it the overdone nodding of the French devotee that encouraged this change?

I knew Girona wouldn't be right for my children – in London they had a gang of friends, mostly from split homes, and this company of divided children was strong and supportive. Bringing them back here would lose them that. For a moment he was horrified – there was no way fate would allow my children, whom he loved, to be deprived of their heritage. Their proper life was in Spain. He promised I would not get tickets to London, the planes would be full.

In the chaos of it all I forgot to ask for Lucia's letters.

25

In February 1976 my book *Having it Away* was optioned for film and I showed the American director the coastline around Begur, where the story had taken place. When she left I took the coach into Girona – I knew that José had been intent on restoring the Cabbala site and had a great deal of support. Apparently even his enemies were fascinated. He belonged to the artists. He was the conscience of the painters and writers and kept the past alive. I was fascinated to see it, too.

I waited until dark to go to the mother's flat and bang on the door. The mother said he was away, many kilometres, for many weeks. I sank onto the stone landing and the automatic light clicked off. He was gone. Downstairs I heard running in the street. I was almost knocked over by the stampede going up the carrer de la Força towards the cathedral, and stepped back into José's doorway. It seemed as though the city was filled with the sound of running.

That night on a hill, near the Frenchwoman's garden, a vision of the Magdalene had appeared, *La Dama de la Copa*, or 'the Lady of the Cup'.

Lluís said over a hundred people had witnessed the appearance. It was like a rainbow and lasted nearly an hour. He said according to Lucia it could only happen in certain places, depending on the power of the ley lines and the pulses of energy in that precise area. It seemed to be above the hill further up from the Frenchwoman's house. I asked if he had seen it and he said he was busy with all the customers who'd poured in, and when he'd got the chance to go outside it had gone. A waiter said it had the effect on him of the Teresa of Ávila miracle. He believed he had seen a vision. 'The form was beneficent. Holy. I can't imagine I'd ever forget it.'

A friend from the old days, Gerard Ruiz, left his book-shop because so many people were running past. There is a vision, they said. When he got to the space in front of the cathedral he could see a patch of light in the sky. It didn't move, then faded and was gone.

His bookshop was filled with rare books, old magazines, postcards and prints. He had thick auburn hair, an ageless face, and he was always in a good humour. 'Years ago, people passing up there on their way to the countryside said they'd seen visions by the house with the tower.'

I asked what happened.

'Nothing. They weren't curious, and anyway, did not believe in visions. They're Catalans.' He laughed.

'What will happen about this one?'

'Depends on the Church. Whether they want to claim it or not. They always said up there,' he indicated the area where the tower had been, 'that a secret ceremony of some sort provoked changes in the atmosphere and that called up the vision. But that was years ago, not in this century.' He looked amongst the mass of books. 'If I find anything about it I'll give it to you.' Then he laughed. 'Of course, they'll say it's José's fault. Digging up the past. Disturbing the spirits.' He looked at the morning sky, which was bright and normal. 'Perhaps she came to protect us – the Lady of the Cup.'

The owner of the Hotel Centro said the city would be divided. Those who believed and the rest who refused even to discuss it. 'Catalans only like what is real and can be felt. Stones. Water. The appearance of a sudden fountain.' She said many of the spectators talked of a sense of lightness beyond anything they'd known. She said Carmen Aragó had been there with her husband and associates. And Dr Baró the psychiatrist. And the mayor.

Had it happened before?

'Years ago, on the lake of Banyoles, a nun had seen the vision.'

The concierge came in, very excited. The night before he'd been on the hill and there were dozens of people. You could hear a pin drop. And then a dog started growling. 'I thought it was evil spirits trying to approach, and I prayed to St Michael who symbolizes the unknown from the other world. He protects against evil.'

I asked the owner if it would be in the newspapers.

'Oh, no,' he said, 'they won't print that.'

26

Four Cabbalists performed an experiment detailed in a work called The Nutgarden, *where they transcended the four earthly dimensions, so travelling into the fifth and further towards the tenth dimension. One Cabbalist went mad, the second died, the third ran away forever, an apostate of Judaism, and the fourth survived and documented the experience.*

In Girona this experiment and others similar were conducted in the medieval age in the buildings José had now acquired. It was recorded that those taking part were over forty, had studied Cabbala assiduously, were initiates on a high level, could fast, meditate, and transcend their physical existence by control of the breath and continuous chants, producing a hypnotic state from which they could ascend 'Jacob's Ladder'. In this heightened condition, spiritual changes occurred. The four dimensions of this planet – the three physical plus the fourth, time – were traversed, and experience in other realms was achievable and became part of the Cabbala discoveries. Reaching these states of being gave the participant enormous power. José believed this allowed the city its dynamic atmosphere. He even told Rafel Pons:'There has always been something compelling and magnetic here. I think the pulse of that magnetism comes from this courtyard, the Cabbala leaving an undying imprint. The marvellous atmosphere is its legacy as well as the real contribution it has made to the development of human thought.

I wrote this in the first article for the *Jewish Chronicle* on the Isaac the Blind centre in 1976. Many others followed. What had happened to the Cabbala documents? José said they were buried in the synagogue below the street; they were in Toledo; the Church had burned them; he had them.

Girona 'the immortal city' had another title, 'the Mother City of Israel'. Nachmanides, the principal Rabbinic scholar, was a Talmudist of the highest order, renowned for his commentaries on the Bible and his 'Sefer Emuna', describing the twenty-two letters of the Hebrew alphabet as the image of God. Nachmanides drew attention to the Cabbala in medieval Spain, but it was only a part of his work. Other celebrated Cabbalists of Girona – Ezra ben Solomon, Azriel, Jacob ben Sheshet – wrote books and commentaries, and Jonah ben Abraham opened Rabbinic schools in Barcelona and Toledo. José called the centre after a revered Cabbalist from Provence who, with many mystics from other parts of Spain and southern France, gathered in Girona to form a nucleus of discovery and experiment. North of the Pyrenees in those days was part of Catalonia. The expert on Cabbala, Gershom Scholem, had devoted much of his writing to the Girona School and considered Nachmanides the master, 'the inspired one', 'the most elevated of mystics'.

The classic book of Cabbala, *The Zohar*, appeared in Spain in the thirteenth century. At first it was believed to have been written by a devout sage of the second century, Simeon ben Yohai. However, Gershom Scholem and modern scholarship attribute *The Zohar* to Rabbi Moses de Leon, living in Girona in the thirteenth century. The inspired work gives an esoteric key to the Bible. José called it by another name – *The Book of Light* – and was in possession of an early manuscript.

It seemed today there were no practising Cabbalists or mystics, only Rabbinic scholars and writers on Cabbala. José was told the last known Cabbalist had just died in Safed, Israel.

I asked Rafel Pons if he had participated in any Cabbala experiences. He had no idea what I was talking about.

'So you're happy doing this restoration?'

'Very.'

He was respectful and pleasant, but there was one drawback. I couldn't hear what he said. It all flowed together with not enough consonants and I realized it was due to drink. The after-lunch brandies had simply washed them away.

'But it must take a lot of money, Rafel?'

'What is money when something like this is at risk? You can't equate money with history.'

That sounded like one of José's lines.

'Has he put money in?'

He nodded.

'I didn't think he had any.'

'His cousin underwrote his loan. And there is some land.' He meant the *barraca*.

'But surely your family, your father, must be worried about your investment. This is an unconventional business scheme.'

He said his father wasn't worried, on the contrary, he was proud. José had spoken to his father. It had begun as a quite ordinary venture. A bar casino. Then they found coins, Passover bread, scrolls. I wasn't sure about the bread. I thought I'd been part of finding that. He had another drink and the list grew. I hadn't missed the reference to risk. Why was the project at risk?

'The money's run out.'

I had a good idea. 'If it's for the Jews, don't you think the Jews should be involved?'

'They will, at the right time. When José says it's the right time.'

The unblocked eighth-century street led to a dark stone entrance containing the *miqwe*, or bath house, and a wishing-well gleaming with coins. A choice of stairways led up to exhibition floors, where paintings and photographs by Catalans were already displayed, or down to the ongoing excavations. The brightness of the courtyard, dominated by the beautifully laid Star of David in coloured mosaic, was only half visible from the entrance. The building was structured so that only a part was seen at one time, unconsciously echoing some aspect of the mystical practices initiated here. Newly restored staircases and balconies formed two sides of the courtyard where Sephardi concerts had been introduced. The third side formed the ritual arch and the towering palace of Nachmanides, and the fourth, a covered seating area, led to further courtyards and unfinished excavations.

The natural lighting was always dramatic, near darkness into immediate piercing sunlight. At night people from the town gathered in the courtyard because of its peace and coolness. To meet the debt, so far three times the original investment, José had opened a bar and restaurant, serving food and drinks until three or four in the morning. The Catalans loved anything unusual, and flocked to the bar. Especially unusual was the fact a local figure had given up his life to a cause that might or might not succeed.

163

José had uncovered the synagogue, the mortuary, the ritual slaughter block, and the oven we'd found together for baking matzos. A hospital and dormitory was next. Financial distress meant only ten per cent of the excavation had been completed. I thought I recognized the huge stone in a place of honour amongst the excavations.

He was showing around a group of businessmen, possible investors, and I joined them. A network of private *salons* with subdued lighting made them a little quiet. Marble floors, sofas in rich fabrics, too obvious mirrors. It looked like a house of rendezvous, but I smothered my first impression and tried to approve of everything. The house with the terrace loomed over the patio and the businessmen were interested in that.

'It belongs to our patron, Carmen Aragó. She made all this possible. She gave permission to open the street and did away with all the dreary legal procedure, so we could rent the area and start buying some land.' He would not specify what was bought or rented.

'But who is she?' I asked.

'The goddess of Girona. She's lived here all her married life. I'm surprised you ask. She is our patron and has given more leases and licences.'

'What was here before?' asked one of the men.

'It was closed. But the whores who couldn't get a place in the Barrio Chino could get in through the broken wall and bring men. Gypsies slept here. A man and his son dug for treasure.'

I could see the point in letting José have a few legal points for nothing. At least the patron slept nights.

'But we have found the treasure of the Jews.'

This was what the men in suits were here for.

'What does that mean? Gold?'

'Oh, something far more valuable. Their heritage. In this courtyard they travelled further into the outposts of human experience than anyone before or since.'

The men would have preferred gold.

Then I saw the French girl hanging a cage of doves at the side of the courtyard. José watched her assessingly.

'The birds of peace,' he said. 'But only two.' She didn't know what he meant. 'You only ever have two doves. Surely you remember the directions.'

Then she turned and saw me, and her eyes were far from peaceful. 'We have concerts here and the whole town comes to listen,' he said.

'I hope they pay.' I couldn't resist it.

'They pay 300 pesetas a ticket. They would pay 3,000. It is their heritage. There are so many, the courtyard is over-flowing. Even the birds join in.'

She nodded fiercely and clung to his arm. Together they took us around the buildings like a couple showing off their house.

The excavation would yield the real stuff, the testaments, vessels, jewellery, gold. People didn't spend all night digging for nothing.

'Here is the area where they slaughtered the animals, this, the bathing area.' We trod over stones, passed through broken chambers, and there again was the real treasure, the stone. 'But of course you know it,' he said to me. 'It's the reason you came to Girona. It pulls to it what is desired. It has for centuries. It sends out its invitation.'

It was pale, marked with symbols, lying tilted. I asked if it was Jewish?

'Before. It belonged to ancient practices.'

'The Romans?' asked one of the men.

'Oh, long before.'

And I remembered it from the Frenchwoman's garden. He'd lost the businessmen. They made a brief farewell and José slumped onto the nearest chair, ran a hand across his forehead. I think for a minute he was looking for someone to blame for the failure with the moneymen. His eyes stayed on mine.

'I'm just here doing this interview,' I said. 'I have to be in Madrid.' I explained about the company from LA preparing to film *Having it Away*.

I asked if any Jews had actually visited. 'The Jews will come. The vibration of this centre will attract them from all over the world.'

She couldn't nod her head ardently enough.

'Are you going to be converted?' I tried not to laugh.

'I must have been a Jew,' he said. 'How else could I find the key to all this?'

'Talking of miracles, I hear there was a vision behind the cathedral.'

He crossed the courtyard and deftly lifted back a branch loaded with blossom and fixed it against the wall. He secured the branch and in that moment I saw what he was. He could show even nature to advantage. He could make the least moment significant. He remained, his hand lifted, making sure the blossom would stay, and we watched him, riveted.

He listed the local visitors, the messages of support, the huge plans for the autumn. He still hadn't referred to the vision.

'It was near where the house with the tower was. Do you believe it?'

'Why not?' He shrugged. 'Just because we can't comprehend something doesn't mean it doesn't exist. I'd hate to think that what we understood was all there was.'

I'd been in the building over an hour and so far no one had come. He sat on the bench in the shade, away from me, and I realized it was difficult for him. He automatically reacted, as he'd always done when he saw me, as if we were together. But there was a third these days. He was trying to balance the scales and not succeeding. He smiled at her encouragingly. That got nowhere. It was clear the way in which he responded to me was different to what she got, and she didn't like it. He was polite with her. We sat in silence. Finally I said, 'Where are the Jews?' as if that would solve it. 'It's very impressive what you have done but it's nothing but a beautiful cradle. Without the baby.'

'We have found it again. The centre of Cabbala is here with us.'

'I thought it was in New York, or Jerusalem?' I was sure about that. I'd asked Hyam Maccoby, the Rabbinic scholar in London.

'No,' he said, decidedly. 'The Cabbala is here.' He thought going up against me would kill off any familiarity. It made it worse. I wondered what he had told her about me. His eyes stayed on mine, like the old days.

'Are you our investigator?' she asked. 'All these questions.'

'No, I'm your interviewer.' 'You'll get a lot of this,' I wanted to add, 'so get used to it.'

I turned to him and he stood up ready to leave.

'Are you going to get in touch with the existing groups?' I said.

'Why should we? We have it here.'

And then I wondered what his mother thought and what was she going to do about this ardent, too young, non-Catalan girl.

And she moved her head emphatically. I asked who would teach Cabbala. By now I wouldn't have been surprised if he'd said himself.

'The right teacher will come.'

'Don't you think you should let them know?' I held the pages of my *Jewish Chronicle* interview for authority. 'I know this must sound ordinary, but what about letters to synagogues and foundations in ...'

'It's not necessary,' he said. She gave the tiniest laugh in the world, but we all heard it. I'd been through too much for this scene.

'I think you're crazy. You're spending his money' – indicating Rafel Pons, who was by the wishing-well not daring to open his mouth – 'to build an institute of Cabbala and Rabbinical studies and you haven't involved one Jew. How do you know what a Cabbala centre is like? They may not even want a building. I'm not too sure about the bar. It seems Cabbala is in books and it's passed from person to person, even now. It's secret. It's an initiation.' Hyam Maccoby's words again.

'It was here. It is still here. Nachmanides opened up another dimension in this space.' He tapped his foot on the courtyard.

It seemed to me it had already been done. A perfection had been reached and recorded. Who today could better the mystics of the medieval time?

'How will you make money out of this?'

'Money!' José scoffed. 'I do not want money. If you can buy it or sell it it's not interesting to me. I'm only after value beyond price.' He paused and said I could print what I wanted. 'I am returning to the Jews what is theirs. I regret I have to go now.' He stood up.

'But you're out of money.' I didn't want to even look at Pons, to drop him in it.

The French girl joined José and took his arm. 'Let the Jews come or not. Do we have to do all this and crawl after them too?'

Was I listening to another investor?

Then she added: 'You know nothing about Cabbala, so how dare you presume to write an article on the subject?'

Late afternoon, and José had spent time looking for me. I had only one thing to say, an expletive, and I turned and walked through the hotel dining-room up to my room. I should have known that if you try to get rid of someone you've got them forever. I didn't realize he was behind me until he kicked the door open and started making love to me before it was even shut. I'd made sacrifices in my time, known crippling anxiety, fear of consequences, but for once in that hotel room I was able to hold happiness for as long as it lasted. The magic came in after we'd made love. I felt rich and full and alive, and a tray of awards couldn't have given me that. The sun coming through the shutters made a shadowed staircase on the wall of our room. It filtered through onto the ceiling and gave it arches and domes. I'd never noticed that before. It was as though we were in church as we lay side-by-side on the bed, hardly touching, looking at the lovely domed ceiling. That was our wedding. Transitory, yes; just as long as the sun lasted.

I made the *Jewish Chronicle* piece attractive, and it provoked interest.

27

Lauren Bacall was one of my favourite stars of all time, one of the adored ones of my adolescence who got my mind off Albany Park. I'd seen *The Big Sleep* and *To Have and Have Not* so many times I knew each frame by heart. When she was starring in the musical *Applause* in London, I'd put my third book *Harriet Hunter* through what I'd believed was her door. It turned out to be the wrong door, but the house owner knew her and re-posted it. Six months later I got a letter from her agents in New York to say they and the star herself had read the book, and wanted to option it for film immediately. Lauren Bacall was coming to Europe and wanted to meet me.

At lunch in Knightsbridge she looked incredible. If she wore make-up, it didn't show. Her voice was husky, low, and magnetized everyone in the place. Her two English agents sat at the table to hear what was agreed. She loved the book. She'd get it made. Oh, yes, it was for her. A writer in Hollywood, Ivan Moffat, told me he'd once asked her how she felt now when she saw the old movies with Bogart. Desperate? Nostalgic? Perhaps she couldn't bear to watch them? 'Oh, I watch them and think wasn't I beautiful?' And she'd laughed, a real, full of humour, generous laugh.

Perhaps because she'd had such a wonderful love affair, it stirred up the old feelings for José. It seemed age, even maturity, couldn't take the joy from those first years and sent me straight back to the carrer de la Força.

Train stations had played a big part in our affair. In the old days the train from the frontier to Girona took over two hours and was always late. He'd be waiting on the platform, black coat, white silk scarf, warm smile, bright eyes, hopes, deceits, and before the train stopped, before my body moved, my soul would leap out to his. The hours of travelling, all the difficulties, would be shrugged off as soon as he touched me. He opened up a new world full of colour, and I used to believe entry into this bright place was only possible through him. It turned out I was right. I'd climb down from the smoking train and the deceits would begin before the first kisses were over.

Lucia waited for me in her car. 'Imagine how she felt, Maria Tourdes, when she waited for the French priest in those days. He used to come, like you, from Perpignan.

'The train was as slow as a horse and kept stopping and no one knew why. Of course there was no money to run anything in those days.'

I asked which days were these.

'She was certainly in that house before 1900.'

But how old was she? I'd seen a woman of sixty-five, seventy at the most, lying ill in Paris.

'She was eighty-four. She looked good for her years and could always get herself up a bit. The mayor wants to talk to you. Naturally about José. He's getting into trouble. But that's to be expected. He won't answer to anyone.' We went first to the Jewish Centre.

Rafel's father, Papa Pons, was in the courtyard, sweeping falling leaves off the Star of David. He was bowed over, frail, his smile angelic. He was doing a beautiful thing. I realized he'd had to capitulate and throw in his whack of money. He said there was nobody around.

I went to Lluís's bar and told him about Bacall. At least he knew who she was. I asked about José. Would it work out? I meant, was she still there?

'If the banks don't foreclose and the landlords don't sue for their unpaid rent and the personal creditors don't lynch him. He doesn't even own the lavatories. Well, just one. By the bar. Those few metres are his. And he owns one stone. The ritual sun stone. Does he know Jews don't eat pork? I hope it does work because it's good for this town. But it's just a bar restaurant until the Jews come. I think it must be supported and you could be a help. I read the article in the Jewish paper, and people wrote to him after that. Get rid of the pig meat.'

Back at Isaac the Blind, José came out on to the patio of the bar wearing a blue-and-white striped shirt and brown cords, and his eyes flickered with remembered fire, then became normal. He told me about the fantastic far-reaching success of the establishment, how visitors were as though blown in the door and had found paradise.

'Any Jewish ones?'

Then I heard a cackling laugh. Old Papa Pons gone senile? But it was a strange bird mocking. I hadn't seen José for months and he looked tired. Everyday worry made him like anyone else and I so regretted the change. We both agreed we loved the autumn, and the bird did its jarring laugh.

'It calls to me,' he said. 'Even flies to my bedroom window. It comes from the mountains. Mount Canigou.'

The French girl's stained glass pieces, here and there in the corners, like detectives, watched our every move.

I leaned forward. 'So how are you?'

His eyes demanded silence. So she was only out of sight. I told him about Bacall and my visit sounded like some movie location hunt.

'You always have such success.' The French girl was in the courtyard. 'When will it reach Girona?' Her voice was hard as the bird's.

'About the time the Jews reach Girona.' I looked at the joint of ham on the counter. 'You want to get rid of that.'

'We don't need advice,' she said. 'This isn't Hollywood.' As she appeared, she pulled a chair close to his and took his hand.

How I wished Bacall could just walk in. Then Rafel Pons walked in and said that Isaac the Blind, the entire building and the courtyards, had been put up for auction.

At first, José couldn't believe it. He laughed. 'Not the sun stone. They won't get that.'

'The banks have foreclosed.'

Everybody was silent, even Papa Pons stopped sweeping; even the bird stopped laughing.

Lluís had given me my means of revenge. By my journalism I'd be the saviour of the centre. That would take the smirk off her spoilt face. I had another Coca Cola and put off killing her. 'I'll do another piece for the *Jewish Chronicle* right now. It'll go worldwide before auction day.'

The mayor, Joachim Nadal, represented the new Girona and wanted to establish a university and expel 'elitist ideas'. He'd studied history at Liverpool, so we spoke English. His message was simple. The town did not want foreign shrines run by José. José was running up debts Hollywood could be proud of. He did not want a political scandal. Finally, he waved the article that had drawn attention. He suggested I should have all the facts before I ever thought of doing another one. José had no idea what he was presenting. Since when was he a Cabbalist?

The French girl either saw me with the mayor or was told about it. She assured José that people knew 'I was thick with the mayor' and was probably his mistress. I knew she wanted him absolutely and in all ways. Because he was charismatic she would always have rivals – people were drawn to him – and that would never change. My crime? I'd known him before she was even born. The other crime, as far as he was concerned, was that I'd never had his child.

What did he know about Cabbala? Rather a lot, as it turned out. He opened his mouth and didn't stop talking for some minutes.

'It goes back to Talmudic times when individual mystics, while in a state of trance, received a vision of God. Cabbala in the Middle Ages is a complicated system where the nature of God and His way of creation are explained through the concept of the ten 'Sefirot', or emanations mediating between God and the world. Mastery of this system allows a mystic to achieve a powerful manner of prayer in which he helps God to become reunited with His exiled bride, the female principle, the Shechinah, and so to mend the universe and bring about the Messianic age.'

'How did you know this? Who told you?'

'I've always known it. From a boy.'

I remembered his months of spiritual work at the seminary with the master near Ripoll.

'It is when you rise above dualism, the positive and the negative, that existence becomes interesting. That is what the Cabbalists achieved. They helped God mend this flawed world.'

He stopped talking and frowned at the cage of doves the French girl had placed in the entrance. 'There you have it – the white dove and the black dove. The black is the messenger of darkness.' He walked over to the cage and one of the birds was darkly coloured, although not exactly black.

'How could this happen? This dark bird. There were two white ones yesterday.'

'Maybe someone painted it?' I suggested.

He saw it as a sign of ill omen. 'Like the church in France. By the porch are two doves, one facing east, the other west. One turned dark. Nothing was right after that.'

I didn't want to start thinking of that church now. I wanted to ask him about the Messianic age, what it was, but he opened the cage and only the white dove fluttered away.

'Maybe it's ill,' I said. 'That's why it's gone that colour.' These were London thoughts and not acceptable here.

I wrote about 'a remarkable Catalan poet and local gentile' devoting his life to restoring the school of the great medieval mystics. 'I want to return to the Jews what is theirs. It is a thing of destiny.' I wrote about the cost in time, energy, and at the bank, and explained away the restaurant as the only way to meet the interest on the huge bank loans. I was even nice about the French girl. I included the refusal of the municipality to become involved. José had said they only come in when they see it's a success story.

On the day of the auction a group of Americans who'd read the *Jewish Chronicle* arrived in the courtyard from Los Angeles. They were led by Zelman Goldstein, a lawyer; Moshe Lazar, a leading Ladino scholar; and Aaron Cohen,

President of the Sephardim Community in California. The sum to stop the auction was quickly raised and the centre was saved.

It was possibly the worst thing that could have happened.

Over the next five years I did a BBC Radio 4 documentary on the project, 'Don Quixote Is Not Dead', features in the *Listener*, the *Guardian*, the *Los Angeles Times*, and the *New York Times*. I went to fund-raising dinners for Girona in LA, supported by Henry Kissinger, Barbra Streisand, and pharmaceutical billionaires. Jane Fonda wanted to make a film with Barbra Streisand about the project. With Moshe Lazar I appeared on talk shows, which I dreaded, and set up evenings in New York and in Leo Baeck College, London, hosted by Hyam Maccoby.

José came over as a visionary restoring a vanished past, which had valuable lessons for the modern age. He was a figure from another century, giving everything up for an ideal. And beside him was the French girl, her sell-out exhibitions sacrificed in the daily toil to raise finance, serving kebabs until long past dawn to the locals. José, throwing his life away on a cause that may or may not succeed, thrilled them. So what? The food was exorbitantly priced. Turning kebabs today, he could be in jail tomorrow.

Hundreds of offers of support came in. People offered their time, money, skills, collections of Cabbala books. Fred Zinnemann, the movie director, was very taken with the idealism and sacrifice, and wanted to meet José immediately. Well-known people were drawn to this idealism that belonged to a bigger era.

I felt, because my writing had thrown light on the place and saved it, that somehow a piece of it was mine. I phoned José to say Fred Zinnemann was interested and would probably visit. And Hyam Maccoby, who happened to be a world authority on Nachmanides and the Jews of Girona, wanted to help. José sounded breathless, as though his nerves were on edge. 'Finally they have come. I knew they would. The strain has been terrible.'

The Americans formed a Foundation and Zelman Goldstein announced it to the press. 'This is more than a shrine. It is a living, breathing history that is very much present. It is one of the most important Jewish sites in the world. We will pay off the bank loans, continue the excavations, establish a School of Rabbinic Study. We will buy up the buildings that are currently rented. José is a poet and a fighter for truth.' In the *Los Angeles Times* a journalist described Moshe Lazar's take on José's find. He had said that José

> had uncovered a huge stone – 'about half the size of this room,' Lazar said, referring to his spacious university office – in what would have been the basement of the synagogue. 'It might be an ancient altar stone,' Lazar said. He said a druidic sign was found carved on one spot.

José's new love affair was on. I got a call from him and he said Leonard Bernstein was on his way. 'What shall I do?'

I didn't think he'd be overfazed by that visit. I had talked to Leonard Bernstein in New York and he was fascinated by the project, even talked of writing music to celebrate its story.

'I'm going to get married.'

I didn't answer. I couldn't answer. My voice was never the same again.

'Well, you did it,' I thought he'd said.

I remembered the beach at L'Escala, years before. The joy of that day had been such that I'd never looked at boats and sand in the same way again. Fishing boats brought back instantly the winter sun, the loud wind, his beauty, his flapping coat. I'd been so happy that morning on the beach that the only thing to do to give it expression had been to try and fly. The wind could have lifted me if I'd found the right way to let go. Gravity could somehow be overcome. Happiness could do it.

What would his mother do? How would she try to stop it? I realized it was an odd thing to think at such a time. And then I understood that she not only approved of this girl, but had chosen her.

I sat and wrote *From the Balcony*, a play for Radio 3 and the Cottesloe at London's National Theatre. I wrote books, short stories, radio plays, film scripts, made documentaries. I wrote about Jeanne Hébuterne, the last friend and mistress of Modigliani, first as a novel *Forget Me Not*, then as a biography *Into the Darkness Laughing*. I produced it for radio, then it became a stage play, being performed in London, Norway, France, and, finally, Spain. I wrote *Albany Park* about my life with José. That was bought for film immediately, but never made. The book came out in Spain, so did the Modigliani book, so did the film *Siesta*. The Modigliani stage play was put on in Girona and accompanied an exhibition of Modigliani paintings at the Fontana d'Or.

The Americans had taken José and his wife to Israel and New York. My journalism meant I got many letters asking where Cabbala was taught. All I knew was that it contained a 'Tree of Life' in its teaching, and that Carmen Aragó had planted one in her garden. It was spread out on the patio, made up of shrubs and flowers, and showed the ladders of evolvement from earth upwards and occasionally downwards. José had given me a diagram showing its different paths of evolvement.

Tree of Life

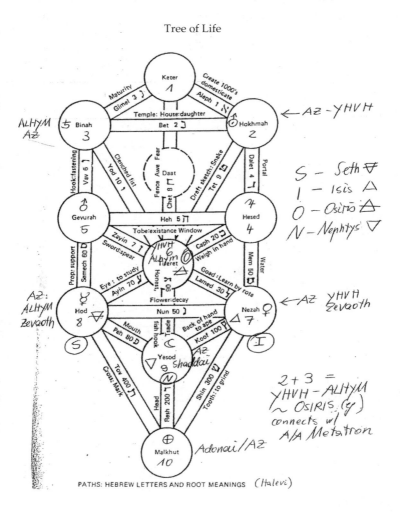

PATHS: HEBREW LETTERS AND ROOT MEANINGS (Halevi)

I'd recognized some of the same symbols from the documents in his room but it was annotated with words I couldn't understand.

My elder son had his birthday in Isaac the Blind. Old friends came to the table and for a while the good times were back.

Patrice and José soon after they met

The Residencia's bar in 1955

How the Residencia
Internacional looked in 1955

Patrice in the Savoy bar

José and Lluís

Lucia

Old postcard of Girona with the Torre Magdala on the right

Girona station as Saunière knew it

Maria Tourdes writing at her desk

Maria Tourdes with some of the men she helped during the
Second World War in the Free French campaign

Roger Mathieu in front of the tower in Girona

The courtyard at José's Cabbala Centre

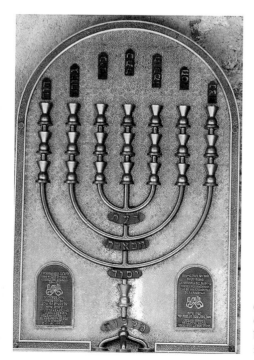

One of José's exhibits at the Cabbala Centre was this menorah belonging to Nachmanides, a founder of Cabbala

The Sun Stone

Shrine to the 1976 vision

The punishing crucifixion scene at
St Sepulchre, outside Besalú

The 'House of the Canons' sign over the arch into Maria's garden

Painting of two towers titled 'La Nuit' by renowned
Catalan artist J.C. Villalonga

28

It went wrong. Zelman Goldstein asked me to Girona, urgently, and said the battle was on. José had used the Americans' money but not their ideas. They wanted him out. The mayor wanted everyone out. Zelman sat in Lluís's bar and put forward a proposition. He and his clients felt ripped off. It would not happen again. He personally wanted Isaac the Blind. It was there in his eyes. He was intelligent, knowledgeable, a good lawyer. He knew about Cabbala and could really explain it. But his eyes – I knew I should be careful of that look. He'd been decorated in the Israeli War. He was a tactician, a fighter. He would never let go. Because of my articles in the *Jewish Chronicle* he'd found Girona and was grateful. For him it was a coming home. All he had to do was get José out.

Zelman's associate journalist, Max Kander, was also someone to be reckoned with. He held down jobs in tough places, and was working as a journalist and broadcaster in Israel. The way he looked at the stones, the stairways and arches, it was his, all of it. He just had to get rid of José.

He walked with me along the Rambla. 'Zelman does not trust you. The Americans have been told not to speak with you. Support for José now could be ill-timed. We have formed a group to restart the centre. The politicians, the university in Barcelona are on our side.'

'Where does José fit in?'

'He fits in very well if he's sensible. He can be artistic director with a privileged place on the board and a monthly salary. He can have plenty of time to write poems.'

Was I suddenly looking like an agent? I asked why he didn't approach the wife.

'She only sees it through his eyes.'

I thought he was finished with me, but he stood by the deserted building that had once been the Residencia Internacional. It was covered with decaying adverts.

'Where are the documents?' Kander said, softly.

I didn't know what he meant.

'I've seen the plan of the twenty-four houses and had it verified. I mean the experiments. And he has the key.' A pause. 'You don't know what the key is?' Another pause. 'The activator.'

So I asked what it was.

'An object.'

I thought back over the years, trying to recall the objects I'd seen. The scorched ring. The dirty, ill-defined goblet. Of course the ritual sun stone. What was I missing?

'What does it look like?'

'A cup.'

The goblet then.

'But with additions.' And he drew a picture in the dust of the street of an object with three legs and two balls attached. It looked like something that had just landed from outer space. I had never seen that.

'You know what *samael* is?'

I did not.

'But you have seen the Tree of Life?'

'No.'

'You have heard of the Ark of the Covenant?'

He gave up on me. I started to leave.

'Did you know the Rosicrucians came here?'

Yes. I remembered those pages from Julien Sacaze's 'Writings on the Rose Cross' all those years ago. I didn't tell him.

He drew another sign in the dirt. 'This is the Rosicrucian pentagram.' He thought I was dumb. I was. I said I'd seen it years ago in José's room, in the book by Sacaze.

And then Lucia was there, dressed in white, her face hidden beneath a large floppy sunhat. Enormous dark glasses did the rest. She looked fragile and sheer, like a character from a Scott Fitzgerald book.

'Have you seen José?' she said, immediately.

She pulled me to one side and Max Kander was obliged to leave.

'They won't get him out,' she said. 'They'll try everything, but this is Catalonia. They don't let outsiders just come in here and take over a whole chunk of the town. José may be stubborn but he is one of theirs. In ten years from now he'll still be serving kebabs on the patio.' She watched Max Kander going back towards the Rambla. 'I wouldn't talk to him.'

'Who is he?'

'I don't know, but a lot of treasure seekers are suddenly learning Cabbala.'

I knew she'd say, 'Stay out of it.'

He came in as the church bells chimed midnight. Everything in the room jumped, and lace doilies on the armchairs slid to the floor. He was enclosed in his marriage, part of her world as the Jewish excavations were part of his. History was being taken in large doses and recycled through his poet's mind.

'The right Jews will come. They are the future of Girona. Girona can no longer be a place of perfection if it does not fulfil its destiny. Hundreds of years ago Nachmanides and the mystics designed its future, and I have the key.'

'Why you?'

He replaced the doilies on the chairs almost apologetically. They were dusty. The old hotel was showing its age. 'Because I am a poet. My style is a memorial to the time past. So through me the voice of Cabbala is transmitted.'

He wouldn't even discuss the Zelman offer. 'They're speculating on the land. That's what they want. They'll bring Disney in here next.'

I wondered if we'd be together if he had found nothing behind the Roman wall. The mystics might have mapped out Girona's fate, but I wasn't sure about anyone else's. It all seemed accidental.

'What about us?' I said, my voice shaking.

'We fucked up.'

He kissed me briefly and started for the door.

'Where did your mother find her? Your wife.'

He paused and thought back through all the meetings over the years, until he arrived at the moment those pale green-yellow eyes that showed two colours at once, like traffic lights gone wrong, met his.

'I believe she came to the Residencia Internacional,' he said. 'Yes, now I think of it, my mother was on social terms with her father.'

He went out slamming the door and the doilies slipped gracefully off the armchairs onto the floor, like debutantes fainting. Normally such a sight would make me laugh, but I was a million miles from laughing.

He'd said 'key'. Wasn't that what Max Kander had said?

I missed the fight. It had a wonderful effect on the town. José weighed possibly eleven stone and Zelman, a professional fighter, possibly two more, but José had lifted his enemy up in the air and thrown him over a wall. He'd landed sprawled across Carmen Aragó's Tree of Life patio. Calmly José said he would tolerate no more speculation. Some said it was like Jesus clearing the temple. The courtyard had never been as crowded. The overflow sat in the windows of the *salons* or on the stairs. There weren't enough hands to take the money.

Lucia said it was like a three-star restaurant in Marbella. She'd been against it since the start, and laughed as waiters dashed around the tables serving huge colourful ice-creams and drinks. 'They're made by a German photographer. She does the cakes too.'

A middle-aged woman with a careless assurance greeted me. This was Carmen Aragó, and she was trying to find somewhere to sit. I offered her a place at my table, and she was the one calm presence in the courtyard. Her hair was curly and hung like curtains on each side to her shoulders, making her a little like a bewigged judge. She had a strong face and sensitive eyes, and really looked at the person she was speaking to. She knew all about me, I had no doubt. 'We're having a course in Cabbala,' she said. She introduced the teacher, her friend Ingrid, a German who'd lived in the US. Had she, I wondered, met Zelman, Max, and the new official owners of the site?

'Yes,' she said. 'Face down in the Tree of Life. That has to mean something, but what I don't know.'

Two men of importance came out of the bar and José gave them his fullest attention. Carmen said they were local men, both psychiatrists. Dr Baró and Dr Colomer.

185

'Send them over here,' I said. 'I could give them some work.'

Ingrid touched my arm soothingly. 'You're just pushed into an uncomfortable position. Don't be in it.'

The psychiatrists, it seemed, looked after José.

'Does he need two?'

'The society here,' said Carmen, 'they're on his Board. With me. Dr Colomer is also in politics.'

Forbidding and resourceful, they looked as though they could take care of things. One was short with a dangling black moustache and busy eyes. 'I'd hate to crack up in their company.'

Ingrid laughed. 'You couldn't afford it.'

And then from a table behind me, a voice I thought I remembered. 'So you're not wearing the cross.'

I turned, but did not recognize the man. He was attractive. That was the least I could say. He was agile, feline, as he crouched beside Ingrid and picked up some dropped coins.

'At least they're not Jewish,' he said.

She laughed, a wonderful open generous laugh, making her bosom shake, her face flush. When it was over she patted him. 'Coming from you,' she said. And I realized it was not what was said but who said it.

His hazel eyes held a challenge, ironic, perhaps cynical. They implied he knew me better than I knew myself. Their beauty made me shy. Their expression, quick, assessing, suggested he wanted my good. I wasn't often looked at so appraisingly. He was tanned, thin, with dust on his coat and shoes. He looked well travelled. He said he'd just come back from South America, an hour ago. He'd been away over fifteen years.

'So what do you think of this place?' He looked around. 'Everyone thinks this is mysterious. Well, at the bank. It's the only word for it. How does he keep going, this Don Quixote, tilting at banks as though they're windmills? But there are more complex mysteries beneath this one. This is just the façade.' He was talking to Ingrid, but I felt he wanted me to hear it.

'Have you seen the sun stone?' asked Ingrid.

He nodded. 'And talking of stones, not a stone's throw away' – he looked in the direction of the path behind the cathedral, '– there was a house with a tower. Madame Mathieu. Perhaps it's her money he's losing here. Not his own.'

'It's Rafel Pons's money,' I said, always ready to defend José, although I knew he was talking about the Frenchwoman – Maria Tourdes to her friends, Madame Mathieu to others.

'Oh no. A little nearer than that.' He gestured back towards the cathedral. 'I think we'll find it's her money in these walls.' And he smacked a stone and dust fell. José was still engaged with the psychiatrists, the visiting group, and looked across at our table, frowning. I thought if only he could he'd join us, making it safe. And then I thought again of the Frenchwoman. I hadn't for years. I remembered her saying, 'Focus on the mark on the tower.'

'So what happened to the cross and chain?'

I wished I had Lucia there to answer for me.

I said I didn't know.

'I see he's got hold of the ritual sun stone,' he said.

'Isn't it his?'

'Not exactly.'

As he talked to Carmen about her Tree of Life development – she meditated each day on one step – I watched his reactions. He was calm, understated. His face was well-boned, fine, the lips exquisitely etched, teeth even and white in spite of his continuous smoking, and they gleamed briefly during the quick rare smiles. The hair black, glossy and streaked with grey, almost touched his collar. He was graceful with beautiful effortless movement. Life had been generous to him. He was used to it being on his side.

'When are you leaving?' He was talking to me.

Had I said I was?

'Oh, you'll have to leave now.'

So I had to ask why. Did he know everything? His voice was expressive and true and, listening to it, I thought he knew how to excite – to give pleasure and stir things up. I was getting too much from a voice. His eyes stayed on mine, provoking a response he needed and I looked away.

'Because now he's fallen out with the Americans someone has to be to blame. It can't be his fault or the wife's, so it'll be yours.'

'I didn't bring those Americans.'

'Oh, but you did, *ma cherie*.'

'I spent hours working on his behalf.' My voice was shaking. 'I brought Leonard Bernstein.' I listed the others.

'He'll tell you these newspaper articles brought those Americans and disaster.'

José was apparently having a decisive conversation with the group around him. His eyes were uncertain. The police chief stood at the bar having a drink. Had he come to arrest him?

'Is he in danger from the Americans?'

'He's got a nose. He can smell it. Don't you remember?'

He laughed suddenly and I saw that he was Quim Carreras, the priest I'd met with José before he sent me to Paris. He'd lost the puppy fat.

Cautiously I watched José introduce his wife to the visiting group. I saw the way he kissed her cheek, and it seemed he didn't behave with the intensity we had shared for all those years. Perhaps he didn't have it any more. And I breathed in the hot air. If he'd shown her that I'd have run forever. I'd have left him with whatever grace and proper respect for his choice I could drag out of myself.

I managed to get close enough to him to say, 'I must see you.' And then I left.

Quim Carreras followed. And then José.

'They've made a little shrine on the hill up there.' Carreras pointed to the path behind the cathedral. 'I heard something about a vision.'

'Oh, that.' José was off-hand. 'It was in the winter. A few years ago. Some workmen got excited.'

'No,' Carreras said, with deliberation. 'A woman saw a vision of the Magdalene. The Lady of the Cup.'

'Do you believe it?' I asked.

'I deal in miracles every day, so why not one more?' José cleared his throat. He was nervous of Carreras.

I held his hand, my love for him back, visible to the whole street, to the intruding eyes of the enquiring priest. I looked down. Carreras almost laughed. He patted José. 'We'll have to have a little truth. See who was doing what on 4 February 1976.' And he started off towards the cathedral and José watched him until he was out of sight.

Suddenly we were alone, one on each side of the strip of street.

'Do you remember Chez Béatrice in the alley?' he said. 'That was a special time.'

'Do you remember it?'

'You know I never forget the past.'

189

'Well, I'd start, because your present looks good to me. You've got an establishment, a wife.'

I heard the trees rustling then, the way they used to in Puerta de la Selva. There was so much I didn't notice any more. He crossed over to my side of the street.

'Sometimes I think about you,' he said. 'Rather you come into my mind. It's strange because I may not have given you a thought for … months.' He spoke as to himself.

'Do you love her?'

There was an awkwardness now.

He should go back but didn't move, and I realized the street for once was empty and not one person had passed in any direction. 'I think when you are happy in a place that happiness goes on existing.' He held my hand quite openly. 'What do you think?'

I wanted to mark the moment with some sign, write a message, leave a token, so it would be remembered for always.

'I'll find some way for us.' And he ran back up to the blue door. And suddenly life moved again and the street was filled with people walking to and fro.

I went around Girona, praying he'd leave with me. I prayed in all the sinful places. Not the cathedral or the churches. Too many prayers got sent up from those. Mine wouldn't get a look-in. Then I walked reclaiming the town, all the streets and cafés where I'd been happy, even the ones that had gone. I'd got him back.

But she found the way for us. In the night she told him she was having his baby.

What had started as a dream, just something in José's head, had taken over until it was bigger than he and he was trapped in the dream. He'd win or die. The Americans might have the moral right to get him out, but his lawyer wasn't asleep on his feet. His skilful handling of the law wasn't quite clear to Lucia, but it was clear in Catalonia. No one could get José out. For perpetuity. He owned the lavatory.

Lucia couldn't understand why I believed José had chanced upon the site. 'He always knew it was there. If he says otherwise he has a reason. Believe me. The Cabbala business is a cover for something much bigger. He used to talk about the time of the Jews at school. He knew all the stories.'

Zelman started buying the land around José, pinning him in as once the Spaniards had pinned in the Jews. But he didn't allow for one thing. You couldn't buy Girona.

'José's lawyer is the real hero.' Lluís polished his glasses and waited for night. Daylight never did suit him. He had a house in the country, another by the sea, and a shop in the centre. Each year he stayed a month in the Waldorf Astoria, New York. He still hadn't written a word. 'He's got José such a deal. Who would think of renting your bar to yourself? The town will always forgive him because he does what the Catalan bourgeoisie cannot. Through him they live dreams. And in Catalonia there's a saying: "Wolves Never Eat Each Other."'

Then the mayor got involved. The municipality didn't want a Jewish scandal, frustrated Americans buying properties, a bad name in Israel, nor José in a privately owned palace, grandiose, elitist, in debt. The mayor tried many ways to get him out. He even suggested I take the place over.

Then one day José was gone. The sun stone went with him. It was in the late 1980s. Whatever he'd been there for was completed. The mayor turned it into a Jewish museum.

29

In the late sixties my brother-in-law had told me of a book by a Frenchman about a poor priest who became rich overnight and nobody knew how, and they still didn't to that day. He had become phenomenally rich after finding a secret hidden in his church at Rennes-le-Château. At the time, I didn't associate my brother-in-law's description with my time in Girona, or my unresolved experience in that church, which I'd kept quiet about for so long. As the book was in French and my earlier good grasp of the spoken language had never been matched by sufficient reading, I couldn't understand much. I didn't connect it with the people I'd known because I had never heard mention of a huge fortune and, of course, there was no reference to Spain. I was preoccupied and trying to build a career.

My brother-in-law spoke of the story with such a fascination. Why hadn't it been known about before? When did it take place? Was it a hoax? My brother-in-law didn't think so and decided to go to the village, but even that was unknown, not marked on general maps. The mystery had never been solved and, even in France, was completely lost in history. The nineteenth-century priest had one morning become the recipient of a great and continuing wealth and it possibly came from alchemy – about which I knew nothing.

The slim book that had captivated my brother-in-law was *Le Trésor Maudit de Rennes-le-Château* (1967) by Gérard de Sède, but it sank without a trace. The best seller *The Holy Blood and the Holy Grail* came out in the early 1980s and, because it seemed to focus on a possible Jesus bloodline, a faked crucifixion, the secret society of the Prieuré de Sion and an attempt to re-establish the throne of France, I still didn't make a connection. As the authors stated, their book had come into being by the casual finding of the Gérard de Sède story. But I did notice that Jean Cocteau was purported to be the last Grand Master of the Prieuré de Sion.

In the late eighties I lived on and off for some years in Céret, a Catalan village in the foothills of Mount Canigou on the French side of the Pyrenees. Visitors passed through on their way to Rennes-le-Château, in search of gold, the secret of the universe. So I went there myself again. It was overrun with sightseers and treasure hunters. The inhabitants were dismayed, furious – the village was in disarray.

Winding up the steep hill to the tower, I remembered the journey with José and Arbós over twenty years before. My visit to the church was short, and I was glad there were droves of agitated seekers and so many flashing cameras that it was like a fireworks display. There was not a sacred moment to be seen or felt. The church was much smaller than I'd remembered, and sinking into the ground crookedly. The Stations of the Cross were too forceful, as though insisting on a meaning that was different from what would be expected. The imagery was clear and disconcerting. The devil by the door was not a figure of spiritual celebration.

The view from the Tour Magdala was awesome, right across to the Pyrenees. I shared the turret with a dozen chattering Japanese. Nobody knew the point of the tower or why it was there. Neo-Gothic, it was constructed in 1903. But what struck me immediately and with great force was its direct similarity to the Torre Magdala in the French-woman's garden.

I went south to Girona for a few days because my literary agent and his wife wanted me to show them this city that had so influenced my writing. I hadn't seen José for over two years and I asked Lluís, established as usual in his bar, if he was around. I needed to avoid any painful meetings. He said José was out of town with his wife and son, somewhere in France. The Isaac the Blind building was closed and being prepared as a museum. He had a wife, a child, and I had my own life.

I led them up behind the cathedral along the stone passageway that had once been the dusty track, and as I passed the approximate place where the peeling brown door had been, I did consider how I could be here at all in this city that had once given me something so glorious and still survive its loss. Hadn't she, the Frenchwoman, felt that? I'd seen it in the letter to José's cousin.

'The stone passageway and the gardens were created in the late sixties,' I said, a true guide. And then I saw what was left of the Frenchwoman's land, which now had a plaque, 'The Garden of the Frenchwoman'. The wall was still broken but the garden was partially restored, and as I climbed the steps onto the city wall with its defensive slits, the sacred mountain Canigou could be clearly seen. I remembered her coming into the garden and watching me walk the wall. My eyes had been on a mark in the stone of the tower. I'd openly admired the structure, for something to say. 'Oh, it's not very important. It's only a hundred years old,' she'd said. The house, although in its infancy compared with its Roman neighbours, had certainly been built more than a hundred years before. The tower had then been added, and, idly, I wondered why and on whose instructions, and the thought passed.

The heat was suddenly terrible, burning, sweltering, sickly, and because I knew José wasn't there I said I'd take them to his *barraca*. We started towards the little hut in the countryside where the garden was cool. If it hadn't been for a little breeze that was so delightful, I wouldn't have stopped. I turned to check its direction – a wind from the south, always lucky for me – and there in the distance was a figure I'd know anywhere, coming towards the track that led to his *barraca*. 'It's José,' I think I said, as I hurried towards him. For a moment he seemed insubstantial. I put it down to the heat. And I increased my pace, so before he turned down his path towards whatever waited for him, he would see me and we would say again our names in greeting.

He was carrying a large string-bag of oranges and a huge plastic bottle of water from the fountain. I said, because I had to say something, 'I've been to Rennes-le-Château.'

He put down the oranges and water and kissed me on both cheeks, politely, but his eyes fixed on mine.

'But Rennes-le-Château is here,' he said. 'You'll find nothing there.'

He took us to the *barraca* and I asked who was there. He was alone. My agent and his wife were quite amazed by the meeting.

'Oh, he's always the first person I see,' I said.

And José explained it away. 'We're on a magnetic path, aren't we?'

He was more passionate about the subject of Rennes-le-Château than I'd seen him about any other for years. His eyes were bright, and he was fervent and engaged as he claimed the priest and the mystery for his beloved city. In his defence of his city he was open, almost careless, as he revealed what he had never mentioned before. 'Of course, Rennes-le-Château was here in Girona. That's why the French priest came here. Girona always had the secret. A place like this with all its resonance. Of course it would have something as powerful as that.'

'So the priest came here?' we asked.

'But yes. He came to see Maria Tourdes. It is well known in Girona. My cousin Geli knew about it and looked after her. He did not know Saunière. My grandfather did, and my great-uncle was his friend. He came here to get the secret. It was never in Rennes-le-Château.'

'But what about the parchments, the ones that were found in the church?' My agent knew some of the story of Rennes-le-Château.

'The original ones were coded instructions, indicating the location of the material.'

'Material?'

'Documents, the secret, the …' He asked if we wanted an orange. Nobody wanted anything, just him talking. 'It's unlikely those parchments are the originals. They would have been copied and changed many times since 1891. Saunière would have seen to that.'

'Who left them in the church? I mean if the secret isn't in or around the church?'

'Abbé Bigou. He was the priest in Rennes-le-Château in the eighteenth century and got out before the French Revolution. He had certain documents and material, but the secret was here.'

'Where did he go?'

'Here. He came here and to a village nearby. He had to get the material out before the new regime got hold of it.'

José was different. I would have said proud of his claim, of the importance of his city. Was it because of the loss of the Isaac the Blind centre?

'Is there any documentary evidence?' asked my agent, carefully.

'A correspondence exists. Between Saunière and Maria. And others.' And then he said no more. Suddenly.

And I realized that we'd seen each other daily during the PR work on the Cabbala Centre when *The Holy Blood and the Holy Grail* had come out to great attention in Spain, and yet he'd not said a word.

'How did he get the secret? What happened here?' My agent asked the questions and we all wanted the answers, but we got an orange each, a cup of fountain water, and a sightseeing journey through the old part, and that was it.

José and I stayed together in the streets and the bars and ended up by the Frenchwoman's garden.

'You knew all this. Why didn't you tell me?' I asked.

'I don't think it's a subject for casual discussion.'

'Why not?'

'It's not resolved. It's safer to be discreet.' And then he asked about my life, and I asked about his. They were living either in her studio in Sant Daniel or in his mother's apartment. She was now with her parents at their house in France. He was busy with the running of cultural events, especially the Flower Exhibition every May.

That night I read the books I'd bought in Rennes-le-Château. In prehistoric times the little village was named Rhedae and considered a sacred site by the Celtic tribes who lived there. This could have been because of the ley lines and meridians understood by those pre-Christian dwellers to harbour great energy currents and pulses converging on that spot. The area became a large and thriving community during Roman times, important for its mines and therapeutic waters in nearby Rennes-les-Bains. The Romans also considered it sacred. Its strategic height in the middle of the plain gave it military advantage.

Ruled by the Visigoths in the sixth century, it became their stronghold, and for the following five hundred years was fought over by the Franks, and then the Arabs, being sold in the eleventh century to the Counts of Barcelona. It was given the status of Royal City with nearby Carcassonne after the marriage of Visigoth Prince Almaric with Clothilde, a royal Frank, and became popular as a court with entertainment and troubadours.

It would seem that various treasures were buried in the area and could partly account for the priest's wealth: the Visigoth gold plundered from Rome in 500 AD, including the solid gold seven-branched menorah from the Temple of Solomon; the treasure of Blanche of Castille; the treasure of the Cathars, of King Dagobert. In the thirteenth century the Northern Knights under Simon de Montfort stamped out the Cathars and claimed the Languedoc. In the fourteenth century the population of Rennes-le-Château was almost extinguished by plague and Catalan bandits. The area then became agricultural and the hilltop town shrank to a hamlet, which I recognized today.

The church was built on what was a Visigoth place of sanctity, and consecrated to Mary Magdalene in 1059. Some miles to the southeast lies Bezu, another peak with the remains of a medieval fortress, belonging to the

Knights Templar. The Blanchefort family were mentioned frequently, especially Bertrand, the fourth Grand Master of the Knights Templar, and his descendants, prominent land-owners, until the Revolution. Abbé Bigou, the eighteenth-century priest that José had mentioned, was the confessor of Lady d'Hautpol de Blanchefort, last in the Blanchefort family line. After her death on 17 January 1781 he erected her tombstone, which was to become a focal point in the later discoveries of Saunière.

Was it this rich mystical and bloody past that gave this quiet agricultural region its disquieting atmosphere today? In 1891, the impecunious and charismatic priest Abbé Bérenger Saunière became a millionaire overnight with endless wealth at his disposal for the rest of his life. It was never confirmed what he'd found. It was understood to be the Holy Grail.

Now his story linked with the people and the snatches of dramatic events that I'd been a witness to for over thirty years.

José was up working on the gardens around his *barraca*. I told him what I'd been reading.

'You won't find much in the books. The priest covered his tracks.'

I asked about Saunière's visits to Girona.

'He certainly stayed in the house with Maria. He needed to be here. It would seem there was a relationship of some kind between them.'

So I asked how he knew, and he said it was always talked about in his family when he was a child. He was going silent again, so I asked the same questions as my agent. What did the priest find?

'A secret.'

'What did he do?'

'He copied the tower.' He pointed to where it had been. 'Why?'

He shrugged. 'He built the same in Rennes-le-Château.'

'For what reason?'

'Well, there must be one.'

'What is the secret?'

He carried on cutting back foliage.

'Do you know?'

He frowned. 'You have to be an initiate, otherwise it's unsafe.'

I felt he would tell me more, but he changed his mind.

'Who else knows?'

'It's not about digging for gold.'

The trouble was I still felt the same with him as I always did. I asked about his son and their lives, and he said everything was going well. I asked why he'd left the Jewish Centre just like that.

'I'd done what I had to do. Then I could go.'

Was his wife involved with the business of the French priest, the secrets from the past?

'She hates it. Won't have anything to do with it. She's busy with her work.'

I said I was glad he was happy, and he didn't answer. There were so many things to say on both sides, so many questions, so I said, 'Was Cocteau in it? This secret society mentioned in the books. Was he the Grand Master?'

'I'm sure he'd be a marvellous Grand Master if it exists.'

'Why didn't you tell me this before? When the Holy Grail book came out here?'

'It's not for me to tell.'

'You talked a lot yesterday.'

'That was because I was taken aback to see you. It made me say things I wouldn't say normally.'

'Pleased to see me, do you mean?'

'I knew I'd see you again.'

We walked together towards the town, and it felt strange, awkward. 'Why does your wife hate it? Rennes-le-Château?' It now had a name.

'Because it has its dark side.'

He stopped and pointed at a small shrine. 'That's where the vision was said to have appeared.'

The shrine was dedicated to Jesus, and there was a copy of His footprint as it had appeared in the dirt. The shrine was well kept up and filled with flowers. It was only when I'd said goodbye to him that I was sure the vision had been the Magdalene, the Lady of the Cup.

He didn't say much until we were down the cathedral steps and opposite Lluís's bar. Lluís was radiant seeing the two of us together. He was the perpetrator of surreal rumours and he didn't like it if the town was at peace. He had the yellow disquieting eyes of a wolf, camouflaged day and night by tinted glasses. His manner had become excessively gentle and encouraged confidences. No one ever saw him eat, drink, or sleep. He seemed to survive on cigarette smoke and gossip.

José had to leave, but said instead, 'Maria Tourdes was a kind woman. Exceptional. She had everything and said that wasn't even the beginning of the real riches.'

'Who did she marry?'

He said he didn't know.

'Shouldn't we do something for that time?' I said, quickly.

'A testament to Maria? I've often wanted to write something about her.'

'We could get people to write what they remembered.' Quick, quick, keep talking, and my mouth opened and more ideas stopped him from going.

Then we said goodbye and he made the parting very quick. I thought careful, practical thoughts. A train to Figueres, then I'd get a car to Céret. I will not cry. My thoughts were quick and jerky. My face was damp and running with what I thought was sweat. It was tears. I went into the nearest doorway, and was inside Gerard Ruiz's second-hand bookshop. For a woman of the world I wasn't doing very well.

A man, slim and agile, was standing at the counter, looking down at an open book. Grey streaked hair reached his collar and was swept back at the sides. He wore sandals, his feet were dusty. I told Gerard Ruiz I'd been to Rennesle-Château, and Quim Carreras looked up from his book.

'No good going there.'

I asked Ruiz if he had any photographs or books on that time.

'Why?' asked Carreras, casually. 'What have photographs of Girona at that time got to do with it?'

I made it appear that I had suddenly thought of something. 'Perhaps the priest came here?'

'Abbé Saunière never came here.' He said it absolutely and conclusively. There was no doubt. The French priest had never been in this city.

'You've been listening to the wrong information.' He went on turning the book's pages. I said I would still like anything on the period – 1890 onwards.

'He died in 1917,' said Carreras. 'Surely José told you that.'

Was he a friend? An enemy? I didn't answer. He looked at me over his glasses as though I was a member of his flock straying. 'Everyone's jumping on the Grail bandwagon. But it can't reach across the Pyrenees.'

Gerard Ruiz was stuck between a possible sale and the priest's disapproval, but he put several books on the crowded counter.

'Who did Maria Tourdes marry?'

'A Frenchman. Roger Mathieu.' He looked at Ruiz. 'It was Roger?'

'I never saw him. I was too young.'

'We were all too young,' said Carreras. 'He was much older than her and died after the Civil War.' He shut the book and put money on the counter. 'Forget Rennes-le-Château. It's Disneyland. If you want mystery beyond your comprehension, and excitement and power, read the real story.'

'What's that?'

'The Bible. What else?' And he stepped lightly out of the shop. I couldn't help watching him.

Ruiz laughed. 'It's a pity he's a priest.'

'I bet a lot of people think that.'

The old Hotel Centro had too many shadows, was too full of memories. I turned on the lamp and a stream of mixed and rather showy insects rushed through the open window like women into a Harrods sale. Out in the narrow street, little more than an alley, the yowling cats arrived. Being here was like the dream I used to have of the old poster, but less substantial because, as I heard the cathedral clock chime the quarter hour, I experienced the punishing solitude that belonged in my present life. A secret unrelenting loneliness, because I'd been torn from that which I loved and to which I belonged. Like other people who existed in a state of ruptured perfection, I made the best of it.

30

Born 11 April 1852 in Montazels, an agricultural village in the Aude district in sight of the Pyrénées Orientales, Bérenger Saunière became a strong, energetic, and handsome man, with penetrating powerful eyes. As the oldest child he went into the Church, as so many did from large, poor families. He was used to the life of the countryside, walking, fishing, climbing, hunting. Highly intelligent, he seemed destined for a promising clerical career but, after only a few weeks in the seminary in Narbonne, he was placed in the run-down and unlikely parish of Rennes-le-Château. He was thirty-three and had been on the way to better things. What had gone wrong? It seemed his powerful stance had displeased his superiors, and he was too political in his support for the return of the monarchy.

From his arrival he tried to restore the decrepit, leaking church. His income was only just sufficient for survival. He read and perfected Latin and Greek, and began an intensive study of Hebrew. An eighteen-year-old hatmaker from the village of Esperanza, Marie Denarnaud, came to work as his housekeeper and cook. His social contacts included Abbé Henri Boudet, from Rennes-les-Bains, and Abbé Gelis of Coustaussa. He was helped to finance the restoration by monarchist sympathizers, especially the

Habsburgs. The Comtesse de Chambord – originally a Habsburg who had been married to the Pretender to the French throne, the last descendant of the Bourbon family – allegedly gave him 3,000 francs. Johann of Habsburg, Archduke of Austria-Hungary, and cousin of Franz Joséph who was assassinated before the First World War, brought considerably more. It was said that Johann sometimes helped to oversee the work, disguised as a 'Monsieur Guillaume'. The villagers called him 'L'Etranger'. José has said that the Habsburgs were keen to receive material secreted within the church.

In 1891, while removing the altar stone (as it was claimed by his verger, Antoine Captier), Saunière discovered four scrolls in hollow Visigoth altar columns. These were the parchments hidden by Abbé Bigou. There were two coded messages: 'Shepherdess no temptation. That Poussin Teniers hold the key. Pax 681. By the cross and this horse of God I complete this demon of the guardian at noon. Blue apples', and 'To Dagobert II, King, and to Sion belongs this treasure and he is there dead'.

The mayor and municipality wanted to claim the find, but Saunière took the scrolls to Monseigneur Billard, Bishop of Carcassonne. He sent Saunière to Paris, to the director of the seminary of St Sulpice, Abbé Bieil. It was understood that one of the messages on the parchments referred to St Sulpice as an esoteric temple copied from the Temple of Solomon. It was also noted that St Sulpice and Rennes-le-Château were on the same meridian line.

In Paris, Abbé Bieil's nephew, Emile Hoffet, introduced Saunière to various groups and secret societies. Hoffet was in his early twenties, training for the priesthood, and had an impressive reputation for scholarship and the occult. He had also made extensive studies of Freemasonry.

Through him the country priest met intellectuals, celebrities, and aristocrats his path would never normally have crossed, such as Stephen Mallarmé, Maurice Maeterlinck, Claude Debussy, and Emma Calvé, the opera singer – the Maria Callas of the time. A priestess of the occult, she was an associate of Joséphin Péladan, who with the Comte de la Rochefoucauld had founded the Cabbalistic Order of the 'Rose Croix Catholique et Esthétique, du Temple et du Graal', the Rose Cross of the Temple and the Grail.

While the scrolls were being examined, Saunière visited the Louvre and bought several reproductions – a portrait of Pope Celestine V, a work by David Teniers, and the painting *The Shepherds of Arcadia* by Nicolas Poussin.

The visit to Paris is said to have lasted some weeks, and Saunière made strong connections with people who were to become regular guests to Rennes-le-Château and then Girona. He was even reputed to have had a liaison with Emma Calvé.

On his return, he continued the restoration of the church. He discovered the eighth-century 'Dalle des Chevaliers', the Knights' stone, with its two riders on the same horse, the origin of the Templar emblem. He also disfigured the tombstone that had been designed and installed by Abbé Bigou for Lady d'Hautpol de Blanchefort. The inscription was erased but had earlier been copied by Ernest Cross, an archaeologist spending his holidays in Quillan. The inscription had read: *'Et in Arcadia Ego'* – 'Even in Arcadia I exist', with 'I' in this context considered to refer to death.

After finding the scrolls, Saunière became wealthy beyond belief. There was never an explanation and both he and Marie Denarnaud left no evidence after their deaths. Saunière restored the church in a manner that provoked curiosity. He built the Villa Bethania, a substantial house in the Renaissance style; he built the Tour Magdala; and he collected rare china, precious fabrics, books, postage stamps. He created a park, a zoo, an orangery, built a road down to Couiza, and installed running water in the village. He designed each of these works himself, and the architects Elie Bot and Tiburce Caminade had to follow his details precisely. He lived a sumptuous and extravagant life with parties for renowned guests, especially the Archduke Johann von Habsburg. Bank statements revealed that Saunière and the Archduke had opened accounts with consecutive numbers. He guarded his terrain fiercely and reacted with a fury, quite out of place, when firemen entered his property to warn him about a nearby fire.

There were many symbols relating to the Rosicrucians and Judaism in his church, which would not have found favour with the Vatican. Bizarre in much of its decoration, it had the devil Asmodeus in the doorway, custodian of secrets, guardian of hidden treasures, and, according to ancient Judaic legend, creator of the Temple of Solomon.

The priest behaved oddly, the parishioners said. With Marie Denarnaud he walked for miles, collecting rocks and stones. Under cover of darkness they were seen digging in the cemetery. He conducted a traffic selling masses illegally. He spent hours in the secret room behind the altar.

The Bishop of Carcassonne enjoyed his hospitality but died in 1902, followed a year later by Pope Leo XIII, liberalminded and protector of the Habsburgs. Saunière's scale of expenses and projects raised the interest of the new pope, Pius X, and the new Bishop of Carcassonne, Monseigneur de Beauséjour, who called Saunière to account. What was the origin of this wealth? Saunière took an arrogant stance and delayed time and again answering the charges. It became a legal matter. Accused of selling illicit masses he was suspended, and the Bishop demanded the return of all the buildings purchased by Saunière. Too late. It was all in his maid's name. He said he'd purchased land and buildings because he feared that the municipality could always turn him out and he and his maid would be left without a franc. The Vatican reinstated him, and he went on to sign a contract for another huge tower. He suffered a stroke on 17 January 1917 and died five days later. As far as anyone knew, he'd left everything to Marie Denarnaud. By today's standards, he had spent several millions.

I'd read and heard about the murder of Abbé Gelis of Coustaussa in 1897, a murder without apparent motive or gain. It appeared to be a ritual murder. Gérard de Sède had mentioned other murdered clergy in the area. He had also written about the secret room behind the altar and the rituals carried out there nightly.

Marie Denarnaud dressed in the latest Paris fashions and the locals called her 'the Madonna'. After inheriting Saunière's properties and money, she never revealed the source of his wealth and sat daily by his gravestone, 'fearing the devil and demonic deeds'. She said, 'I could give you a secret that would turn these streets to gold.' After the Second World War the French currency changed, and everyone was required to account for their money when exchanging new francs for old. Marie Denarnaud chose to burn the entire fortune rather than declare the source of her wealth.

Other books mentioned the priest's short travels for days at a time, but to where and for what? Later, books stated the parishioners suspected that he crossed just across the border into Spain.

The conclusions so far were in favour of his having found a secret with which he blackmailed the Vatican. It was thought the secret was that of the bloodline of Jesus and the Magdalene existing in France, ready to claim the throne, protected by a secret society. If Jesus had married and produced children, the Vatican would pay highly to keep that a secret.

I wondered why with all that money the priest didn't travel and have a more adventurous life. He liked the grand things, style, important people. Why stay in a back-water? Why didn't he buy an island? Was it because he couldn't? Did he even want to be a priest? He must have expected some inspection by the Church of his lavish life and spending. He would have been prepared for that. As José said, the priest covered his tracks.

Finding gold, treasure, money, didn't seem enough. Not for this story. Whatever it was had to be a secret. Marie Denarnaud had not said one word. Was she terrified to speak? Had someone done a very good job on her? There was much mention of the Habsburgs. What part did they play?

The story lent itself to many possibilities. Alchemy, blackmail, proof of the bloodline of Jesus. It was as though the money was too big for Saunière and he didn't know what to do with it. So he spent it on extravagant follies, in the small area where he seemed to constantly reside, had to reside. And the tower – what else but a folly?

That's what I thought that night, full of what I'd read.

A knock on the door, and the old furniture shook. Every sound in the hotel was dramatic. I thought it was him. It should be him. Lucia came in with a bottle of white wine, some glasses, ice.

'I didn't think they'd have room service here. José rang with a message. He said he will start the testament and you would understand. Also he will talk to a woman who has letters and photographs. He is busy for a few weeks preparing the flower show.'

So, he was prepared to talk after all. But I'd have to come back to hear it.

'They've put this hotel up for sale.'

'Oh, please, don't say that.' I sank onto the bed and wished I could buy it. But would owning the building mean I could keep the memories?

'It's a shame you're not married to him,' she said. 'Something happens between you two even when you quarrel.'

I realized Lucia was the same age as José. She looked thinner, serious, even gaunt. Although we'd been in each other's company over the years we didn't know each other. I asked her about the chime he'd heard, because I remembered she'd been a witness.

'It was in José's head. I didn't hear anything.' She still had her lovely laugh.

'What is it?'

'An energy stirred up on a certain meridian.'

She changed the subject. I asked if he was happy.

'Not like the old days. But he has something quite exceptional. A love of life. He'd have it anywhere, whereas my light is going out.' She said she'd been ill, but the operation was successful. 'I remember I heard sounds when I was a child, playing in Maria's garden. And I didn't like it and didn't want to go there. José used to come. Sometimes the atmosphere was edgy and that's when I heard these voices. Always in the same place. If I moved further away they weren't there. I thought it was ghosts. I think my mother thought it was schizophrenia.

But José heard it too. It was beautiful in that garden and the view of Canigou ...'

I said I wished she would come and visit me in Céret.

'I'll say I will, but I won't.'

'It's closer to Canigou.'

'Oh, I don't like mountains.' She said it as though she was frightened of them.

'A bad experience?'

'Definitely. I never go near them.' She didn't finish the wine and seemed ready to go.

'There's so much I want to tell you, to talk to you about,' I said.

She went to the window and looked out.

'How did you meet Maria?' I said.

'My mother was her friend. Took care of the money. Sort of looked after her.'

'Didn't she have any? Money?'

'Too much. My mother had to get it invested.'

'Did she lose it?' I remembered José saying she never had any when we were in Paris.

'She always covered up everything. Like all of them.'

'Was your mother from here?'

'Paris.'

'So why did you come here?'

'Why? Because Maria was here.'

I asked how her mother and Maria had become friends.

'Through the private society here. The society needed someone to take care of Maria.'

'Before she married Roger Mathieu?'

'Exactly. And afterwards. My mother was suitable and well off and all that.'

'And would take care of what Maria knew,' I said, all of a sudden. 'What was she like?' I meant her mother.

'You met her.'

It turned out to be the thin, brown-skinned, rough, smoked-out woman on the doorstep of the house in 1955, and in the *salon* in Paris in the sixties, whom I'd assumed had fallen on hard times. How could you look like that and be rich? 'What happened to Maria's money?'

'I got a lot of it,' Lucia said, simply. 'But I'm radical. I want things known. That way we have progress in this world. Secrets are not safe.'

She looked at the books I'd been reading. 'You're not afraid to ask questions. Question the story. Don't accept it. He built a tower. Why did he build a tower?'

She said she'd see me in May, and her feet were light passing through the empty building.

I didn't see her next time. She was dead.

31

Much of the investigation that came out of the mid-eighties interest concluded that the priest's secret was the Grail. It was something to be sought that would improve life immeasurably. It was mentioned in pre-Christian rituals, often with Judaic connections. The Grail power was also mentioned in the ancient worship of Isis, the Roman/Egyptian/Graeco female deity.

Some accounts dated the Grail from the time of Jesus, as the cup at the Last Supper. More popular was the theory that it was a vessel used by Joseph of Arimathea to collect Jesus's blood at the Crucifixion. The Grail is bound up with the rumour, opposing the male-dominated Catholic Church's doctrine, that Jesus married the Magdalene and that she, pregnant with Sarah, fled to Marseilles, carrying Jesus's blood in the Grail and his genetic imprint in her body. This bloodline was continued in France by the royal heritage of the Merovingian Kings. According to the Church the Grail could not exist, but the Church still looked for it. By order of the Vatican the Merovingian dynasty should have been extinguished with the assassination of King Dagobert in the seventh century, but Dagobert's son Sigisbert escaped, so continuing the lineage which later included King Godefroi de Bouillon, who conquered Jerusalem in 1099.

The Grail was said to be amongst the lost treasure of Jerusalem's Temple of Solomon, plundered by Titus of Rome in AD 70. In 1099 Bouillon created a group of nine Knights – 'The Order of the Poor Knights of Christ and the Temple of Solomon', which became the Knights Templar – to retrieve the Grail secretly from beneath the Temple. Yet four centuries earlier, when those great Teutonic warriors from Central Europe, the Visigoths, toppled the Roman Empire in the sixth century, it is said that they brought the Grail or some of its related documents to their stronghold in France – Rennes-le-Château.

Whether it was carried by the Visigoths or the Knights Templar, tradition agrees that the Grail was secreted in Rennes-le-Château. In the twelfth century the Vatican perceived the Knights as guardians of an ancient secret, one that made them unaccountably power-ful, a secret so explosive in its nature that the Church would do anything to claim it. Pope Clement V supported the massive execution of the Templars by Philip IV of France in 1307. This was the end of the Order as it had been, but the Vatican did not find the Grail. It was poss-ibly taken by escaping Knights to waiting boats at La Rochelle.

The Cathars were said to be at one time its custodians, again in the Rennes-le-Château area, before their an-nihilation in 1244. The Grail became the source of legend and folklore. The Bavarian knight, medieval writer, and best of the romancers, Wolfram von Eschenbach, placed the castle of the Grail in the Pyrenees, composing an epic poem *Parzival*. A Grail document provided the source for the Grail romances of Chrétien de Troyes, *Le Conte del Graal*, and of Robert de Boron's *Roman de l'Estoire dou Sant Graal*.

I'd heard of the Grail from the tales of King Arthur. Galahad was identified as Gilead which meant 'Mount of Witness' (Genesis 31.21–25). He was descended from Nahor, brother of Abraham (I Chron. 5–14). I knew that it appeared in Celtic legend and poetry in Ireland and Scotland.

But what was it?

As well as the Knights Templar, King Godefroi de Bouillon had also founded the Prieuré de Sion in 1099. It was said that this society became the guardian of the Holy Grail and its documents. Possessor of a secret which had been in his family since the time of Christ, and fearing its theft or disappearance after his death, Bouillon charged the brotherhood with the responsibility of protection, passing it on from generation to generation. Based in France, it was described as a discreet society, privileged, not materialistic. Its Grand Masters included Jean de Gisors, 1188; Marie de Saint Clair, 1220; Sandro Botticelli, 1483; Leonardo da Vinci, 1510; Isaac Newton, 1691; Victor Hugo, Debussy, and then Jean Cocteau. Today's Grand Master is not named.

The members swear absolute allegiance to the nature and integrity of the Grail, its information and effects. Those who have had knowledge of the Grail include Poussin, Mozart, Bernini. The significance of the treasure was spiritual, not mystical. The Church was keen to stamp out the bloodline rumour, whether heresy or fact. Jesus was *on* the earth, but not *of* the earth. The Church was clear on that. There was no royal bloodline and the Magdalene was not from the royal family of Benjamin as suggested, but a whore. The second hypothesis, that Jesus was not crucified but travelled with the Magdalene to France and spent the rest of his life in the Rennes-le-Château area, had less support.

The Grail was said to be in Scotland, to be in Chartres, and then Saunière made a discovery in his parish church.

I had read the material, but the actual form of the Grail was unclear. In one instance it was described as not being a chalice at all but a huge collection of documents, a stone tablet, a mythological concept, a precious cup, the Ark of the Covenant. I remembered José's vessel and the extra-terrestrial shape that the American, Max Kander, had drawn in the dust of a Girona street.

'It's a key,' said Ingrid, the German Cabbalist teacher I'd met with Carmen Aragó when Isaac the Blind was still going. We were standing outside the building, which had been reopened as a museum and renamed Bonustruc ça Porta. At first I didn't recognize her, but the energy and good spirit were unchanged.

'Shall we go in?' I dreaded it.

'But of course.' And she led us up the steps I'd trodden a thousand times. At first sight nothing much had altered, except there was an entrance fee. The Star of David, the wishing-well, the lemon trees, the lights, the excavations, the Cabbala books, were all still there. In the main *salon* was an audio exhibition of the Jews' history in Spain. Downstairs, facing the carrer de la Força, was a shop selling Jewish books and lamps. I thought the bar was still there but reduced. The atmosphere was squeezed of life. It was cold. I found the door.

'Walking out?' It was Quim Carreras.

'Running.'

Ingrid, not a regular of Lluís's bar, not an insider from the past, preferred to drink in the Bar Arcada on the Rambla. Carreras asked if he could join us.

'It's better for Girona,' he said, and put his arm around my shoulder. 'It's clear what it is. It's on a small scale, but safe.'

I understood I must have been looking upset. José's enterprise belonged there and this new concept, forced upon all that energy and drama, was a shock.

'It's dead.'

'Museums tend to be,' said Ingrid.

It was a shoe that didn't fit. 'They've got all José's things.'

'Not all,' Carreras said. 'They haven't got the sun stone.'

I was upset about a lot more than a stone. This transformation represented the loss of what was now the past and all that had been happy.

Carreras had an edgy charm. He was the one person I'd met who was not confused and didn't waste life. His voice could seduce just by the sound. He was certainly seductive. Sex and death were his influences, and I thought he understood them and seemed to carry them inside him. He was intuitive, sensitive as a weather vane, but cold. He was sun on snow, nothing much in between. He'd written prize-winning scholarly works on politics and ecclesiastical reform, and had been offered a key job in the Church. 'I prefer not to be in a fixed position, labelled. I'm more dangerous when they don't own me.'

I wasn't sure what he did. He certainly didn't have a parish or conduct services.

'He's a scholar,' Ingrid said, and waited for him to disagree.

'So did you find the Grail?' he asked.

I blocked any more provocation with a question. 'What is it, the Grail?'

'What do you think it is?'

I told him what I'd read in books.

His answer surprised me. 'It's in existence, but it's not here.'

Ingrid laughed. 'A minimalist definition.'

'Can you do better?'

'Oh, I expect so. Find the key.'

'Maybe there are several grails,' I suggested.

He said there were several traditions but not grails. The pursuit of the Grail gives a spiritual change, an evolvement 'That is perhaps more important than a material object.'

I asked Ingrid what she meant by 'a key'.

She gave me a card with her address. The house was in the middle of a wood on a hill overlooking the sea near Begur. 'I have many things I can show you.'

Lluís told me about Lucia's death. I'd assumed it was a health problem. We sat in silence for some time drinking whatever he'd put in our glasses.

'She always said she'd have a wild death,' he said.

I asked when she'd been buried. Her husband had come from Italy and taken her home.

'They had to get her body down.' Realizing I didn't know any of this, he said, 'Lucia died on the mountain. On Canigou.'

I didn't believe it. 'That wouldn't happen to her.'

'At the top.'

'She hated mountains.'

'She was very ill.' That explained it. For him.

I asked what she was doing there.

'She had to go back. Up there. That's what she said.'

'But what's up there?'

He didn't know. He'd never been. He said that on St Jean, the longest day, there was a ceremony on the mountain. Catalans went up to the peak carrying flames. But it wasn't the longest day when she died.

'You should ask José. He helped bring her body down. The priests rang bells throughout their descent.'

'What happens to the money?' asked a man at the bar.

'She had no children,' said Lluís.

The man staring at me turned out to be Dr Arbós, who'd driven us to Rennes-le-Château all those years ago. He worked in Barcelona now and came to Girona to see his estranged wife and children. I thought he'd aged better than me. He'd seen me with the German woman in the Rambla.

'Ingrid,' I continued.

'Do you know what family she comes from? One of the richest in the world. So what does she do living alone in a cabin in a forest?' asked Dr Arbós.

I thought Dr Arbós was a little obsessed about money, and when he'd gone Lluís said it was because he felt cheated.

'The ex-wife?'

'No, some deal he's involved in here that doesn't happen.'

I went to look for José to ask for Lucia's letters, the ones she'd put into his care some time before. He was waiting for me in Ruiz's bookshop. Lluís had arranged the meeting. José now lived in a village in the Empordà, the most sought-after countryside in Catalonia. He preferred to meet in Girona. He didn't especially remember Lucia's letters and, because he'd moved, everything was harder to find. He promised to look in his cartons and send them to London.

He was looking through books and clearing his throat. I could see that being with me in a town full of gossip was difficult. I said we should get a taxi out of town. His moustache was longer over his lips, his hair white. The eyes, as he looked at me, eventually became as they should. He was busy with his secret society.

'We organize the Flower Exhibition. It's becoming so popular, ten thousand people passed through this year.' Of course, I knew there were other responsibilities.

Private courtyards and gardens, streets and public places were opened up for this event, which combined flowers and trees with local artists' work.

'Do you know what the Grail is?' he asked, suddenly.

'King Arthur and the Knights of the Round Table. A myth.'

'If only.' He sighed and looked at me as though I could provide an answer. He stayed silent and left the shop. I ran after him, clattering on the cobbles. I still hadn't heard what he had to say. 'What do you want me to do?' I shouted, and the stone street echoed my words endlessly.

He gestured I be quiet.

'Is it the ritual? I'll do that. You asked me once …'

He said the heat had got the better of me, and took me into the nearest bar. The heat certainly affected me as it hadn't in the old days. I said a lot of things. I think I said I'd do anything for him.

'The ritual doesn't exist any more,' he said, gently.

Quim Carreras passed by and smiled at me.

'You get on with him?' José sounded sharp. Was he jealous?

I was thinking, at the same time, was Lucia's death suicide?

32

Monsieur García, a Parisian taxi driver, had the apartment next to mine in Céret, and one day in the early nineties we decided to drive to Rennes-le-Château. Visitors swarmed between the presbytery, the church, the cemetery, expecting what? They didn't know, and they left empty. Celia, an English girl, eager to rectify the chaos, had formed a society. The villagers were resentful of the intrusion in their lives and of media people descending on their world, making TV programmes and plenty of money, yet not giving one sou in thanks to the village.

García pointed immediately at the tower. 'It's mock-medieval. Why he should choose that I can't imagine.'

'Why did he build it at all?' I asked.

'To get rid of some of that money, mad money. Some people say it's a landmark. It's all very run down. Why doesn't the municipality step in?'

Celia explained that the tower and the villa were privately owned by a Henri Buthion. She pointed at a depressed middle-aged man walking mournfully towards us.

'He must have *des frics*,' said García, rubbing his fingers to indicate money.

'That's what he hasn't got,' Celia insisted.

Henri Buthion had bought the properties in the mid-sixties from Monsieur Corbu, the hotel owner José and Espriu had talked about at Arenys de Mar all that time ago. He in turn had tried to turn it into another hotel. He was now desperate to sell and get out. He was financially and spiritually exhausted.

Just to keep his hand in, García asked the price. He hungered after property in beautiful places. 'My dear sir,' he said, 'not even l'Abbé Saunière could afford that.'

The church worried García as it had me. 'It's blasphemous.'

Like the church, the inside of the tower was vividly painted, disturbing, exotic, hinting at pleasures, experiences beyond the average comprehension. Who was Saunière? A madman? A dangerous megalomaniac?

Henri Buthion, eyes red-rimmed after nights of financial worry, spoke slowly. The church was decorated in such a manner that it became a code. At the top of the tower, with uninterrupted views in every direction, the wind carried off his words.

'Why did he build this?' I asked.

'To hold his book collection.' He added, 'Really I have no idea.'

He allowed us inside the Villa Bethania, where it was clear he was somewhere between moving out and sinking down. He gave us the household accounts kept by Marie Denarnaud. 'You can see a sharp difference before the scrolls and after. The same can be found in my household accounts but the other way round.' The priest had kept a regular account book in small private writing, which stopped abruptly when his fortunes changed in 1891.

Why did Buthion come here? If it had been for the treasure he didn't look as though he'd found it. He'd heard about the place from a Spaniard travelling through Africa. Buthion and his wife decided to take it on. 'I searched for treasure day and night. I found only debts.'

I noticed some of Saunière's original lavish wall-paper with hand-painted landscapes, young trees, inlaid with gold, birds, butterflies, and white flowers. I thought I recognized it from Maria Tourdes's house when we'd peered through the shutters with Cocteau and the French crew. It came from Duchesne. In what resembled a shrine stood tinted photographs of a lovely woman at different ages. 'My wife.' The way he said it indicated she wasn't any longer.

'Is she deceased?' García asked, respectfully.

'I don't know. I'm not mad. I should be. I came to this place with that beautiful woman and our children. With the money from the sale of my business I bought into hell. One day a group came to the door. This was in the mid-1970s. They were from a mystical cult and they took my wife and children away. I never saw them again. Naturally I went to search for them. I think I even found where the cult was located. On the other side of the Pyrenees. They had me arrested for, as they described it, trying to kidnap my wife and children. I was in prison for four months. My life is in ruins.'

'You have had too much bad luck,' said García.

'Were they Spanish?' I asked.

'I don't know, Madame. They wore white. According to the police my wife and children wanted to be there. She said she felt safe there. She did not in this place. I need just one small part of the treasure to make up for some of what I've endured.'

He sounded like a serial loser in Las Vegas. I asked him exactly where the cult was based, but he didn't or wouldn't remember. I was remembering José had been sent by his mother to the seminary near Ripoll.

'The treasure is here. Every night when I lie on my bed I feel it below me, below this house, and it has a presence. It mocks me.'

García said he should get away from this terrible place. 'It is terrible. It even says it on the church door.'

'I have debts and loans.'

García waved his arms. 'Your life is more important.'

'It gives off a pale greenish glow. The place has brought me bad luck,' he added, somewhat unnecessarily. 'But I'm scared to leave. The owner before me sold up and left. He'd got only a few kilometres before dying in a car crash. Another packed up to go and died of a heart attack. There is a curse on this place.'

'Some can't get here, some can't get out. I'll drive you.'

Buthion was doubtful.

'No one has ever died while I'm at the wheel.'

It seemed the unknown he knew was preferable to the unknown he did not.

'There is nothing to find there,' said García, and we drove away, circling down the hill.

An Englishman passing through Céret said the treasure was an equation that provided the 'archplan' of human life, placed on this planet by extraterrestrial beings, the discovery of which would make the finder master of this world. It was stated that this 'archplan' showed how to transcend death, to become invisible, to link with past and future, to see the blueprint of your life purpose. It was hidden because in the wrong hands it could be lethal. He believed the Vatican had always known.

225

We were in the bar, where these things could be said without objection.

'Considering what I've heard over the years, that sounds quite sensible,' said García.

'Saunière knew, and a secret society, existing for hundreds of years, also knew. Saunière, in his extraordinary church with its tantalizing imagery, may have found it. Did it help him?' the Englishman asked.

I asked what part the tower played.

'A landmark,' he said.

He didn't, it seemed, know about the tower that had been in Girona. He was a professional-seeming person, a specialist in map-drawing.

My neighbour, Madame Barat, looked through the window. 'Canigou is gay today.' She ordered another *Crémant de Limoux*. The snow-covered summit was sharply etched against a blue, sun-bright sky. A good sign. Although not Catalan, she came from Toulouse and she paid heed to the mountain's moods. It was sacred and the Catalans sang songs praising it, asking for its blessing. They made pilgrimages to its lower slopes and told it their secrets. She said spiritual healers came to the mountain to claim energy. 'It recharges everything,' she said.

The Englishman asked why.

'It contains precious minerals. They say the Phoenicians came in ancient times in boats and took minerals and salt, and the Germans were here digging mines. Hitler sent the Nazis here looking for treasure. Planes won't fly over the summit. There have been many crashes.'

'Because it's full of iron,' said the local pharmacist. 'It magnetizes them. Iron and other metals. It's a savage mountain. It will claim its sacrifice.'

As he said it, I shivered.

'You aren't allowed to ski up there,' he continued. 'It always takes its price.'

Sometimes you couldn't see the mountain, the cloud around it was so thick. The worst clouds were black and morbid and, if the sun should shine, they turned a sinister green. Each day I made sure the mountain was the first thing I looked at. You can get too used to things, even beautiful things. Often, the light changed around the mountain and all in a minute white clouds fluffed up, yellow in the sun, like a soufflé mixture. Overheated, they disintegrated and drifted off, mere foam, leaving the vast scarred body of the mountain exposed.

Before I left Céret that time I went to Madame Barat's apartment. The first stars were out in the near-turquoise sky. The sunset still flamed over Canigou. I watched stars come on, hundreds of them. A clear pitted sky. She pointed to a light that moved visibly around the mountain's girth.

'A comet.'

I watched it speed off towards Spain, then disappear.

'They say many strange lights are seen around Canigou. They appear and suddenly flash off. They say they're spirits, and the mountain attracts them. And beings arrive from out of space. That's what they say.'

The flower show was over and José was clearing the Frenchwoman's garden. He barely acknowledged my arrival. I started to tell him about Rennes-le-Château.

'I want nothing to do with it.' He stopped digging and looked out at the mountains.

I thought travel weariness had affected my hearing. I started again about the testament for Maria Tourdes.

'I want nothing to do with it.'

So I asked why.

'Rennes-le-Château belongs to the devil.'

On my way back down to the town centre I knew someone had got to him, had stopped him, forbidden him to go near the subject.

By chance I took another street off the carrer de la Força, and José's mother was coming out of the fruit shop. She was just recognizable, with the cinder-black dyed hair obligatory for every woman over eighty.

'Oh, so you're back.' She chose to speak clearly this time. 'He gave up his spiritual vocation because of you.'

Beyond surprise, I waited for her to continue.

'You kept coming back. He fell for you and decided he wasn't strong enough for the spiritual service and his vows.'

'Oh no, Señora.' I had never been so full of dignity. 'You've got it wrong.'

'I doubt it,' she said, preparing to pass me.

'He fell from grace long before I started coming back. The moment we met. That's when he fell.' And I walked on. Her bitterness came from a more personal place than even religious beliefs.

A man had been hovering near the drinking fountain. Seeing me he looked twice, then turned fast up a side alley. It was the journalist, Max Kander.

33

I didn't see José for over ten years. Since the old hotel had been closed down I couldn't face Girona any more. Nowadays I stayed 30 km away, in the spa village of Caldes de Malavella at the Hotel Balneari Prats. It couldn't be more different from everything I'd so far experienced.

In the autumn of 2004, José suddenly arrived at Caldes. He simply got off the train and walked back into my life. I looked less than my best and he was barely recognizable. He was old. He'd had a heart attack after the last Flower Exhibition. He needed to speak to me.

I had three grandchildren, I'd written books, I was involved in running a charity, my Modigliani play was on in France. I came to Catalonia quite frequently over the years, when it had something to do with work. This time I'd been in Barcelona and Girona, giving talks on Modigliani's life before an exhibition of his work. They put the play of my book *Into the Darkness Laughing* on in the Fundacion Vila Casas in Barcelona. I was now in Caldes to get the play ready for performances at the Girona Festival. It was a privilege to be included, but if it, or any of my work, reached his life I never heard.

I didn't mix with the old crowd any more. Now it was writers, artists, and a publisher in Barcelona. My good friends included Miguel Berga, Dean of Humanities at the university in Barcelona, and Lidia Arias from the Catalan government. Most of these people were younger than José, and for some of them he was a legend. As I started working with Clara Mascaró, a local actress, I was amazed to discover how many people in Girona I didn't know. I'd always concentrated on just one.

José had written a well-received collection of poetry, and been given awards for his work on the Jewish Centre. He'd been preparing a garden in his *barraca* for a Jewish ceremony. His wife was busy with her stained glass and his son grown up, getting married.

What he was really doing should have surprised me, yet in truth it did not.

'You said once you'd do anything for me.'

I said yes, thinking what a dangerous thing to suggest.

Certain material had been in the care of Girona, privately, for many years. A society had been formed to protect it and one of the main members was near death. Others wanted outcomes different to those originally agreed. He was worried because the heart attack had reminded him he was mortal.

'Why me? What about your wife?'

'It has nothing to do with her. You knew Maria Tourdes and she liked you.'

'What do I have to do?' Suddenly the thought of Lucia on a mountain, dead, stopped any enthusiasm. She'd always said keep out of it. She'd used the word *danger*. Not one she'd be casual with.

We sat in a peaceful place under the trees. It was siesta time at the spa, and there were no clients by the hot pool or fountain.

'The society is under threat. The material could go in any direction. And Maria's story with it. I need to protect that.' His eyes were still a rich brown, but his skin was not olive any more but flushed. He seemed tired.

I told him to lie in a chair and rest, but he wanted to keep my attention. He talked about our life, always in the past, for nearly two hours. It seemed he was making it clear to me that it had importance. Perhaps he was making amends to me.

I asked what he wanted me to do about the society.

He explained that for years he had held material that was originally hidden in that house. He said he wanted to tell me because he owed it to me. For the past.

I asked what he meant by 'material'.

He said the Grail, or cup. Was he saying he had it? That it was an object in his possession?

He claimed he needed me to know.

And he got up to walk back to the station. I said I'd go with him. He wanted to go alone. But how would I contact him? He was still living outside of Girona.

'Through Gerard Ruiz at the bookshop.'

That night I dreamed I was in front of the old chocolate poster in the alley. 'I don't have time,' José said in the dream. Did he ever? I asked if he felt joined to me. I needed to know his side of my story.

'We have at best a state of harmony. Don't we?'

And he called me Maria. And it wasn't José's voice.

'They will come for me,' he said. 'And I have so much to do.'

I sat straight up, legs reaching the floor, ready to run. But I had no one to be terrified with any more.

In the morning I understood. José was alerting me. Not telling me anything.

—\~—

Ruiz tried the number again. 'It's been cut off.'

I wanted Lucia's letters, and José had them. Ruiz gave me a postcard of Girona in the fifties with the house and tower clearly visible.

'Have you any of Madame Mathieu? Or the French priest?'

For once he wasn't smiling. 'Don't go into all this as a journalist. Just play tourist or treasure-seeker.' And he tried to make his advice sound light. I still asked questions. 'José is the only one who knows the story. But plenty would like him not to,' he replied. And he handed me a letter to do with *sardana* dancing.

I started to leave, and he said, 'Remember Lucia.' He kept trying to stack books in the crowded space. He wasn't smiling and didn't look at me. Even his hair was dark, not red these days. 'What would she be doing on a mountain?' He spoke softly. 'Mountains? She was frightened of them.'

'Vertigo?' I wanted to be sure we were on the same side. For the first time I sensed the danger she'd talked about.

'Something happened up there. In her childhood.' A small gesture of his head northwest. 'Stop José. He knows the story of the garden. It would be unwise to reveal it. Worse to use it.'

To make safe whatever it was, I said nothing had been revealed.

'But he's spoken to you. What will he do next? He's always a wild card. Look what happened to that,' pointing across the road to the Jewish museum, with its lines of visitors. Someone was making money. The municipality?

'I should be on a percentage,' I said.

'Keep him quiet. He might listen to you.' He made it clear he admired José for the inventiveness and courage he'd shown in the fifties. 'But they want to forget that time now. It's a wealthy city.'

I asked why Ruiz didn't speak to José's wife.

'For José the past was the best time. So we who belong to that time will have more effect.'

I was out of the door and into the street because I'd heard footsteps I'd know anywhere. Ruiz called me back. 'Lucia once said "I wouldn't be caught dead on a mountain."'

José's step was light, life-loving as he'd always been. He was surprised I'd been alarmed. His phone was cut off because he'd recently moved to a house near the Pyrenees. Ruiz should know that. He'd dialled the old number.

He'd dialled any old number because he wanted to alarm me first.

I walked with José to Carmen Aragó's doorway and asked for his phone number.

'I have a meeting here.'

'That secret society of yours?'

He said yes.

'Who runs it now?'

He hesitated. 'Still Carmen.'

I said that if he didn't tell me what was happening I couldn't help him.

'But I don't want help. I just wanted you to know certain things.'

'So that if you end up dead on a mountain like Lucia I'll know why.'

He laughed. 'That won't happen. Mountains are my friends.'

'You're in trouble. Even your friends think that.'

He hesitated at the door.

'So if you give the story to me they won't do anything to silence you. Because I'll have passed it on, won't I?'

'I really don't know.' He pushed open the door. I could see a huge medieval hallway with magnificent lamps, stones standing on their sides in the corners, and a partially visible garden behind a grille.

When the door shut I stood remembering Lucia. She'd said, 'Don't accept the story. Question it. He built a tower. Why did he build a tower?'

What was the society? Was it only a group protecting history? What was the French priest if not history?

I still asked questions but not of him. I wanted to know what was really going on. To know half the story was dangerous. I had to know as much as they did and be quick about it. Did the Grail exist and, if so, where was it? What was it?

Ruiz wrote a name – Josep Luna. He thought I should have a talk with him. He worked in the Motel Empordà in Figueres, one of the best restaurants in the province. I'd been there for special occasions over the years. Señor Luna had given up the Church and become an accountant. As I was in the shop I wanted to know what part Ruiz played. Was there a society protecting information? Who was for José? Against? Today he didn't know anything.

'Catalans tend to be reserved,' he explained.

'They say that about the English. If you want him quiet you have to talk to me.' I suspected he had a part in it and needed to be safe. Also, he seemed ill at ease. His eyes flicked to and fro, watching as much of the street as he could while he spoke.

I'd often heard people saying that José's mother and her family belonged to the Rosicrucians, but they always denied it. From what I knew about the Rosicrucians, they didn't exist in Spain, except perhaps a small group in Madrid on a low level. It was said the mother belonged to a society of Rosicrucians in France, and her father was high up in the Order. The French society included some of the most powerful people of the time. This was at the end of the nineteenth century, beginning of the twentieth. The Order was meaningful at the time, and wealthy. Including European royalty, its structure infiltrated religion, finance, politics. It was subtle, little-known. In those days if you followed the Order you had to follow it. José's mother was born in 1907. The central group was in Paris, but had a branch in Narbonne. The story went that she placed José in the Rosicrucians' care to be spiritually prepared for a high position, that he was sent to a retreat for months at a time. The mother had died some years ago.

I asked Ruiz if he knew about any of this, about José's supposed high position.

Ruiz shrugged.

'When did you come to Girona?'

'I was born here.'

'How did you start in bookselling?'

'The business was left to ... to someone who chose to do something else. I took it over. It originated ...' Another shrug and a smile, and Quim Carreras was with us. The subject was instantly changed and Ruiz, again the laughing bookseller, concentrated on the customer. He was in no hurry, the priest, as he looked along the shelves. He had been to see a Señora Guilini who was very ill.

Ruiz mumbled sounds of dismay.

'So what have you found in Rennes-le-Château?' said Carreras.

I wanted to say a rail timetable from Couiza to Girona, 1901.

'You can't find anything except seekers like yourself. It is over-sensational and should not be encouraged.'

Ruiz nodded in all the right places.

My turn with the questions. What was she doing here? Madame Mathieu?

'Doing?'

'I remember some years ago your saying she'd had a marvellous affair.'

I could tell Ruiz wasn't happy with this conversation.

'She was trying to sort out her spiritual life and she found help here. She came to a decision.'

'Which was?'

'To hand her life over to God. And to work on her spiritual progress assiduously. If you just leave yourself open, if you're casual, you don't have a spiritual direction and you can let in all sorts of things, especially darkness. Go towards the light and you are safe.'

I hadn't thought about it like that, but didn't tell him.

'It was the process of finding her priorities that was important, not so much the result. She was very unhappy.'

'So you knew her well?'

'No. That was Geli, José's cousin. He looked after her.'

'Who was the lover? I don't remember you saying.'

His eyes on mine were not without humour.

'Gossip could not help what I do.'

'Was l'Abbé Saunière good or bad?' I remembered she'd asked that, in the letter.

'I am not a judge of the clergy in France.'

His eyes were no longer laughing. I went to the rehearsal of my play.

My actress friend Clara and other friends from the production got into the car for Figueres. It was just a group going for a good meal at the Motel Empordà. Why did I feel uneasy? I used to go there with José. There was a lot of 'used to' these days.

There was a Dutch painter, who liked to drink and to laugh. He had a scorching wit and took care of the mood of the evening. At some point I sought out Señor Luna, and he came to his office door, blushing and smiling and saying he'd got the message I was coming and he was thrilled to meet me. Was this the right Señor Luna? He said he'd finish his work and join us for coffee.

'I've come from Ruiz's,' I said.

He nodded, approvingly. More laughter. It was an evening of laughter – for them. When he joined us Señor Luna brought a bottle of special wine and the talk was about art, my play, Catalonia, and then he got up to go and he still hadn't spoken to me. He did say he had been preparing for the priesthood but it wasn't right for him. He came to the car and opened the door for Clara, and then said he had some books for Ruiz and would I take them. I offered to go with him to his office but he didn't want that. The carrier bag was heavy.

Back in Caldes I felt safe and opened the bag. Between the two large books was a note. A Señora Juncosa would be helpful on Girona and the past. She'd like to meet me and would come to the play. Señor Luna had enclosed her phone number and address. 'There are significant changes forecast for Girona. That which is held back in the dark is coming into the light.'

Inside one of the books was a letter from someone named Micheline relating to José and Jean Cocteau. It said that Cocteau had called José 'the key' but that he, Cocteau, 'must find the lock'. It mentioned 'the affair of the two towers'.

Paris le 2 avril 1971

Cher Josep,

J'ai vu "Madeleine Cocteau" hier et elle m'a dit d'envoyer ses amitiés à son "maton de Gerona".

J'adore vos photos de Cocteau. Est-ce vous qui avez fait celui de Cocteau en Napoléon? Il correspond ainsi vers de Cocteau.

Cocteau a souvent parlé de vous et a dit que vous étiez la clef, mais qu'il devait trouver la serrure — Il a dit que vous lui avez dit précisément

Conservez-moi jusqu'à ce que tu aies découvert ma serrure — L'affaire de deux fous?

Avec toute mon admiration et mon amitié dans le souvenir de "Jean".

Micheline

Translated in full on page 324

It reminded me that Ruiz had given me a letter, too. The top part was about an engagement. The bottom, in another hand, was about more urgent matters. It said, 'Forget *Sardanas*. I want these things out of my house … these things are bringing bad luck. Ask José to move them. And now the Frenchwoman went to take the cure in Caldes and left more things and never came back. And people here have eyes. Do something!'

Cobla-Orquesta
LA PRINCIPAL
Representantes: Alfonso Mercader y Ramón Cortada   Teléfono 107

Cassà de la Selva 19 julio 1954
(Gerona)

Sr. Presidente
Agrupación Sardanista
Caldas

Muy Sr mío:

Teniendo libre la noche del sábado 7 de agosto, tengo a bien ofrecérsela como le prometí, esperando que de interesarles, se servirán comunicármelo lo antes posible.

En tanto me reitero su SS

A. Mercader

Sr. PONS—
OLVIDA LAS SARDANAS. QUIERO QUE ESTAS COSAS SALGAN DE MI CASA. TODO EL MUNDO USA A ALFONSO Y ESTAS COSAS TRAEN MALA SUERTE.

PIDE A TARRES QUE LAS MUEVA. Y AHORA LA MUJER FRANCESA TOMO LOS BAÑOS EN CALDAS Y DEJÓ MAS COSAS Y NUNCA VOLVIÓ. Y LA GENTE AQUI TIENE OJOS. HAZ ALGO!
MERCE MERCADER

Translated in full on pages 324–25

The next morning I phoned Señor Luna and asked him if he'd met Madame Mathieu. He'd heard of her. Did he remember the house? It had always been in the care of the clergy. She was the first secular person to be there. What was so special about the house that the clergy had let it go? Someone must have paid a lot of money. And why did whoever bought it agree to have it knocked down?

'Things were different in those days. The Church didn't keep records. They just did a cash deal, a handshake. It was their business.' He said he had to go. Someone was waiting for him. I wondered why he'd left the Church.

34

Carreras was waiting for me outside the Planeta Theatre. We walked by the river and I thought he seemed concerned for me. 'The fact José is married must be hard for you.'

I said I was best free, a voyager through life. It used to be true. He didn't believe it.

'It must be hard because he was yours. I can see it in your face.' He sounded caring. I wondered if he had had women during his travels. He talked about his work in South America. He felt he was more an academic than a priest. He'd obviously applied himself to his profession seeking excellence. I sensed he dismissed José as a poet lacking discipline.

'It's all about the Grail, isn't it?' I said. 'Madame Mathieu believed in its existence because the writer she talked to before her death wrote a book. How else did he find out all the information?'

'Did you know him?'

'There was a writer there in Paris when she was ill. José says it was Gérard de Sède. What is the Grail?'

He said it was present in many traditions since the twelfth and thirteenth centuries. It contained white powder of high-spun gold and platinum metals. Its power was used in the worship of Isis, the goddess from antiquity.

It was certain the Cabbalists in Girona had discovered the properties of the Grail, and from this time came their experiments transcending physical life. That was possibly why José had been so interested in the Jews, because of the accounts they left behind. I asked if he had lost Maria's money on the Centre.

'Well, he wouldn't lose his own. He doesn't bother with things like money.' He wasn't sure I understood what he'd said. That made two of us.

'Who is Isis?'

'The greatest of all ancient deities. From Ptolemaic Egypt worship spread throughout the Graeco Roman world. Only the birth of Jesus stopped its continuation. She was the goddess of 10,000 names. Victorious over fate.'

'What does the Grail look like?'

Just as José had, he described it as being made of the most remarkable physical matter in the universe. It was purported to give powers beyond human reach including physical longevity, immortality, invisibility. Who holds this, holds the world. It has power of projection and takes the bearer out of time. It produces levitation. Objects move out of the dimensions as we know them and reappear elsewhere. They've not disappeared. They've just travelled beyond our sight and come back. He mentioned transmutation, teleportation. It is a gift from paradise, known since the beginning of time.

'Has anyone seen it?'

'In a state of elevated super-consciousness, yes.'

'Is that what the ritual does?'

'That's what it attempts.'

'Have you seen it?'

'No.'

'Do you believe it?'

'It doesn't fit in with the world as I understand it. Or the doctrine I subscribe to.'

It seemed he had nothing more to say to me. I didn't dare say anything to him. He was cold, skilful, and that alone made me believe José was in trouble.

I hadn't finished the vegetarian dish that was always plate no. 2 on the spa menu when José was in the dining room, undeniably drawing every eye. He gracefully nodded at guests who recognized him, and bestowed a wonderful smile on Rosa Quintana, the proprietor. Once opposite me, he stopped all smiling and said the Americans were trying to buy the material from the society and a lot of money was involved. It would all come out in a year or so. The focus would be on the priest and his secret. It would be worldwide. That was forecast. It was cosmic. The revelation had a purpose – to challenge man's belief in God. You had choice. That's what you were here for. The level of our existence was known as dualism.

'What Americans? And who gave this forecast?'

'It is in the records relating to the Grail. I don't know how it happens. The Americans are buying for someone else. The offer is beyond price. But then what they want is beyond price. And that's why they won't have it.'

'Who are they buying for? Is it political?'

'Oh no. Beyond political.'

I wondered if these were the Americans who'd been interested in Isaac the Blind. I described, as best I could, Max Kander.

'He has another name these days, but he is one of them. He approached Dr Arbós again; he wants us to sell the material. He's always wanted money. Not for grandiosity but to do medical research. And now he has a good argument, because things are predicted which bring light to the whole business.'

'In America?'

'Worldwide.'

'About this?'

'No. They haven't got "this". That's the point. But it will rouse attention to "this". And then the cosmic plan comes into being. It's even in the Cabbala message.'

'The woman who is ill – does she have an Italian name?'

'Guilini.'

'Yes. Is she important in the society?'

'Very.'

'Carreras goes to see her.'

'He would.'

'Is he in this?'

'I'd rather not say.'

'How many are there? In the society?'

'Madame Guilini, two other women, two doctors, a lawyer, a French businessman, two members of the Church.'

'And you. Who are you?'

He called himself the custodian. He'd said that before, that his family had always been its custodians.

He put Lucia's letters on the table. They were dirty with discoloured envelopes.

'Was Lucia in it?'

'Of course.'

He wouldn't give me the other names. It seemed the divergence of interest was serious, its outcome unknown. Lucia had wanted the secret known for the benefit of the world, its future.

'Shall I write about it?'

'If one or two of them want to talk, then listen. Make your own decision.'

'Are you frightened of dying?' I spoke roughly in my fear, my absolute incomprehension that anything as unnecessary as death could choose to snuff out all this life. His eyes were still glowing. Was it the wine? I thought, he must be seventy-five.

'I'd like to know it goes to the right person,' he said.

'You've never spoken about it before.'

'I always thought it should be hidden until such a time when the world was more optimistic. It doesn't seem to happen. Perhaps I've waited too long.'

'Where is the material?'

'They won't find it.'

'The sun stone?'

He shook his head.

'What purpose did that have?'

'It was essential for the ritual.'

'Is the ritual a ceremony of worship?'

'Never.'

I asked who he trusted, so I didn't have to waste time trying to work out people's real intentions.

'I trust you,' he said.

From all this I understood that, after his heart attack and own brush with mortality, it was time to pass certain things on. The society felt other people were getting too close, and they were starting to feel the pressure. The main members, now old, feared for the material. José made it clear he trusted me, and the others trusted him. Did this explain why men like Ruiz and Luna were willing to talk? It seemed I was part of it all now.

—◊—

He must trust her. The letters were in Catalan. I understood that sentence, but very little else. José sat beside me and kept saying he'd read them to me. I didn't trust what I'd heard.

Lucia had said these letters would explain the whole affair started by those in the past. The danger began by … wasn't it her family? But surely these few notes would hardly even explain the change of weather or their state of health? There was plenty of that. He said he had to take them back.

'Lucia gave them to me.'

'Her possessions belong to her estate.'

Where were the rest? He said he was in a hurry, took the letters and read them out fast in French. A letter from a Pepita to Dolores, which I thought must be Lucia's mother, told of things being paid for by the 'Belgian Congo'. And also:

> *The French priest must have trusted her not only in terms of investment but also on a scientific level. I saw a note he left her on the energy produced between two towers. She was there when the ring was thrown into the fire. She has seen too much … he frightened her to death.*

Hotel des Italiens. Gerone Espagne.

16 - 6 - 51

Chère "Dolores".

J'ai rencontré Maria à Paris et nous nous
sommes bien amusées.
Une petite fête chez Schiaparelli. Et elle a eu le
corps de joie pour une création "Shocking Pink,"
une couleur criante. Malgré son insistance à vouloir
aller à un thé dansant et même rue de Lappe, je
pense qu'elle était fatiguée et même malade.
Elle est encore obsédée par des bas de soie et de rouges
quantité en cheveux ainsi que par de jolies choses
payées par le "Belgium Congo". À ce sujet l'abbé
François a dû lui faire confiance, pas seulement
en matière d'investissement mais aussi en la chose
scientifique.
J'ai lu une note qu'il lui a laissée sur l'énergie
produite entre deux tours. Elle était là au moment de la bague jaune dans le feu. Elle en a
trop vu. Yorcisse a dit que bien sûr il pouvait la
croire mais en fait il la terrorisait.
Je vous avertis que c'est son opinion personnelle.
Ma chère Dolores, ayez confiance. Je crois que
vous pouvez attendre des temps meilleurs. J'ai
vu à Gerone, ce n'est pas facile. Vous discutez
à chaque rencontre. Meilleurs souvenirs de
Gloria.
Affectueuses pensées Pepita.

Translated in full on pages 325–26

In another, dated 1904, to a Narcís from a Rosa, there seemed to be suspicion:

The young Frenchwoman is delightful but people are talking, saying that Guillem is not her brother and that he is not even Catalan. Nobody understands where the money is coming from. She says she's writing a book of poetry but I think that the money is coming from him – the French priest. He's using the house. The gardener told Jacint that he has seen him there twice. May God watch over you.

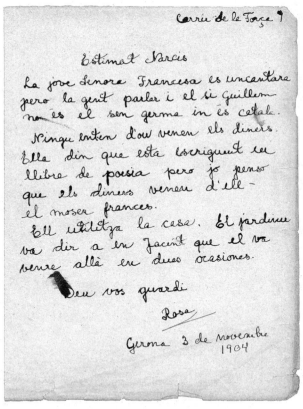

Translated in full on pages 326–27

Rosa had changed her view in a second letter, dated 7 January 1905, when Jacint had spoken to a cultural group, the *Revista de Girona*, and the Frenchwoman was mentioned. She might be published in their next edition, so there was no need to worry. Jacint had found out that the French priest was a student of texts. 'God watch over you for many years.'

'Who is Narcís?'

'There was a Narcís who was one of the founders of the *Revista de Girona*, a magazine which brought in Catalan writing and art in the nineteenth century. It might be him.'

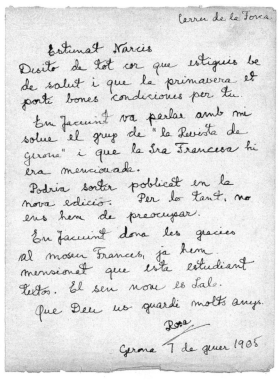

Translated in full on page 327

Did Maria publish any work? José didn't think so.

A part of a torn letter described Maria's love for the priest:

Recently she told me that she still thinks about the French priest, that there would never be anybody else like him, but he did not want to give up his ...

i ja no se la veu pel carrer, em preocupa.
Fa poc em va dir que encara pensa en el
mossèn francès, que mai li tornaria a
haver ningú com ell, però no volia
deixar córrer la seva vocació. Em va
demanar si era bo o dolent, però no
el coneixia prou. Podries anar a veure-la
quan puguis?

El teu amic Narcís

Bonastruch de Port-, 20
Girona
Maig del 1951

Translated in full on pages 327–28

The word looked like 'vocation'. She wanted to know if he 'was good or bad'.

'Well, it's not us,' I said, as he folded the letter.

'Oh, but it is.' He laughed. I'd got used to him looking old.

A letter from Maria to Dolores talked of investments, the maid, the significance of the 'Shepherd's Crook' being placed with the Magdalene and how Berenger 'never did anything by chance':

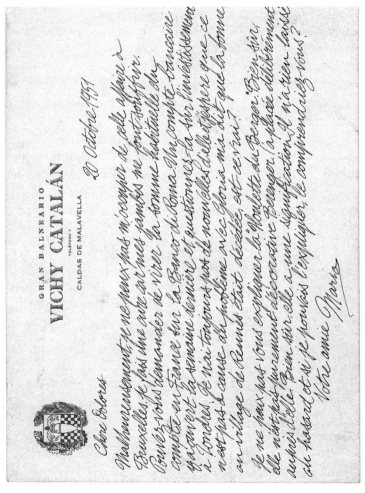

Translated in full on page 328

In the final letter there was a reference to the priest's fall from grace, into the darkness of unsuitable passion. The chocolate advertisement was mentioned and underlined. The letter said the priest seemed to be between Maria and another woman. He loved Maria's young looks, her quick transforming smile. The writer understood the priest felt safe with her. Also a large part of the money had been invested in the Belgian Congo.

I asked José where she'd met him.

'In Quillan, with her parents and Ernest Cross, an archaeologist. Then he saw her in Paris. He paid for her to go there at least twice.'

I read again the portion of the letter referring to the two structures. José explained that travel through further dimensions was possible by means of a vibrating power governed by the force of light. He also gave me postcards of duplicate towers, apparently sent to Maria. One said 'Be

prudent'.

'Are the experiments the Cabbalists made the same as the ritual?'

'Saunière came here to get the Cabbala documents and the key. The key unlocks the gap or tower. Through that you are positioned beyond these four dimensions of this planet.'

I must have looked doubtful.

'It was common knowledge in Paris in the occult and Rosicrucian societies. In this era it's all forgotten.'

I checked through the letters. Saunière was never mentioned by name. José had seen letters in his cousin's possession, mentioning the priest's arrival in Girona.

He stood up unexpectedly. 'It's occurred to me we have to complete all this somehow. Otherwise we will never be free.'

I watched him walk off through the ornate gateway and I thought of all the years I'd known him and how that should be celebrated, and here we were stuck in other people's lives.

I read the latest books from the mid-nineties and didn't see anything new about the priest or the secret. The first account by Gérard de Sède was still the main source. It had the facts. The poor priest woke up rich and no one ever discovered why. Was the Jesus lineage story true? I could see that at the time, 1891, it would upset the entire structure of the Catholic Church and that it would be suppressed at all costs. The reception of the Grail books seemed negative. It was fake, Harry Potter grown up. Did anyone believe it? No. It was entertaining bullshit. The protecting society, the Prieuré de Sion, was now judged as false. The Grail was put back in mythology and interest waned. World focus coming next? I didn't think José need worry.

An Oxford friend, working in physics, said the subject belonged in the fifth dimension. He hated that term, preferred 'an adjacent reality', but change the names as you liked, it could not be proven. Some scientists were trying to push forward the possibility of a tenth dimension. It did not conform to the laws or structure of the universe. Therefore whatever was written on the fifth dimension had its own reality and could not be challenged, and you could say anything. He used a word like 'twaddle'.

What did I actually have? The vision in the church in the sixties. I could see it as clearly as the evening it happened. I'd seen photographs of Saunière in the books. Was it him? I thought the man I'd seen was older and shorter with a bull neck. Could I prove my experience? They might listen in a shrink's office. And Lucia's death?

I phoned my friend Miguel Berga at the university in Barcelona. Although born in Girona, he couldn't remember the Frenchwoman or the house. He vaguely remembered a tower.

I asked Rosa Quintana, from the spa at Caldes. She was old enough. Did she remember the Frenchwoman? She had to ask the other guests. The garden of the Frenchwoman, if they thought about it, was so named because of some French visitor in the past.

Rosa asked the editor of the local Girona newspaper and he knew nothing of it. It wasn't relative to their lives or history. He told Rosa he'd look into it. So I asked Clara and her friends at Girona University. It was as though it had never been.

And then Señora Juncosa, whose details had been given to me by Señor Luna, returned my call.

'You'd better hurry there,' said Rosa. 'She's over ninety at least. The butcher's family.'

She lived on a main street, relentless with fumes and traffic, in the new part of Girona. Some disquiet in me these days made me turn and just see what was behind. This time, a priest. I'd know that agile walk anywhere: Quim Carreras. The hair must have been cut or tied back. My turning made him stop unexpectedly, almost jolt into a doorway. I kept walking. I stopped to face a shop window. He wasn't following. I kept on into the high nineties, the hundreds, only thirty-five doorways to go and there he was on the same side of the road, now ahead of me. He was watching me in the reflection of the windows.

Why did Lucia die? Lluís had said the mountain was too much for her. Like an ailing animal that senses death and needs to find a place to die alone, she had gone to the emptiness of the mountain. But her operation had been successful. Was there anything else? 'You mean, was she attacked? Hard to determine with a mountain death. José was quite clear on the cause. Shock.'

Opposite the doorway now, and the old lady possibly at her window, shuttered against the heat, waiting. The priest increased his speed accordingly. There we were, one behind the other, in the scorching fumes, he following from in front. Should I cross the road and get on with the business of the day? I suddenly turned round, walked in the other direction. He did not follow. Furious now, sweating, I ran and caught him and shouted at his black-clothed back. I shouted his name. He wasn't buying that. So I ran past and stopped and came towards him. His eyes met mine without doubt. It was almost him.

Exhausted, I sat on the roadside. My nerves were not up to it. I was too old, too everything. This wasn't even my business. I got onto my feet (arthritis was now in my life), and crossed to Señora Juncosa's doorway. An elderly man opened the door, jovial enough. I was late and his mother, thinking I wasn't coming, was taking a siesta. Another day?

35

Gerard Ruiz slipped an envelope across the counter. He said it contained two photographs, one of Madame Mathieu and some others. I should put it in my bag. Then he included a map and other documents.

'What is José doing?' he asked.

'What is the worst he can do?'

'Do what Lucia wanted and reveal it to the world.'

'What do you think?'

'Too many people don't want that and they're not fussy how they get their way. I think José's life is more important than whatever he's got. We've lived without it so far.'

I asked what he thought it was.

'Something on the edge of good and bad. That's what I heard years ago.'

I asked where Carreras was. I hadn't seen him for days.

'This is his family's business. I took it over from Quim because he decided to go into the Church. The other day he gave me this.' He lifted up a large copy of a painting of a tomb. He said it symbolized death, and that by finding Arcadia death had no dominion. And he said Arcadia was what they were all looking for. 'The Holy Grail.'

The painting by Poussin was mentioned in all the books, which began with Abbé Bigou putting '*Et in Arcadia Ego*' on the last ancestral tombstone of the Blanchefort family. The painting was constantly used as a key to the mystery. I realized I'd used the word 'key'. That's what José called the Grail. And Saunière in Paris had purchased a copy at the Louvre. So what did Carreras have to do with it? He was adamant Saunière never visited Girona, and that the Grail did not fit with his concept of reality. José believed the priest had visited Girona. Lucia did. Did Gerard?

'They say it's a story José cooked up to make Girona more interesting. He never mentioned it before these books came out.'

But he had. The visit to Arenys de Mar with Paco speeding on the empty roads to deal with Noël Corbu's hotel PR plans. The visit with Arbós to search for careless evidence.

'They might have meant Bigou. He came here. He was French,' said Ruiz. 'But there is no argument.' And he pointed at the envelope of photographs. When I opened it later there was one of Maria Tourdes, or Madame Mathieu as she was then, writing at a desk.

'Did Bigou bring this mystery?'

'It was always here,' said Ruiz. 'Arcadia is part of Carreras's story. He is sixth-generation Catalan. His ancestor studied in Paris in the late 1820s. He came from the north of France and had a career ahead of him. I think it was in law. He used to visit a bookshop specializing in old texts and rare books near the Sorbonne, and the owner, who was from the west coast of Turkey, let students use these books privately for free. Carreras's ancestor learned something of immense value in that shop, which brought him immediately to Girona. He gave up his career and stayed in this provincial city just as it was recovering from the Napoleonic War. Whatever he wanted he didn't find, and on his death he passed the secret to a young Catalan, Joaquim Bocher, and to one of José's family in the cathedral. Bocher set off for Greece to Arcadia in the Peloponnese and was murdered. It was at a time when people travelled. The bookshop owner – who by now had established a collection in Paris of earliest editions, ancient texts – before his death arranged for the entire library to be taken to the foot of Arcadia. Thousands of books were sent by ship to Andritsaina, below the mountain at the top of which is Arcadia.'

'Is it a real place?' I asked.

'Most definitely. It seemed a strange bequest, and the mayor had to go down to the coast to bring the books up by mule train. Andritsaina was not intellectual but full of landowners, and the library was a problem.'

'Who was the bookshop's owner?'

'A bibliophile. Nikolopoulous. He had started from nothing, was poor, and must have discovered mention of the secret before Carreras's ancestor did. Or maybe they shared it. Whatever it was, this text, it clearly showed Girona held the key.'

Our meeting place was the Frenchwoman's garden. José was sitting on the wall looking over at the countryside.

'I love this place. I never feel alone here. She wrote about that. Finding tranquillity instead of all that quite hopeless passion. And when I sit here I feel she's left its imprint, and I can be part of it too.'

'What have you decided to do?' I asked.

'Leave it to the right person.'

'Then that person has to know all the facts.'

He said that, if I knew, I'd be compromised. And he didn't know 'all' about anything.

These days I questioned the accepted parts of the given story. That Abbé Bigou fleeing before the Revolution must have stirred everything up. It was said he came to Spain. Where? And surely he brought the items of value with him. It was thought he died in Sabadell near Barcelona. Was this true?

'He came here. This did not begin in Rennes-le-Château. It was always in Girona. Even before the Romans. It goes back to Egypt and the ancient Jews. Some documents and ritual artefacts passed to and fro between Rennes-le-Château and Girona, over the centuries, depending on the state of warfare or plague. There has always been a line of evolved priests, rabbis, doctors, mystics in a private society here or near here, taking care of the secret. In 1792 Bigou brought all that was existing in his church, and it was hidden here below this house by the society. In those days there was no tower. Inundation of water and land shift meant it had to be taken somewhere safer. It went to a church in the middle of a wood in Besalú. The work on the experiments had to be carried out in the form of rituals. The church was used for this. Artefacts that the Cabbalists had left in the closed area were already in the care of the society, so for the first time in 1793 all the material was in one place.

'Where did it come from?'

'Ancient Egypt. It was said the Magdalene carried it here after the Crucifixion and landed in Marseilles. There are documents suggesting she did land south of Narbonne. There are stretches of inland water and lakes and it has a powerful atmosphere.'

I remembered it stretching on either side of the train track to Spain.

'Lencate is just level with Rennes-le-Château, and this is where the Magdalene was received on that waterway. Others say Isis worshippers brought the secret when they arrived in boats at L'Escala on the coast here 4,000 years ago.'

I was certainly increasing my knowledge of history if nothing else.

I wanted to know what the material was that was stored in Besalú.

He talked of a ritual or sun stone. A menorah from the second Temple, a cup made of stone and gold, but he passed over that quickly. Amulets for protection. Documents, records of experiments, chants, sacred texts, the instructions, the equation.

I had no idea what he meant. I expected E= and then a string of numbers.

He explained it was pages long and takes the ritual participants into each level of experience. It was originally in scrolls. Dozens of them. The rituals were carried out and perfected in Besalú, and the transformation work began. Abbé Bigou was hidden in the house adjoining the church. There were many searching for him, especially the Vatican. After his death it stayed in the care of the descendants of Count Tallaferro.

'How did he die?' I asked.

Possibly in the performance of a ritual, he thought, that produces a stimulus of the nervous system to such a degree the normal defence of the brain is lowered so that the range of perception is much larger and too vivid. He explained this is now considered dangerous, and only initiates are given the ritual process, but Saunière's brother Alfred may well have died through this participation. The material was moved back to Girona after the Napoleonic War in 1820. It was kept here in this house.

Did he mean by the Rosicrucians?

All he said was that they'd been around since the time of the temples in Egypt. The Church saw them as the enemy because they believed in direct contact with the divine through no intermediary. They are gnostic as were the Cathars. *Gnosis* means direct knowledge of God. Which, of course, the Church sees as heresy.

'Then how do you have the Church involved?'

'The members in the society understand that there is other matter outside the ruling of the Church. The Catalan priest and poet Jacint Verdaguer was involved to some degree and used mediums and occult practices to exercise the powers of darkness. He believed illness was caused by demonic intervention. The Church suspended him and he was sent to a retreat near Ripoll.'

'Where you went?'

'No. I was in the mountains.' He pointed to Canigou. 'He was the greatest Catalan poet and wrote an epic poem about Canigou. He was born around the same time as Saunière, and it's quite likely they would have been aware of each other. Of course the Carreras family knew Verdaguer, because of their interest in the resurgence of Catalan culture and its emphasis on the countryside and the peasants. The poor family believed the material was on Arcadia.' He spoke simply, from a serious place in his memory. I believed him, all of it. I trusted him. I asked if he'd wanted to be involved in all this.

'Never.'

A bird drew close to him and settled on a branch and made the calling, jarring sound of the one in the Jewish courtyard. Was it the same bird?

'It always comes to me and calls me to go away.'

'To?'

'The mountain.' He closed his eyes and I thought he slept. 'But I have my son.' And the bird sang its heart out.

The responsibility had come into the care of his family – the canons in the cathedral – before 1851. And his mother had sent him for instruction. In what?

'The life of the mystic,' he said, and got down from the wall. 'It won't happen to my son.'

I re-read the books on Saunière, and tried to do what Lucia had suggested. The secret seemed to pass to Bigou as Lady d'Hautpoul de Blanchefort lay dying. It was suggested the secret had been in the Blanchefort family since the Knights Templars. I noted she died on 17 January 1781, the same day and month as Saunière suffered his fatal stroke. It was the Day of St Sulpice. It was also known as the 'alchemist's day', after Nicolas Flamel conducted the first successful alchemy experiment in Paris on 17 January, some time after 1382, and became phenomenally wealthy. I felt that Saunière had a lot of luck stumbling upon parchments with secrets, especially as the secret was probably known of to some extent in the area. What if he had not stumbled upon it, but searched for it? For me that fell into place with the man I was reading about. 'Intelligent', 'ambitious', 'designed for higher things'. How could he fail so badly that he ended up in a run-down church in a backwater, miles from the good posts? Unless he contrived it. He left Narbonne quickly. Had he discovered the secret there, or searched for and found it?

The Rosicrucians were mentioned. They were probably his paymasters. The Habsburgs had Rosicrucian links. Why else would he flout the Catholic faith by placing Rosicrucian signs on his property, in his church, unless it was to acknowledge something for him more powerful? In the later books his constant trips away from the parish were taken up. He had composed letters for Marie Denarnaud to send to cover his absence. He contrived always to seem present except when on a retreat. He was often 'indisposed'. The parishioners were well aware of his desire for secrecy when leaving, and the rush to return for his Sunday sermon.

Claire Corbu, the daughter of Noël, wrote in *L'Héritage de l'Abbé Saunière* (1985) that the rumour in the village was that he went to Spain or Paris, 'but we haven't found one trace of proof where he went or what he did'.

To me, the story of Jesus leaving, after a contrived Crucifixion, to live with Mary Magdalene and their family in France fell flat. What were they doing? That Jesus took, step by step, a predecided path and died on a Cross to cleanse sin, to carry our redemption, made far more sense for me. Either way I was interested in Jesus alive on earth, what He said and did, what He gave to us.

When I next saw José I asked about the early days in Girona. Who was Julien Sacaze? He was an antiquarian and Rosicrucian, and a friend of his grandfather. 'He worked on meridians, especially the Rose meridian.'

I remembered Cocteau's desire to enter the house and to climb the tower, the loss of the cross and chain, the ritual I'd seen a part of through Maria's window. And the man with North European looks who flitted through Girona unseen, with the sudden disconcerting visibility of a ghost, whom nobody could identify. He'd offered Beryl money, which she'd taken.

He was trying to get the Grail to clean it up and sell it to the highest bidder. The Habsburgs were after it. 'A man was sent to watch me quite obviously when we were in Puerta de la Selva. Just to let me know I should be careful. There have been many like him over the years.'

—᱈᱈—

'Still searching for the Grail?'

I was looking through a register in the cathedral and had arrived at 1891. Who had visited and from where? Slim, brown fingers turned the huge pages for me.

It was Carreras. 'Nothing from the Aude, but then there wouldn't be. End of the nineteenth century. People passed to and fro across the border, especially the ecclesiastical order.'

I had Clara with me to help with any language hitches. Carreras asked for a bigger book and then for the director of the Registry. According to Clara he had asked for records of visiting priests from France. There were no records.

He led us out by the side door of this official building. 'Don't be disappointed,' he said, teasing. 'I know what. I'll tell you a better Grail story. I'll tell you about Arcadia. That's much more interesting.' And we sat outside Lluís's bar, which now had a forest of tables on the pavement and an English speciality – 'sandwitches'.

'The Catalans came to Arcadia in the 1300s, led by a Catalan count. They battled with the Franks who were here and there in the region, and returned to Spain. In the middle of the countryside there is an unexpected Gothic cathedral. It is south of Olympia and supposedly built by the Catalans. There was a substantial crusader influence in the area. The ancient site of Arcadia was written about by Pausaniaus in the first century AD. The Arcadian cult of 2000 BC mentions Zeus and his three daughters, and before them a wolf cult and tradition of human sacrifice. So no one goes up to the site. It is said the animals leave no shadow. It is reputed to have supernatural powers. There is also a well-preserved temple nearby, the temple of Bassae. This, too, is in the middle of nowhere. What is its purpose?' He looked at me. 'It was once known as the home of the Grail.'

Clara listened politely, but I felt she was wary of him.

'The Grail has always had connections with the Catalans. You have heard of the Santo Caliz in Valencia cathedral?'

She had not.

'And you a good Catalan girl! It was a chalice that came from a monastery in St Juan de la Peña. Jaume II of Aragon asked the Caliph of Egypt in 1322 to send him the chalice used by Christ at the Last Supper. And then there's the *Libre de Gamaliel*, a Catalan sacred book about the Grail written in 1300 by Pere Pascual. And haven't you heard about our Catalan thirteenth-century wall painting of the Grail at Sigena? And there is all the thirteenth-century artwork of the chalice.'

'What is behind it?'

'The desire for something we all seek. The immortal, the all-loving, beyond pain, beyond dualism. In reality, money and power.' In case Clara had trouble with 'dualism', he said good and bad, dark and light.

'For a man of the Church you seem oddly interested in this legendary object,' said Clara.

'In the tradition. After all Wagner went to Rennes-le-Château before he wrote *Parsifal*. That has to interest me. Because Wagner's music transports me beyond where words reach.'

When he'd gone she said, 'Why does he tell you all that?'

Later it occurred to me – to get my mind off what it really is.

Before we parted by the bridge built by Eiffel, Clara said, 'It's much bigger than a treasure hunt.'

As I crossed back to the old quarter I was walking through layer upon layer of history. Eighth-century streets, arches, stairways, the Arab baths, monumental churches,

broken walls, disused fountains, excavated Roman ceme-
teries, the remains of a shrine. The past was so present,
if unperceived, still alive – it was no surprise if a visiting
priest with a Grail, dramatic in its time, should have been
forgotten amongst the abundance already there. Absorbed
by the search, I spent more time trying to find information
than rehearsing the play.

I sought out those I'd known in the past, the ones who
would remember the building. Some remembered frag-
ments about the Frenchwoman. People like Eva thought
it a dark subject, best not gone into. People spoke openly,
and then they didn't. I believed a select group around
Carreras had put a stop to it. The atmosphere in the city
felt uneasy.

In my search to uncover the little-known I'd taken what
could be seen as risks, and any questions had alerted Carreras and possibly the society. My search aroused people who
had never spoken, and some who had no idea they held
part of a powerful secret, like the grandson of Maria Tourdes's gardener. I began to sense a beyond-normal darkness around me. Could I end up like the treasure-seeker in
Rennes-le-Château, Monsieur Henri Buthion? Cursed?

Señora Juncosa was always unavailable. I couldn't locate
José. Lluís said he didn't know anything. He remembered
the house and tower, not the woman. He'd never heard
of the priest. Ruiz was busy. I couldn't find Dr Arbós or
Paco. Miguel Berga thought Espriu was dead. Señor Luna?
I phoned him. The French priest visiting Girona? He'd
never heard of that.

Finally, I waited for Ruiz to be alone.

He shook his head to indicate silence. 'It's been so busy,'
he said, and passed me a sheet of paper and an old quill
pen.

I wrote, 'Is José in danger?'

He wrote quickly, 'You could be.'

He tore the paper, and amongst the sound the words: 'Because hurting you would make him think twice.'

36

The play went on at the end of November. Clara was excellent, and there was a lot of interest and attention. The press gave me some space, mentioning my long association with Girona, but I had only one thing on my mind. Girona was considered a mystical city. What mystical things had happened here? I chose the *Vanguardia* journalist for that one. He paused. 'As in legends?'

'Miraculous changes ...'

'Oh, you mean the miracle of the flies. St Narcís, saint of Girona, driving back the invading French?'

'Secret societies?' And I wanted him to keep this conversation to himself.

'Nothing like that. Only the Freemasons.' And then he thought he'd got it. 'The vision in 1976. The woman who witnessed it was locked up.'

José did not see the play. It would show an allegiance with me that his wife forbade. He was busy working on the Christmas Eve event at the cathedral, and about the other matter he had to make a decision. I needed to see him.

Although the vision happened thirty years ago, people remembered better what happened 300 years ago. Miguel Berga had a good idea. 'Don't bother asking anyone in ordinary life. They don't bother unless it relates directly to them. The Catalans don't go for visions. They like it down to earth. The young don't know anything about Madame Mathieu and that story. Go to the archives, the municipality, the press, the architects' society, the museum.'

The archives were run by Albina Barrés, daughter of the filmmaker Antonio Barrés. She remembered various stories of Rennes-le-Château and Girona being linked by the towers. 'The priest copied the tower. They are the same. The Colomer family know about that. They are a leading family in Girona.'

Did she mean the friend of José, Dr Colomer?

'He was very associated with José during the Jewish Centre period.'

She showed me on Google a reference to Torre Magdala. 'Fransec Ferrer Gironès, politician and writer, mentioned the relationship of the two towers in his work. He'd received information from the Colomer family.'

Did Albina know why Saunière had copied the Girona tower in Rennes?

'He'd told José's grandfather that he thought the municipality in Rennes, with whom he often had problems, would throw him out of his house, leaving him and his maid homeless. So he bought the land and built wonderful buildings as an offering to God. The tower gave a view facing south on two levels. He said he needed to keep his books in the tower and spent much of his time there.'

Of course he would have to explain his extravagance somehow. 'Is this true?'

'There shouldn't be a need to copy the Torre Magdala. It was ordinary. He said he built his because of the magnificent view. And he was there to work. But he copied the measurements so the towers mirrored each other. My father knew about it because he made a film in Maria's garden.'

I asked how Maria Mathieu had come into the house, and who was Roger? She found me a folder of documents about the house, filed under the address of 3 Sant Cristòfol. It had been owned by a Señor Massaguer, and in 1851 he'd added a tower 'and paid for it out of his own pocket', although no explanation was given. He left the house to his maid on his death, as long as she remained celibate. The next reference to the house was a Señor Saguer selling it to Roger Mathieu in 1932. In 1940, on his death, it passed to his widow, Maria Tourdes. Albina explained that widows reverted to their maiden names. In 1962 the mayor of Girona applied to purchase the house, and Señora Juncosa carried out the transaction for Maria Tourdes, who was in Paris.

Albina said her mother had been friendly with Maria and the house was quite lively. The bishop lived up there in those days, and there was also a spiritual healer. Was Maria a writer? I asked.

'Nobody ever saw anything she wrote.' Then she looked through another document. 'You should look up the "Occult Circle – L'Ordre Kabbalistique de la Rose Croix, Paris". That should be interesting.'

I looked for information about the vision. There was nothing in the newspaper libraries. I went from church to museum to bookshop and I found nothing, except the previous mayor Joaquim Nadal. He was now in the Catalan government.

Clara introduced me to Dolores Badia, who was married to the producer of the Girona Festival. She had amazing energy and drive, and if something needed finding she was the one to do it. She didn't say no, or I don't know, but simply said, 'Joan Puig will know that. Pep Dalmàs will remember that.' She gave me at least twenty names and contact numbers. I asked if she personally remembered the night of the vision. She thought there were at least a hundred witnesses, but most just accepted they'd seen something and left it at that. But a cleaning woman, Maria Mendez, was insistent she had seen the Lady of the Cup, the Magdalene, and with several other witnesses told the church, the municipality, the press. She was put into a mental hospital for some time. When she came out she was told she had seen not the Magdalene, but Jesus. She wouldn't accept it. I asked if I could see her. Dolores doubted it.

I went to see Joan Puig and Pep Dalmàs.

'What kind of place am I in where things happen and people say they didn't?'

Pep Dalmàs laughed. 'Girona!'

He and Joan were the first gay couple to be married in the town, and they ran the cultural section of the municipality. It occurred to me that, if I continued saying I'd seen the Frenchwoman and a tower, the same would happen as in Maria Mendez's case.

Pep Dalmàs had no problem with the vision. He remembered a strong feeling of calm before the light appeared. 'It was like a silence. I was in Lluís's bar and it was a strange feeling. Other people said the same. And then she appeared behind the cathedral and dissolved like a rainbow. It lasted a few minutes.'

He hadn't got up there fast enough to see it himself, but remembered the effect. 'People said it was not earthly. Some had a deafness or ringing in their ears, like a car alarm. The waiter in the bar said it was a chime that sounded like a gong. No, she said that, Maria Mendez.'

Joan Puig, who was too young to remember, added something else. 'Oh yes,' said Pep. 'The perfume. Many people talked of a scent which was sweet, hypnotic, not of this world.'

'What did they do, these people?'

'Most of them thought in hindsight it was a trick of the light. Others felt free and joyous. Some thought that a group was practising black magic, and it had gone too far.'

Joan Puig spoke soft Catalan, cautioning him. They both looked at me.

'Maria Mendez, and the witnesses with her, felt an approaching divinity, a lightness beyond anything known, a golden honey light, healing, sweet. The feeling lasted hours. So they locked her up.'

I was surprised people didn't go on talking about it.

'It was not encouraged. And they wouldn't insist because people would think they were drunk.'

'What do you think?'

'Those I spoke to said it was an effect like Son et Lumière. People would want to see if the Church accepted this vision officially. Maria Mendez came out of hospital and they had changed her story for her. She stayed with her belief, she'd seen the Magdalene, not Jesus, and she put a small shrine on the hills where the Magdalene had appeared.'

'There were unusual markings on the ground,' said Joan.

'A lightening of the earth and a mark like a sign. She placed flowers, candles, and a simple wooden cross. When she left, her shrine was destroyed. Then a group, The Way of Jesus, took care of her and again changed her story.

They're a right-wing group and the Church allowed them to make a permanent shrine for her. It's on the hill near the Frenchwoman's house and has an account printed of how she'd seen Jesus. The markings were the footprint of Our Lord. The Church is clear on that. But she still remains firm about what she saw.'

'Why?'

'It healed her, changed her life. Dozens of people collect on that hill at that day and time every year.'

'Who was the person who put her away?'

'Dr Baró.'

'The psychiatrist?' And friend of José, member of the society. 'To keep her quiet?'

'Definitely,' said Pep. 'For some reason they didn't want the Lady of the Cup mentioned. Obviously it coincided with something else that was happening. Maybe that something stirred up this appearance. I have heard that a few times from surprising people.'

I thought that was surprising coming from the municipality. Clearly something had happened which they needed to hide.

'The person to see is Marie Corvese, who runs the Flower Exhibition. It's no good talking to José, because everyone dismisses what he says as poetical.'

The storm broke and I ran into a doorway. Wild continuous lightning, thunder shaking the buildings – an apocalyptic war – and the doorway filled up and I recognized Clara. Then the wind started and Dolores from the festival was more or less blown in on top of us, and I saw we were in the entrance of Carmen Aragó's grand house.

'Ring the bell,' I said. But these were Catalan women and you had to be invited. Especially by someone like Carmen. Drenched, the lightning like liquid gold at our feet, we held on to each other. And in one huge illuminating flare I saw a figure coming towards us, the only calm presence around. And then the flare was spent and in the blackness of a lightless city feet approached and Carmen, soaked until even her curly hair was straight, said gently, 'Come in.' And she unbolted the door.

Up flights of stone stairs we went in this medieval palace, unadorned, severe in its denial of softness. The stones ruled here. On into her apartment at the top, with the open terrace I'd gazed up at for years. Windows in most walls gave good views of Girona and the side of the cathedral, all now in darkness from power cuts. They gave a marvellous passage for the immense lightning. At first I tried to appear normal, but all that gave way to shaking fear. Carmen sat beside me and took my hand. Hers was dry and strong. 'You are not frightened, not here with me?' I wished I could agree. Clara didn't look too good either. Dolores said she loved storms, which made me wish she'd go out into it. After a while, I got the conversation off the general, the play, Christmas. I got her attention onto the almost forgotten house just up above her. Why had the tower been built?

She answered immediately, 'Because of what had been found at Rennes-le-Château.' And so she brought up the subject herself. I asked how she knew and she pointed to the cathedral. 'The last bishop was a friend of mine.'

I asked the usual questions, but she said she knew little about it and I should meet a friend of hers. I understood it was a man and he was in Germany. He worked with Cabbala. But the thunder made it impossible to hear anything. In a lull it was decided by these polite interlopers that we should go. I hated leaving this calm, peaceful woman, now in her eighties but ageless. I distrusted lulls. Dolores sang a song to Canigou as we went down the street.

When I was five my father
Took me to the boat and told me
When you are older
Beware calm times.
Mountains of Canigou, fresh you are
And God sent as a present.

Señora Juncosa had been away to visit friends in Millau, France. 'To the house where the singer Emma Calvé retired.'

We sat in a neat, plain drawing room with a table in the middle, two blow-heaters and no air, not a puff of oxygen to be had. She shut the door and everything in me cried out, 'Let me breathe.' She needed the heat as a hothouse flower did. She was at the age where she should have what she needed. She had a story to tell. To begin with she said she knew absolutely no one connected with the story. Not even José, except by reputation. She had known José's cousin Geli, the organist, but that wasn't how I was sitting here. Her family owned the butcher's shop near the Residencia Internacional hotel and she remembered me going in with Eva to buy cutlets. She even remembered that I'd asked the delivery boy about the Frenchwoman. People said I was twelve and a beggar. Others that I was an extraterrestrial. She thought I was a winner and loved my style. Señor Luna's family bought their meat from the shop and that's how she knew 'young Luna'. He'd said recently I was interested in the house with the tower. What a thrill! She looked thrilled. I was still at the stage of needing oxygen and wondered if we'd still have the story if I opened a window. I forgot that when she said, 'Maria talked about you and your friend Beryl.' That made me stop worrying about breathing.

'When did she come to the house?'

'I don't know. But before she married Roger Mathieu.'

I told her I'd looked in the Registry of Properties and she wasn't listed until her husband bought it as late as 1932. A Señor Saguer owned it. That made her smile.

'Of course. He was a lawyer and bought the house in his name. She paid black money and avoided taxes and duties, especially for a foreigner. It was common enough.'

I didn't know what to ask first. It was as though I'd finally found the Holy Grail of information. 'Why live alone in that house?'

'Because she wasn't alone. He visited.'

'The priest?'

Señora Juncosa didn't waste time. 'I didn't know her then. I didn't meet her until after his death. She used to describe his visits and how splendid that time was. When he died the world was a darker place.' She paused. 'I don't think he came much during the First World War. I think they closed the frontier.'

I asked when he died.

'I know it was after she married Roger Mathieu and that was around 1907.'

'Why did she marry someone else if she loved the priest?'

'Because she couldn't marry him. The marriage with Roger became unhappy.'

'Who was Roger?'

'A man of letters. That's how he described himself. He liked a drink and I hear he liked the ladies. He had a house in Llançà. He was much older than she. He seemed a man of leisure, but when he died the Vatican gave him a funeral for a man of honour. So he'd worked for the Vatican but never revealed it.'

'And the priest visited from France while the husband was there.'

She nodded, definite about that. She'd looked after the house and the business matters when Maria had gone to Paris. It was 1955. It was supposed to be for a month. She never came back.

'I understood she returned to Girona from time to time.'

'Girona! It was as though she feared it. I used to visit her in Paris.' And then she asked why I needed this information and I said I was writing a book about the house with the tower. To get her mind off worrying thoughts, I asked why the tower was built. It did not fit with the house or the surrounding architecture. She had no idea why it was first built but she seemed to know a version of its history. She scribbled it down on a scrap of paper for me:

Massaguer acquired the tower on 3 December 1851. It was Joaquim Massaguer Vidal who had the tower built.

On 8 June 1922 the Massaguer family sold it to Roger Mathieu for 2,500 pesetas.

On 5 December 1932 it was acquired by Joan Saguer for 1,250 pesetas.

On 9 December 1932 Joan Saguer sold it – to Roger Mathieu and Marie Augusta Bertroz.

On 9 December 1940 Roger Mathieu died and Madame Mathieu became the sole proprietor.

On 31 August 1962, against the wishes of Mme Mathieu, the property passed to the Municipality of Girona.

'What was Maria's life like when she first came here?'

'I heard she was very chic and pleasing. So unlike anything the people here had seen. She wore the latest Paris fashions and kept to herself.' She described Maria much as José had, giving sophisticated evenings for visitors from Paris, intellectuals, artists, musicians, an opera singer, the aristocracy. It was the talk of Girona.

'And she was friendly with the priests?'

'Oh, she liked priests.'

I asked if Señora Juncosa happened to have a memento.

She opened a cupboard and out came bundles of correspondence and photographs. 'You can have it,' she said, generously. 'As you're writing a book.'

'Did she have any children?'

'I often wondered if she had had a child. She never mentioned one, but I had the feeling there was something. She was very proud of her looks and kept herself up, in spite of having no money.'

If I could, I'd have frozen at those words.

'No money?'

'Roger didn't leave anything. There were bits and pieces of investments. Some in the Belgian Congo. I think that's why she kept going to Brussels. She was always hard up, so she'd get a bit and then spend it on silk stockings and chocolate. She loved chocolate.'

So I remembered the chocolate advertisement. And I asked the question I should have asked at the beginning. How did Señora Juncosa know Emma Calvé?

'Through her. Emma Calvé did the famous chocolate advertisement in France. We used to laugh about that. She

278

bought a castle in Millau and practised mysticism. She's dead of course – years ago – but I knew the family.'

She had nothing more to say and put the letters and photographs in a bag and gave it to me. 'They'll only throw them away when I'm not here.' She could have been as young as seventy or as old as ninety. She was alert, responsive, with a wonderful memory.

Then, as I was going out, she said if I cared about José I should remind him to be prudent. More questions from me were left unanswered.

'Is it that he needs money?' she asked.

I was stunned. She said it pointedly.

'There are powerful people looking after that priest's affairs, and José is only a poet.'

Could I come back in? I could not. Her son was now beside her. Weakly I asked if there was anyone else who'd known Maria.

She said there were three who had information, but she doubted they'd see me. 'People talk to you because you've been in the city on and off for years. You've written a beautiful play. You've written about a certain time in Girona. You're not an outsider.'

'Did Maria believe in the Grail? The Lady of the Cup?' I had to know that.

'She must have because she talked to the writer Gérard de Sède before she died, and he wrote a book about it.'

'Her whole story?'

'Maria never told her whole story.'

I sat on a bench with my head in my hands. Nobody was who they seemed to be. It was too big a subject for me. I shouldn't be in it. And then I remembered the warning about José. I got out of the new part of the city and over to the well-loved streets with the main vein, the carrer de la Força. I phoned José from Ruiz's shop and got a woman I didn't recognize. I did a lot of clicking with the receiver and hung up. I got Ruiz to ask for him and to give a message. He must come to Girona now. Suddenly it was cold and Ruiz lent me a sweater. Could I talk to Señora Guilini? He doubted it. Was there anyone I could talk to? Same answer. José did not come, I had to go back to London to work, and it was nearly Christmas.

It was summer before I next came to Girona.

37

The trail had gone so far and then ended. I did phone Ruiz to warn José. Warn him of what? Then I received a letter from Girona, with no sender's details. Inside was a cutting from a newspaper or magazine, old and dirty, of a French advertisement for Chocolat Guérin-Boutron. The woman was in the style of the early 1900s, and I could just see *Mme Calvé de l'Opera* at the bottom. It was so frail that I thought it would vanish like the morsel of bread in the Jewish courtyard.

There was also a page from a letter:

Monsieur Abbé Saunière said:
  'They showed it to me, I laid my hand on it, I made it work and I'm holding it firmly.'

MENU

Rennes, 14 de Maig de 1949

Estimada Marta,

He intentat recordar exactament el significat.

El senyor abat Saunière va dir:

"M'ho van ensenyar, lui vaig posar la mà, ho vaig fer funcionar i ho tinc agafat amb fermesa".

Ho vaig veure escrit en la carta que va enviar a Juli Tarrés.

Narcís,
de tot cor.

VICHY·CÉLESTINS
l'eau qui fait du bien...

Translated in full on page 329

Was this the same Narcís as in the other letters? What was its purpose?

In the gathering of letters and cards given to me by Señora Juncosa, I could see the relationship between the two women. Maria needed things done and Señora Juncosa was keen to oblige. A lot of the content concerned money and investments, and queries about the sale of the house. In one letter she wrote, 'I once loved a priest'. In another, to Genevieve, she said of Berenger, 'He is very kind and I feel transformed when he is here – as I should be … and then he always has to leave, oh, so suddenly – and then I feel terribly alone'. She also wrote of how 'North and South … must be unified'.

Back in Girona I stayed in the new hotel by the covered bridge, which had no memories and a good restaurant. I'd left a message with Ruiz for José. Had the society dispersed? Had the material been sold? Señora Guilini was still alive, just, and Carmen, Marie Corvese, and José were preparing the 2005 May Flower Exhibition.

Albina Barrés was busy in the records office and her colleague produced the house registry. The papers on 3 Sant Cristòfol seemed lighter. I read again the document signed by Señora Juncosa for Maria Tourdes in 1962. Where were the papers relating to Roger Mathieu's purchase and before that, most vitally, Señor Massaguer and the construction of the tower that Saunière had later copied at Rennes-le-Château? Albina had no explanation. She said she'd never seen them. She was busy, so I spent the morning with the assistants trying to locate the lost files. I got Clara up to the desk with her perfect Catalan. I did not get the papers.

'They were here five months ago.'

We were told to go to the modern registry office outside of town.

13 mai 1897

Chère Geneviève

Merci de ta lettre, arrivée avec une saison de retard, elle mit encore plus de temps que le train
Je te prie de ne pas te faire de soucis pour moi et surtout de ne jamais jamais faire allusion à ce dont nous avons parlé à Quillan.
J'apprends le catalan, prends des leçons de musique Berenger me donne des livres à étudier

J'adore cet endroit. Je m'y sens si vivante, si fortunée. Il arriva mercredi et nous restâmes dans le jardin bien après la nuit tombée. Il est constamment ravi par le son des cloches, cette cité des cloches qu'il trouve magnifique. Cela le fit sortir de lui-même. Il est plein de gentillesse et je me sens transformée lorsqu'il est ici, ainsi que je devrais l'être en effet

J'ignore qui arrivera et pour une fois je m'en moque. Nous rions beaucoup ce qui va te sembler bien inapproprié, oui, follement inapproprié mais c'est ainsi que les choses se passent lorsque nous sommes ensemble et puis il doit toujours partir, oh - si soudainement - et ensuite je me sens terriblement seule
Guillem l'appelle dans le style catalan. Hier soir Guillem cuisina un lapin: il me montra un papier qui avait été laissé ici et qui était couvert de signes et de mots révélant un message qui disait je connais Sion, Berenger avait en effet parlé du Nord et du Sud en expliquant comment ils devaient être unis, je présume qu'ils doivent l'être aussi en moi.
Je suis un peu lasse aujourd'hui, pardonne-moi mon humeur maussade. Oui, je reviendrai.
Transmets bien toute mon amitié à ta famille

Marie

Translated in full on pages 329–30

'But they were here.'

Perturbed, the women looked along shelves of published works, but found no proof. Finally, Albina produced a small hardback about the city's gardens that included the one with the royal palm tree. Roger Mathieu was described as the owner from 9 December 1932, and he died eight years later on the same day and month. The author thought there was something significant about that.

'I regret there is nothing else.' Albina's eyes were sad.

Clara drove to the building outside town and we queued for an hour. We gave every name known to us. Massaguer, Saguer, Tourdes, Mathieu. They had no details of a house at 3 Sant Cristòfol.

'They've removed it.' I checked every other archive in the city. The house with the tower had simply ceased to exist. It had disappeared into the endless mystery of the city.

'Three months ago I would not have believed you,' said Joan Puig. 'But I spoke to a man here who knows about the secret society connected with the French priest. He says there were rituals performed in that house. A North European of high standing came regularly to Girona.'

I realized this informant would not have a name.

'He said the society had existed for many years and that originally the documents were kept inside stones. Every year in Besalú, in the church of St Sepulchre, at the summer solstice the light falls at a certain point and hits a ritual stone and the Lady of the Cup appears made up of light. The church is in the middle of the woods. It is private. The clergy know of this happening and keep it quiet. The church is not used for general worship.' José had told me

Besalú was one of the places Abbé Bigou had hidden the ritual materials.

Joan had looked into the subject, and had also been told Jean Cocteau knew of the secret and sought the material. There were no records anywhere. He didn't think the tower was necessarily a key component. Many towers were built at that time, because it was not customary for a woman without a chaperone to be out of doors – a tower would allow her to see around a city, into the streets. Up and down the stairs gave some exercise and diversion. From the gallery she could take the air. How could I find out who designed the tower, who'd built it? On whose order and who gave permission? Massaguer had paid for it out of his own money. That was so clearly mentioned in the lost records. He said, sadly, that I'd have to go to the archives of the college of architects. Everyone's eyes got sad when they thought of me trying to make sense of the archive system.

I didn't waste time in that building. They didn't keep documents of towers from so long ago unless they were important structures.

I did go to the church of St Sepulchre, outside Besalú in the woods of Palera. Clara had asked the tourist office if it was open. It was definitely shut. There were a lot of phone calls to private houses including the local priest's before it was agreed that I, as a friend of the former mayor of Girona, Joaquim Nadal, should be allowed to visit.

At the priest's house she asked for the key to the church. He was unwilling. I could tell from where I was sitting. But Clara was charming and had a loveliness about her. And she was Catalan.

The key was small, the directions exact. We parked in the narrow road. The church was two minutes away in the thick wood.

'It's one of the oldest in Catalonia,' Clara whispered as she pushed open the door. There was no electricity, but through the light from a small slit of window we could see something of this austere place of worship.

'Perhaps that's the ritual stone?' I pointed at a stone shape in front of the altar.

'Bernat Tallaferro, the Count of Besalú, brought it back from Jerusalem. He was a Knight.' She was whispering and holding onto the door, keeping it open. 'They say it has power to produce a vision.'

I was sure someone would walk in. A presence disguised in a normal human body, probably smiling, and nothing, absolutely nothing good about it.

In the corner was a wooden cross, rough and almost pagan, made from a tree in the forest. It seemed more significant than any cross I'd ever seen. On this you would suffer.

'Tallaferro brought back a piece of the Cross of Jesus,' she said. 'They used to hide priests from France here. In the house next door.'

I could not wait to get out from that severe place.

There on the naked tree in front of me was a crown of barbed wire. I had never seen a picture of the Crucifixion so punishing. The slim, naked trunk of the young tree, its two branches flung up like arms, the crown of barbed wire digging in on the top of the trunk. I expected to see a head, a face. I wanted to run. I said, 'Who did that?'

'No one comes here.'

We did look in the windows of the house and it looked comfortable, lived in. 'The French priest Antoine Bigou hid here.' And then we saw a fire, still smoking. 'Probably a shepherd,' she said.

She then chose her best advice. 'I know you're looking for something. But there may be nothing.'

'Nothing?'

'My father was a lawyer. He's been dead many years; he was over fifty when I was born. For a while he was president of the society that protects the old customs. There was something special about that work, as though he carried knowledge that he'd rather not have. Guests used to visit privately from France and Germany and I heard their voices, but we, the children, were kept out of sight and my father never spoke about it. Perhaps to my mother. And I remember the atmosphere of our house. You could see he was sad. I felt he had enormous responsibilities, too much for him. We always felt there was something, and before he died I asked him. There was no reason then for him not to clear it up. He said there was absolutely nothing. And after his death my brother went through every document, every diary entry – nothing.'

I asked if she knew who was in the society. 'Certainly Geli had been. And Señora Guilini, who's ill.'

And we drove back through what seemed endless isolation to the reality of Girona.

The first letter was under my door at the hotel. It was handwritten from B. Saunière to Maria.

Rennes-le-Château, 22 May 1899

My dear Maria,

Thank you for your letter of the 12th May. I am organizing a retreat at the end of the month so will place the stones as Guillaume suggested.

Each of them is marked by a sign, which doesn't mean anything. It is no more than a signature of the mason who hollowed and sealed it at that time.

I have studied the text but my grasp of Hebrew ritual is outmatched here.

I have shown it to a very old professor at Paris University and he thinks it might come from the Phoenician.

Take good care of yourself. I think of you pouring yourself a glass of wine in the garden and wearing your silk from Paris.

Your devoted friend,

B. Saunière.

Rennes-le-château le 22 mai 1899.

Ma chère Maria,

Merci de votre lettre du 12 mai.
J'organise une retraite à la fin du mois,
donc j'installerai les pierres comme l'a suggéré
Guillaume.
Chacune d'elles est marquée d'un signe qui ne
veut rien dire, ce n'est rien de plus qu'une
signature du tailleur de pierre qui l'a creusée
et scellée à cette époque.
J'ai étudié le texte mais ma connaissance du
rituel Hébraïque se trouve dépassée dans ce
cas là.
Je l'ai montrée à un très vieux professeur à
l'Université de Paris qui pense que cela vient
peut-être du Phénicien.
Prenez bien soin de vous, je vous imagine dans
votre jardin en train de vous servir du vin,
et portant de la soie de Paris.

Votre ami dévoué

B.Saunière -

The second was in a drawer in Ruiz's bookshop, with a drawing – a plan – attached. 'Someone dropped it in. I didn't know where you were staying.'

Rennes-le-Château, 6 February 1901

My dear Maria,

The storm was very strong, so I thought of you. I was on my way back from Montazels and I didn't stop. You wouldn't have given up!

I will arrive Wednesday late so please wait up for me. Otherwise leave the other door open. I will bring some plants.

Can you find out the measurements of the foundations and if they know how that precise figure was arrived at?

You will have to go and see the architect, or better still, ask Dalmas to go. He must get a copy of the plans.

I think you should have a pretext. Why don't you say you're teaching them French?

Your friend as always,

B. Saunière.

The 'other door' was the one from the city wall above the steps that I had found so long ago. Saunière had been in the house with the tower. They were discreet letters, not those of a lover necessarily.

Rennes le-château, le 6 Février 1901

   Ma chère Maria

La tempête était très forte et cela m'a fait
penser à vous. Je revenais de Montazels et je
ne me suis pas arrêté. Vous, vous n'auriez pas
abandonné!
J'arrive mercredi tard. Je vous prie de
m'attendre. Sinon ne verouillez pas l'autre porte.
Je vous apporterai des plantes.
Pouvez-vous vous renseigner sur les mesures des
fondations et s'ils savent comment on est
arrivé à ce chiffre précis?
Il faudra que vous alliez voir l'architecte ou
encore mieux que vous demandiez à Dalmas
d'y aller, il doit se procurer un exemplaire
des plans.
Je pense que vous devriez avoir un prétexte.
Vous pourriez peut-être leur enseigner le français?
       Votre ami dévoué
             B. Saunière -

The plan seemed to be of a tower, giving details of two angles. Were these the measurements Saunière had been looking for?

I knew José wasn't delivering these documents. He was always one street away, one doorway out of reach. In the end he phoned me from a public callbox.

'How are you?' he asked, softly.

Apart from being scared to death, deep in a search that could risk my life, obsessed by finding the truth, I was fine. I wanted to say, do you love me? What a consideration now.

We sat at the back of the Savoy Bar in the gloom. He looked thinner, more tanned, his hair longer, eyes bright. He didn't look old any more. I showed him the letters and he'd seen several more. Everyone in the society had a part of the whole. I said the only way to make it safe was for the two of us to know as much as 'they' did.

'You didn't just tap a wall and find a wasteland, did you?'

I understood he'd had to uncover what was there and find certain material. It had to seem casual. And he found it eventually.

'Where is it now?'

'Here and there. I've moved to a house up near the mountains.'

I said I'd seen some of the artefacts from Isaac the Blind in the museum.

'No one will think of looking for them there. I was supposed to make the centre into something more mystical and private.'

'I think the priest did what you did. Seemed to stumble upon a secret. I think he was looking for it all the time. And when he found it he went to the society in Paris who

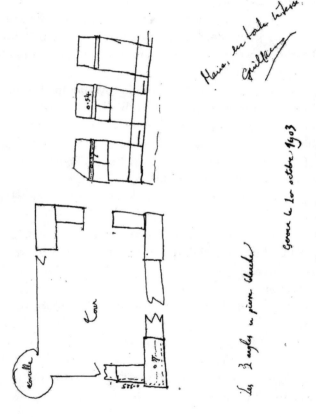

Saunière's drawing of the tower

gave him all that money. Why did he stay in Rennes-le-Château?'

'Because he had to give them a little at a time. He knew if they got it all they'd kill him. They didn't guess it was here.'

'He wanted to come out of it.'

'You're not wrong. He told my grandfather he was in it too deeply to get out. I don't want the same ending.'

'Why did Saunière come here?' I thought I might get a different story.

'To follow the instructions left in code by Bigou. To find the material and to use it. The tower was the key. He gave Maria Tourdes enough money to acquire the house at whatever price from the Church. It was the first time it had passed into the hands of a secular person. A lawyer, Saguer, fronted the deal.'

He brought out a letter from a Tomàs to Berenger, saying Saguer would be the 'ideal person' to help him get the house.

I asked about Massaguer who'd built the tower, and he remembered him as part of the society. José explained that Saunière copied the tower and also called it Magdala, but it couldn't have been perfect because he planned another one. He brought a lot of money to Girona and Maria had to hide it. In her garden he could meet people he could no longer see in Rennes-le-Château. He'd attracted too much attention there. He, or his brother Alfred, brought documents to Maria for safekeeping. After his death nothing was found in his parish. In 1907 she married Roger Mathieu, perhaps to get a better camouflage. He had a dark side. She had no idea he worked for the Vatican, and he didn't know she was in love with Saunière. Oddly, she'd married Saunière's worst enemy. Roger Mathieu's

_- 1888 -_

Cher Baronguer,

la maison est derrière
la cathédrale et facile-
ment reconnaissable à
cause de la tour construite
il y a trente ans.
Elle se trouve près de la
Porte San Cristobal
comme cette Porte
immobile à eux qui
fait partie de l'église
pendant ce qui se peut
pas être ailleurs.
le peu ... j'décide pour
acquérir la maison St
Salvan, lui a la ...

Bonico et une grande in-
fluence de les Travaux
publics.
Dieu ... ... de vos
bons amis et va ... !
Joli Tomás attendra votre
visite.
Félicitations pour les fêtes
de Noël.
Tomás

Translated in full on page 331

purpose was to spy on this maverick priest, find the extent of his discoveries, and deliver them and eventually him up to the Vatican. Saunière was too canny. Watchful, shrewd, he expected enemies. He had to continue to visit the house because he needed to perfect the ritual. José's grandfather had known that.

I asked why, if Maria had so much money, she told everyone she was hard up?

He thought it was because she had to show another face. Just having known him meant people were after her for the rest of her life. He said something about not wanting that to happen to me. She played a deceptive role.

Like everyone else in this story, I thought. It was what everyone wanted to know. Where Saunière had been going to, all those times he started down the hill to Couiza.

I changed tack. 'Why are you telling me all this now?'

'Because I don't want to go on being a deceptive person. I thought I could win. Now I'm not sure. They will tell you a different story. I want you to know the truth.'

'We could just *fou le camp*,' I said.

'We could. But he didn't, Monsieur *le prêtre*.'

When I got back to the hotel, a third letter was waiting for me. It was to Quim, from his grandfather. It was dramatic, and warned Quim that 'Saunière went too far. The ritual does not belong to the Church. He may have started in good faith but he must have done something wrong. Look how he ended up'. Quim's grandfather recommended that he steer clear of this dangerous business.

José had been lent a huge house in the foothills of the mountains near the village of Ravós. On a hill, it had a chapel and a cemetery, and at some time in the future he

Hotel Elysée

1. Juin 1973

Cher Quim,

Saunière est allé trop loin. Ce rite n'appartenait pas à l'église. Il se peut qu'il ait commencé de bonne foi, mais il a dû faire quelque chose de mal. Regarde comment il a terminé.

Ce n'est pas pour rien que l'église a dos l'incident et l'a dissimulé. Pourquoi ne cherche-tu pas la profondeur et la spiritualité au lieu de cette "Magie"? Si les Egyptiens la gardaient secrète, ils devaient avoir de bonnes raisons. Pourquoi ne te tourne-tu pas vers un homme sage et attachant, riche de bonté, qui porte le message de Dieu à tous de manière éloquente, comme le Dr Augusta Vila y Domenech.

Déjà aux Jocs Florals de 1914, il avait dit à mon père que Saunière finirait mal. Augusti a toujours été contre ce rite et contre cet homme. Quel que soit ce qu'il faisait, cela n'avait rien à voir avec l'Eglise catholique. Augusti ne souhaitait pas particulièrement que les prêtres à Gerona deviennent impliqués mais avait de l'argent et de la persuasion.

Translated in full on pages 332–33

Hotel Elysée

CABLE ADDRESS
ELLEESAY, NEW YORK

60 EAST 54th STREET, NEW YORK, N.Y. 10022
TELEPHONE PLAZA 3-1066

El bisbe Dr Boullloch a conseillé
à Maria de retourner dans sa
famille et voulait que la maison
avec la tour soit purifiée.

Augusti a toujours dit que
l'affaire de Saunière avec Carcassonne
était un prétexte. "Ils" ont toujours
su que Saunière devait expliquer
cette extraordinaire richesse sans fin
donc l'ont arrangé de cette manière.
Je sais que Saunière a reçu les
meilleurs conseils du Augusti Vila.
Mais en a-t-il tenu compte?

Regarde les tourments qu'il vit
maintenant. Maria n'aurait jamais
dû être mêlée à tout cela. Bien
sûr elle a changé de nom. Ils ont
fait faire de faux papiers pour
elle. Même son âge a été changé.
La réponse est et restera toujours Non!

Ton Grand-Père

planned to reconstruct the buildings. It was in decline and owned by a lawyer, one of the society.

Here, we talked about the ritual, how it used to be called 'the ceremony'. José explained, 'It transcends time and space as we know it.'

I asked if he'd been part of it and he said he hadn't, so I reminded him of the chiming, unbearable noise in his head – with Lucia. This was no time for avoidance.

'To be part of that you have to be an initiate. I was a witness. The initiates fast and practise rites of purification and sit in meditation for days. They recite texts and incantations endlessly. Their breathing changes and they reach a state of near disembodiment, of sheer consciousness, exalted, and then they call up the highest level, the bearer of the cup.'

'Is the Grail present?'

'Here it is called the cup. It is not of this world but in an adjacent realm, and I understand that it is the spirit of this chalice that appears, not the three-dimensional object in the four dimensions we know. By the laws of this earth the physical Grail cannot leave. It is trapped here, ageing, deteriorating. What is called up is its spiritual essence carried by the bearer. Some believe it was used by Jesus at the Last Supper and that the ritual He performed – wine into blood – may have changed the vessel's nature, so thereafter it could pass out of our vision and by evocation be brought back. This would depend on the energies of the place, and the level of the initiates. Possibly it changes its composition when in an adjacent reality, as many believe we do when we die. It has enormous powers and is instrumental in spiritual change. It is good, evil, dualistic, seemingly depending on the bearer, who may or may not appear.'

I asked what was needed for the ritual apart from the preparation of the initiates. They had to be placed in the presence of the ritual stone, blessed many hundreds of years ago and used in the ceremony by the ancient Jews and Egyptians. He agreed it was the sun stone that had been brought from Jerusalem to Besalú. There were five to eight initiates, and they knelt on the ground, which was covered in ashes. 'The stone is touched by each in turn and some time afterwards a presence is with us.'

'Its purpose?'

'To give ultimate power of all that has been, is, and will be.'

I asked how that made him feel.

'I was chilled to begin with and later serene, as though made up of light. At one point I remember feeling there was a path before me and I was pulled towards taking it. I would not have thought such an experience was possible.'

He described the chime as a huge unearthly sound. The chime opens the door – to the other realm, the experience. People unprepared could have a seizure, and in the past some had died. An inappropriate presence could call up a lower force that would bring an undesired effect.

Why want the powers of the Grail, which could be ungodly and had possibly in the past been smothered by the Church?

I asked what proof there was, and he said the experience – he'd seen it with his own eyes – and the money. Why did I think there could be more? 'It doesn't fit in with orthodox thinking, but very orthodox people would kill for it. Look at Carreras. He would spend a fortune trying to relocate that cross and chain I once gave you.' He said something about how he'd slit him up in the name of God, because he keeps the vows of the custodian. He wouldn't explain more.

'Has he been present at a ritual?'

'Never. He is a hunter and has gone around the world for what was under his nose. He told Geli, my cousin, of a Jewish priest finding a wooden chest under the floor and it contained a silver shrine holding three books in black hog-skin, books of Jewish devotion in Hebrew characters of great antiquity. Saunière got possession of this as well. Carreras believes that this calls up the Grail.'

'Did he find it?'

'Of course not. It's probably in some flea market in Paris with your cross and chain.'

He made a fire and we sat wrapped in coats, and Canigou looked very clear and glacial. We tried to talk of other things, but what compared with all this? José talked about Umberto Eco, and how he referred to the ritual in *Foucault's Pendulum*. He added that, before the calling up, some early texts were read of experiments from darkness to light, and contact was made with those initiated ones in the next dimension or world of spirit. How was an observer included? It was necessary to be concentrated in thought and have understood the incantations. To be protected by light and to wear amulets.

'What is the object they're all looking for?'

'What I've just described.'

So I described the nondescript-looking vessel he'd got back at auction in London and later wrapped in newspaper and hotel towels.

'That is the ritual object of this earth. Its essence is not here. That object is valuable because of its historical passage through this earth.'

'So the cup the bearer carries has the same shape?'

'The spiritual dimension of this dead object, yes.'

'Is this earthly one used in the ceremony?'

'It is not necessary.'

'Where is it now?'

'Lucia had it.'

Saunière had been after it too, of course. José had a letter in Catalan from 1898 saying that Mr Abbé Saunyer – the Catalan form of Saunière – had asked about the cup and describing it as 'an ornate golden chalice'.

He had been present at one full ritual ceremony, in the Frenchwoman's house in the early fifties, and by chance at another that coincided with the vision seen by the people of Girona in 1976. Obviously his mother had been lying to me about his whereabouts that eventful day. The vision had appeared, but was not expected to be seen by passers-by. After that the ceremonies were stopped.

'Who were the initiates?'

He indicated the mountains. 'They're chosen. It's their life.'

'Were you?'

He didn't want to talk about that. He wasn't suited to the process. I'd heard that the Rosicrucians, as Saunière found, did not like disobedience or withdrawal. So supposedly, José had worked for the secret society, briefly in charge and now as its custodian, in line with his family's tradition.

'Why do they want it hidden?'

'Its power in the wrong care could be fatal.'

Girona 26 Abril de 1898

Dr. Pidro Daus i Fontan

Benvolgut amic:

El Pare Nolan va re ordenat, el 25 de Març i la setra ha anat es va tenir a Albor.

Missatger. L'ABRE SAWYER va demanar pel calze.

No se per quina rao a tracte d'un niquelium calle D'OR.

Enrique Bosset i Siso ha acabat. El seu monument que es titularà "LA COSTA DE LLEVAN."

Espero que haguem recuperat la salut i que la primavera us retorni les forces.

Tou amic Emili Talrog or Nadal

D.

Translated in full on page 333

It had always been known about, searched for, and feared. In 1656 Nicolas Poussin, while living in Rome, told a priest, Abbé Louis Fouquet, about the secrets. The priest wrote a letter to his brother in France. José showed me part of the letter quoted in a book:

> *Monsieur Poussin will give you through these things advantages which even kings would have great pains to draw from him and which, according to him, it is possible that nobody else will ever rediscover in the centuries to come. And what is more, these are things so difficult to discover that nothing now on this earth can prove of better fortune nor be their equal.* *

The recipient of this letter, Nicolas Fouquet, Superintendent of Finances to Louis XIV, was imprisoned for life.

I believed José had told me all this because he had made a decision, and the secret of the ritual and the cup would be resolved. By telling me this much he had made me a gift, the gift of his life. Being a custodian meant he could never change his role, his location, nor his loyalty. I always thought that finding him was like finding the Holy Grail. And I was right. We should say goodbye and continue our lives as they seemed to be destined – apart.

---

* Lépinois, *Lettres de Louis Fouquet*, p. 269. The letter was kept in the Cossé-Brissac freemason family, in the eighteenth century.

38

Quim Carreras was envious of José, of his courage in the past, and of the admiration he still received from the city. Cocteau had loved José's uniqueness and courage. Carreras accused José of doing what he believed without due consideration. The Jewish Centre! What a catastrophe. He chose to despise him for not taking a scholarly, rational approach.

By now I knew he did not wish him well, but I made my mistake. I defended him.

'So he still believes in the myth of the Grail – its power to transform, heal, make rich. So you hold a stone, a vessel, an equation and are given the power of sight beyond physical limitation. And you believe in this celestial lottery?'

I had no idea. I said I believed in José.

'If true it would cheat the holder of his path in this life, given by God, and therefore it would deny him redemption.'

He was suddenly cold and looked down, gone into another place where I could not reach him. Absolute. All those years of the Church behind him.

And as I looked at him, continuing in silence, I sensed his disapproval and power. And now I, too, was expendable.

I left a note for José at the bookshop.

'Watch the priest.'

'Well, you have worked hard,' said Ingrid, laughing. 'You have put your all into it and I like that.'

I felt I'd passed a test I didn't know I was taking.

Carmen poured a goblet of water for each of us and closed the window. 'It's always cold. There's snow on Canigou.'

Now I thought of it I hadn't felt warm for months. Not since the chill in Ruiz's shop at the end of the last visit, when I knew I was into something I couldn't see and could never win. And it had to do with the cold of the mountain and Lucia dying. 'I want to know …'

Ingrid cut me off. 'Of course you do. You're fuelled by frustration, like all of them.'

'Can I see the ritual?'

'The ritual, my eager friend, is no longer performed. It stirs up appearances and brings all this attention. It alerts curious people. In the old times, when Bigou tried to perfect the ceremony in the garden, it provoked visions but people thought it was ghosts from the black cemetery. It sent them rushing into church, instantly converted, so the clergy didn't complain.'

As Carmen had invited me for lunch she provided a plate of salad and Spanish omelette. I doubted if this was the reason I was here. Ingrid, obviously a close friend of our hostess, clearly wanted to talk.

'A society looked after the effects and then it was moved to Besalú, to the St Sepulchre church.' Ingrid didn't describe it, assuming I knew. 'A small society including French members kept the secret until the Napoleonic War in 1808 made their visits impossible. In 1820, the material was moved back to the House of the Canons, but part of the city wall had been damaged. Then into the care of José's family. The ground was unstable under that house. There was water, or insects, or animals, so the papers were kept inside stones. The masons, who had built the churches, passed on the skill. A stone was hollowed out, the papers placed inside, then sealed. Saunière learned that. He understood stones. That's why he was always rambling around the countryside with his maid, selecting the right ones. In 1851, the Tour Magdala had been added to the house.'

'Why?'

'Following the instructions in the documents, this was erected facing a certain angle – on N2 49E. Quillan is N2 11E.'

I stopped her. 'Is this angle why the tower was built?'

'Of course. And it also became a fairly suitable hiding place for the material.'

'There was a mark on the tower.'

'Indicating a measurement which must match another.'

'Where?'

'Where the tower was facing.'

'Why 1851?'

'Perhaps because Bernadette Soubirous saw the vision at Lourdes just across the Pyrenees. Also a manifestation was seen here that became the Lady of the Cup. It was believed the tower was built to hide the material safely. It could no longer be subject to climate conditions. War, invaders, a change in the fortunes of the clergy, the constant water shift, theft. So it had a dual purpose. It was difficult to find the right hiding place. José's great grandfather wrote about the problems. The Jewish treasure from medieval times, according to legend, was hidden in the hill over there. Montjuïc. He considered a cave, but didn't dare mark it or others would find it. But if they didn't leave some mark they wouldn't find the location again. The cathedral vaults were no good. It would be in the power of the nosy clergy. So this tower was practical.'

Ingrid was the only person I'd met who actually wanted to speak and possibly might not stop. I asked Carmen if she knew all this.

'I know that in the 1850s the locals here said a secret of some sort provided changes in the atmosphere and that visions were seen by some around the House of the Canons. But they were not curious and, anyway, did not believe in visions.'

I mentioned the loss of the files concerning the ownership of the house and the building of the tower.

Carmen was not surprised. 'Of course that would be removed. It's easy enough to do. Massaguer's name was on the document but the house was still owned by the Church.' She gave me a letter to Maria from a Cecília that put the construction of the tower at 16 June 1851. It said that 'naturally, we have not found any documents' and that 'the work is moving along, but always in secret'.

I asked why they didn't carry out the rituals elsewhere. Ingrid clapped and laughed. It was made clear to me that the calling up of the cup could only happen in certain sites depending on the power of the ley lines and the pulse of energies in that precise site. One is Girona, the other Rennes-le-Château, the third St Sulpice. They have to be linked, one with the other, and energized, so that the ritual process is possible.

I asked how it was known where these pulse places were, and Ingrid said they were marked. I kept looking at an extremely large stone fishpond. The water was shallow

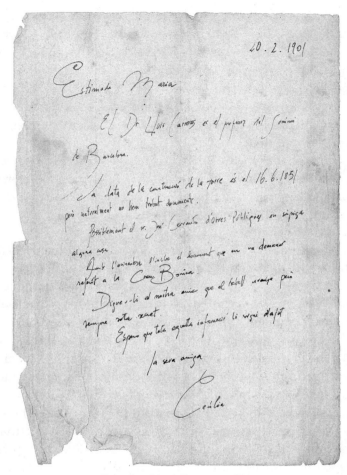

Translated in full on page 334

and collected in a sloping corner at the top and assorted fish swam in a crowd in this small area allowed for them. Below, the huge stone was smooth and pale, and substantial. For a moment I thought I might have recognized it, but I couldn't see any engravings. They watched me watch the fish.

'Did you send me the letters?'

'But of course. You are a seeker. Always have been.'

'But where is it? The Grail?'

By the end of this lunch they would want something from me. My early street smarts had served me up to a point. I was outmatched here. Again I looked at the fishpond, but it was just that, a stone ornament for fish.

I was very surprised back in the hotel room. Why tell me all that? What would they want in return? She'd given me more letters, two about Saunière's appearances in Girona, and one, unsent, from Saunière to his maid, saying someone called Guillem had made a potentially extraordinary discovery and that he'd be held up as a result. He asked her to 'tell the workmen to continue with the stones'.

Other letters related to the society, including one from a Luis Carreras about Saunière's inauguration of his restoration work at the church at Rennes. It had the same symbol at the bottom, with the '130', as the letter from Tomàs to Saunière about getting the house.

She'd also given me an invitation to her house in the forest near Begur where she had more material. I did feel she was testing me. My search was a test. Was I tested enough? And who exactly was Ingrid? Carmen had said she was German. She spoke several languages and had lived in the States. According to Lluís and Dr Arbós she was from one of the wealthiest families in the world. She was small, strong, vibrant, and probably in her seventies. She defied definition – perhaps deliberately – but I trusted her and felt she was on the side of good outcomes. Without question, she had some influence in the society. I understood she was also a high initiate. But I couldn't recall her face. Not even whether

Gerona, Vendredi soir

Chère Marie

Hier Guillem a fait une découverte
qui pourrait être extraordinaire si
c'est en effet ce que je crois – aussi dois-
je demeurer ici et ne rentrerai pas
dimanche. Peux-tu envoyer la seconde
lettre à Carcassonne immédiatement?
Dis aux ouvriers de continuer avec
les pierres. Alfred apporte ceci avec le
document et passera la nuit s'il
est trop épuisé pour continuer
jusqu'à Montazels
En hâte
BSaunière

Translated in full on pages 334–35

Els Amics—

Sembla que ben bé podem
dir el primer fet important
que s'esdevé un cop recent
vicari capitular et Monsieur
L'abbé Larmièu is la inauguració
de la restauració de l'interior
de l'església parroquial à
Rennes le Château amb altres
celebresions preparades per donar
una esplendor mes gràn si
possible à la propia de la
inauguració de les reformes
del temple

Lluís Carreras

Girona 22 de gener de
1897

Translated in full on page 335

she wore glasses. Somehow it was hidden by all her energy and fiery smiles.

When we met again, she confirmed what I had surmised about Saunière. Yes, he had a promising ecclesiastical career, went to the seminary in Narbonne, and within weeks uncovered the information leading him straight back to the countryside. He took over the parish of Alet and then Rennes-le-Château became free. 'That backwater. No one could believe it.'

The way to work out the secret was through Cabbala text, and Narbonne was the second centre in medieval times. He gave what he uncovered to an interested party, a small piece at a time.

'So he wasn't working on his own?' I asked, sounding naïve.

'Of course not. He was run by somebody. Certainly.' Who did I think? The Rosicrucians?

'And behind that?' She laughed. 'The Habsburgs, of course. José would have told you.'

So I asked why Saunière didn't just leave and have a better life?

'They would have killed him. Also he had work to do. He worked with his brother Alfred, whom they planted in Narbonne. He could find anything they needed. He also worked to a degree with the murdered priest Gelis. The two priests left the signs of their master openly in their church. The maid Marie Denarnaud was no problem. Saunière tried to buy her silence by leaving her all his French property. He needn't have bothered. She was scared to death by what she'd seen and never said a word. At some point he would be questioned. They decided to create a sale of masses illegally and say that was the money source. But the money got too big for these small account books to front.' I remembered about the other priest, Abbé Gelis of Coustaussa in the next parish to Rennes-le-Château, who had been murdered in 1897 in what was described as a ritual killing. Had he been used as a deterrent by whoever was behind the money, to keep Saunière on that hill even with all his riches?

But Ingrid had moved on. She drew a picture of the cup, not unlike the diagram Max Kander had etched in the street dust, with the two circles attached and spindly legs and an extraterrestrial look. 'He had to carry out the instructions. He had to build the tower to match the one in Girona. One north, As-Tet (Serpent), Isis. The other south, Nephtys (the vine). These form the Golden Cut. The magnetic path. From Egypt.' She drew two towers.

Reaching for a book about the church in Rennes-le-Château, she turned to a picture of one of the Stations of the Cross. 'He has it here. Clearly marked. Two towers.'

It all went so fast. I was too slow.

'The towers mark a point which is hidden. The chocolate adverts marked the pulses where the rituals can take place. Girona, Rennes, and St Sulpice.' She showed me another advertisement of Emma Calvé. 'And there is the chocolate manufacturer's name and address. Rue St Sulpice. The pulse is exactly there, on that site. Activate these three points and you change the chemistry of what's there. It enables matter and spirit to leave and also re-enter existence. It reclaims the past. In unwise hands its power would send the planet into unthinkable darkness.'

'Where does all this happen?' I asked.

'The towers mark the point.'

'Does the point have anything to do with the figure 130 and the symbol that is on some of the letters?' I asked, thinking of Saunière and his measurements. She told me

the figure related to Cabbala and Jacob's ladder and the symbol was a Cabbala sign meaning 'I want to complete the uncompleted.'

I was so absorbed by the information I could have been anywhere. I asked how Maria Tourdes came into it.

'It's a front. It's all a front,' said Carmen. 'Everything was. He needed her in the house, gave her 'a brother' and 'a maid'. Even an investment adviser. It's unlikely she knew the full extent of what he was doing. Probably nobody knew that. He certainly wasn't digging for gold bars. And whatever he was doing had nothing to do with the Church. He had to complete the work. He invited Parisians involved in the occult and spiritualism to Girona, and she looked after them.'

'Why are you telling me all this?' Again, that feeling she wanted something from me.

'José will explain,' she said. 'There is something he must do. He needs your help.'

Later, José read me a letter written in Catalan from a Celestí Pujol to a friend, Tomàs, mentioning a dinner where he would meet a French priest with a special interest in sacred texts.

I told him he was in danger and should leave Girona.

'I cannot ever leave, except to go up.' Not without irony, he indicated heaven.

'Aren't you afraid to die?'

'We only have the moment but should go on as though life was eternal.'

I asked him about Ingrid's pulse points, about the points marked by the towers.

He explained that if the towers faced each other on compass point N2, the exact middle point, the portal, was the peak of Mount Canigou.

3 de maig 1896

Al Sr. Tomas Ros i de Batlle:

C/del Pou Rodó - Girona

Estimat Amic;

Tinc el plaer d'assabentar-vos que el senyor Dalmau, serà present al nostre sopar del dia 16 del mes acordat.

També he demanat al fill del senyor Prats i Bosch, estudiós i gran intèrpret de música sacre, organista de l'església de Sant Lluc, i expert en ciències ocultes d'origen medieval, la seva assistència al nostre sopar. El reverend francès l'Abbé Saunière, que té un especial interès per els texts de ritual sagrat en llengua francesa occitana puig que per Monsenyor l'Abbé, el francès es el seu idioma.

Em satisfà comunicar-li que sa il·lustríssima, el Senyor Bisbe de Girona està molt interessat i que encara no ha confirmat oficialment la seva assistència al nostre sopar; es molt possible que hi assisteixi.

Esperant retrobar-nos la nit que vostè sap, el despedeix afectuosament el seu amic amb Crist

Celestí Pujol i Pera

Translated in full on pages 335–36

'So what is there?' I asked.

'In early cultures it was believed that gaps existed on the planet, and that in these places entry from other realms was possible as well as exits from this one. They were places of great energy. Mount Canigou is one.' He explained that Sin was the sacred mountain of the Sumerians, but then the sacred mountain-worship moved to Egypt and then Palestine – to Sion. After this, the sacred site moved north – to Canigou. He said seekers had found clues in Psalm 48 and also in Saunière's supposed parchments, in the link between Teniers and Poussin – the letters S-I-N. Even Hitler, it was said, had sent people here to search for answers.

'So what happens there?'

'You should find out.' Ever since Lucia's death I hadn't been keen on mountains. I was happier with the drama at sea level.

He told me how the ritual was similar to one practised by the Cabbalists. It is contained in an equation, pages long. It took between one and two hours to recite. The initiates do patterned repetitive acts and manipulate their bodies, using the normal reactions of the nervous system to such stimuli to arrive at a state of ritual trance. It was described in *The Sworn Book*, of which there were few copies.

'How do you join the society?'

'You don't. You are invited.'

'Who is the Lady of the Cup?'

'She can on occasion come back to this earth. The ritual can bring her, to heal, to save, to empower.' He understood it was the Magdalene.

As he was prepared to answer questions, I asked about the priest – was he good or bad?

'He was between good and evil and his work was never finished. He never managed to unite the north and the south.'

319

I didn't understand. It seemed we were back at the two towers. The north was Rennes-le-Château. The south tower was Girona.

'You have to unite the north with the south. Once they are brought together there is super-consciousness and a higher plane is within reach. Then, the other realms can reach us.'

'But Saunière failed,' he continued. 'He couldn't find the portal. He didn't finish what he had started.'

I did just about manage to ask about it. I was already seeing the wisdom of Ingrid's caution, 'You must be well prepared in all ways to approach this subject.'

'With Isaac the Blind I was trying to complete the plan but I attracted unsuitable seekers. Like Saunière, I failed. And now the material isn't safe and, possibly, neither is this city.'

These unsuitable seekers were getting close and the society had given him his instructions.

'There is only one thing to do. Take the material out of the sight of this American, Max Kander, who is sent here to get it. Take it back to the mountain.'

I asked about the ritual stone. He said that was safe. Where? Right under their nose. He'd simply turned it upside down and made it into a fishpond. The dirty cup? Lucia had gone up with that, herself alone. That's what she was doing. Returning it. Returning it because we'd failed.'

'And the shock of what is there killed her.'

He didn't disagree.

'Where is the equation?' I said.

'We got that out years ago. When we sent you out of Spain into France. We put it in Beryl's rucksack. And across the border it was picked up by a kind person helping her with her bag.'

He stopped. 'Come with me. Let's finish this business.'

I'd been drawn in by the story of Maria and the priest, set against the old city I so loved. I remembered her warning words, and her death. For perhaps the first time in our long association I knew I could not go with him.

José did come back down from the mountain. I asked him what he had found, whether he had finished the business, fulfilled his God-given role. He would not speak of it. Not of Canigou, of Saunière, of the ritual, or of the secret society. He deflected my questions and moved on to other things. I understood the subject was closed. He'd told me only what I'd been allowed to know.

Perhaps if I'd said yes to him it would all have been quite different. For me, my search was about the town and its people, its long and mystical history and strange resonances. And its end brought the absolute understanding that this man had always, and inevitably, been on an unreachable path. And I remembered how Maria, in the kitchen that day, had said, 'You won't stop him doing what he wants. Accept it and love him.'

Appendix

Document, page 40

The World of Light

We can only sense it with a spiritual eye. She reveals herself to him whose conscience has been completely transformed. And she will open wide before thee the portals of her secret chambers, lay bare before thy gaze the treasures hidden in the very depths of her pure virgin bosom. Unsullied by the hand of matter she shows her treasures only to the eye of Spirit, the eye which never closes, the eye for which there is no veil in all her kingdoms.*

Purify yourself – you are the temple.

1, Listen to the highest initiate. He knows how to work with the spiritual force of the group and knows the right sound, colour, ritual, protection. He works with the force of the spirit of the group.
2, Be restrained. Use the force, the energy, but with care. It is powerful so it can also be dangerous to use its energies without sufficient preparation. These are divine forces.

---

* From 'And she will open wide' to the end of the paragraph is from a Spanish translation of HP Blavatsky's English translation of *The Voice of Silence* (1889), a Buddhist text.

3, Use your inner voices to guard you.

4, Art [...]

Letter, pages 135–36

Hôtel Eden au Lac

Montreux

Monday evening

Dear Friends,

Since the death of my grandmother, I have decided the most sensible solution is to give the material to FD.

I am well aware that this may not be what she would have wanted but in today's world there can barely be any question of that.

GT assures me that the Vatican has always known of its existence. The 'friends' here and in Girona have put forward the theory that this is one of the greatest secrets of our time, of all time, and I am intent on burying it. Upon my word, let someone else find it. Furthermore, they're challenging my rights.

Consequently, could you see that the attached instructions and documents are transmitted to the person named above.

Your friend

CCC

and Marie Corvese

PS The scandal that could break wouldn't be good for anyone.

Letter, page 238

Paris 2 April 1971

Dear Josep,

I saw 'Madeleine Cocteau' yesterday and she told me to send her best to her 'tomcat of Girona'.

I adore your photos of Cocteau. Did you take the one of Cocteau as Napoleon? It looks like a Cocteau.

Cocteau often talked about you and said that you were the key, but that he must find the lock. He said you had told him specifically:

Keep me until you have discovered my lock. The affair of the two towers?

With all my admiration and friendship in memory of 'Jean'.

Micheline

Letter, page 239

Cassà de la Selva (Girona)

19th July 1954

The President

*Sardana** Appreciation Society

Caldes

---

* *Sardana*: a traditional Catalan dance

Dear Sir:

Since I am unoccupied on the night of Saturday 7th August, I would be delighted to offer my time to you as promised, hoping that if you are interested you will let me know as soon as possible.

As such I repeat that I am at your service.

A. Mercader

Mr. Pons –

Forget *Sardanas*. I want these things out of my house. Everyone takes advantage of Alfonso and these things are bringing bad luck.

Ask Tarrés to move them. And now the Frenchwoman went to take the cure in Caldes and left more things and never came back. And people here have eyes. Do something!

Mercè Mercader

Letter, page 247

Hôtel des Italiens, Girona, Spain

16.6.51

Dear Dolores:

I met Maria in Paris and we had great fun.

A little rush of blood at Schiaparelli's and she fell head over heels for a 'shocking pink' creation, a garish colour. Despite her insistence on wanting to go to a *thé dansant* and even the rue de Lappe, I think she was tired and even ill.

She is still mad about silk stockings and long kid gloves, as well as the pretty things paid for by the 'Belgian Congo'. Talking of which, the French priest must have trusted her not only in terms of investment but also on a scientific level.

I saw a note he left her on the energy produced between two towers. She was there when the ring was thrown into the fire. She has seen too much. Narcisse said of course he could believe her but in fact he frightened her to death.

I am letting you know that this is my personal opinion. My dear Dolores, have faith. I believe we can look forward to better times. But it's not easy here in Girona. We talk about it at each meeting. Fond regards from Gloria.

Thinking of you affectionately

Pepita.

Letter, page 248

Carrer de la Força, 9

Dear Narcís

The young Frenchwoman is delightful but people are talking, saying that Guillem is not her brother and that he is not even Catalan.

Nobody understands where the money is coming from. She says she's writing a book of poetry but I think that the money is coming from him – the French priest.

He's using the house. The gardener told Jacint that he has seen him there twice.

May God watch over you

Rosa

Girona, 3rd November 1904

Letter, page 249

Carrer de la Força

I hope with all my heart that you are keeping well and that spring brings pleasant times for you.

Jacint talked to me about the 'La Revista de Gerona' group, and the Frenchwoman was mentioned in the conversation.

It could be published in the new edition. In that case, we do not have to worry.

Jacint sends his thanks to the French priest, we have already mentioned that he's studying texts. His name is Sala.

May God watch over you for many years.

Rosa

Girona, 7th January 1905

Letter, page 250

and nobody sees her out any more, I'm worried. Recently she told me that she still thinks about the French priest, that there would never be anybody else like him, but he did not want to give up his vocation. She asked me if he was good or bad, but I didn't know enough about him. Could you go to see her when you have the time?

Your friend Narcís

Bonastruch de Porta, 20

Girona

May 1951

Letter, page 251

Gran Balneario

Vichy Catalan

Telefono 7

Caldas de Malavella

20 October 1951

Dear Dolores

Regrettably I cannot attend to this business in Brussels. I am taking a cure because my legs are giving me trouble. Can you ask [omission in original] to transfer the usual sum from the account in France to the Banco di Roma. A bank account has opened here last week and ask her about the investment in London. I still haven't heard from her and I hope it's not because of the problem with Gloria [omission in original] told me that the maid in Rennes village was dead. Is that true?

I cannot explain the 'Shepherd's Crook' to you. Of course it's not purely decorative. Berenger deliberately put it next to her. Of course it means something. He never did anything by chance and if I could explain it, would you understand?

Your friend

Maria

Letter, page 282

Rennes, 14th May 1949

Dear Marta,

I've tried to remember the exact meaning.

Monsieur Abbé Saunière said:

'They showed it to me, I laid my hand on it, I made it work and I'm holding it firmly.'

I saw it written in the letter he sent to Juli Tarrés.

Narcís,

with all my heart.

Letter, page 284

13 May 1897

Dear Genevieve

Thank you for your letter that arrived a season late; it took even longer than the train.

I beg you not to worry about me and, above all, never ever to mention what we talked about at Quillan.

I am learning Catalan, taking music lessons, Berenger gives me books to study

I love this place. I feel so alive, so fortunate. He arrived on Wednesday and we stayed in the garden well after dark; he is forever delighted by the sound of the bells, this city of bells that he finds glorious. It brings him out of himself. He is very kind and I feel transformed when he is here, as I should be

I don't know what will happen and for once I don't care. We laugh a lot, which will seem very inappropriate to you, yes, insanely inappropriate, but that's how things are when we're together and then he always has to leave, oh, so suddenly – and then I feel terribly alone

Guillem addresses him in the Catalan style. Yesterday evening Guillem cooked a rabbit. He showed me a piece of paper that had been left here and was covered with signs and words revealing a message 'I know Sion', Berenger did talk about North and South, explaining how they must be unified – I suppose they have to be in me too.

I am a bit tired today, forgive my gloomy mood. Yes, I'll come home.

Give your family my kindest regards

Maria

Letter, page 290

Translated fully in narrative, page 289.

Letter, page 292

Translated fully in narrative, page 291.

Letter, page 296

1888

Dear Berenger,

The house is behind the cathedral and easily recognizable because of the tower built thirty years ago. It is near the Portal de Sant Cristòfol known as the Invisible Door where those in the church speak of what cannot be said elsewhere.

The ideal person to acquire the house is Saguer, who has Creu Bonico and great influence in public works.

May God protect you in your good work and help you! Juli Tarrés will expect your visit.

Happy Christmas.

Tomàs

[Note: In this letter the use of an 'o' instead of the correct 'a' in Creu Bonica is a deliberate mistake. The use of the 'o' draws attention to the message of the text – it is a sign to the reader. This technique was quite common in such communications, to test if the recipient understood and also to pass secret knowledge under the nose of the Church. These apparent mistakes were always deliberate. The letter also seems to read 'port de San Cristobel' but the correct Catalan is 'portal de Sant Cristòfol'.]

Letter, page 298

Hotel Elysée

60 East 54th Street

New York

N.Y. 10022

1 June 1978

Dear Quim,

Saunière went too far. The ritual does not belong to the church. He may have started in good faith but he must have done something wrong. Look how he ended up.

It is not for nothing that the church closed the incident and drew a veil over it. Why don't you search for the profound and the spiritual instead of this 'magic'? If the Egyptians kept it secret, they must have had good reasons. Why don't you turn to a wise, engaging man, full of kindness, who eloquently conveys God's message to one and all, such as Dr Augustia Vila y Domenech.

As early as the Jocs Florals in 1914, he told my father that Saunière would come to a bad end. Augusti was always against the ritual and the man. Whatever he did, it had nothing to do with the Catholic Church. Augusti was especially against the priests in Girona getting involved but [omitted in original] had money and powers of persuasion. El bisbe Dr Benlloch advised Maria to go back to her family and wanted the house with the tower to be purified.

Augusti always said that Saunière's business with Carcassonne was a pretext. 'They' always knew that Saunière would have to explain that extraordinary wealth without end so they arranged it that way. I know Saunière received the best advice from Augusti Vila. But did he take any notice?

Look at the torments he suffered. Maria should never have been mixed up in all of it. Of course she changed her name. They fixed false papers for her. Even her age was changed. The answer is and will always be No!

Your grandfather

Letter, page 304

Girona 26th April 1898

Dr Isidre Pons i Fontan

Dear friend

Young Vilar was ordained on 25th March and your presence was dearly missed.

L'Abbe Saunyer asked after the chalice.

I do not know why, it was about an ornate golden chalice.

Enric Botet i Sisó has finished his manuscript which will be called 'La costa de Llevant'.

I hope that you are feeling better and that spring will bring your strength back.

Your friend Emili Fàbregas Nadal

Letter, page 310

20.2.1901

Dear Maria

Dr Lluís Carreras teaches at the seminary in Barcelona.

The tower's construction date is 16.6.1851 but naturally, we have not found any documents.

Perhaps José Cervantes at the Ministry of Public Works will know something about it.

I shall take advantage of this opportunity to include the document you asked for referring to the Creu Bonica.

Tell our friend that the work is moving along, but always in secret.

I hope that all this information will be of use to you.

Your friend

Cecília

Letter, page 312

Girona, Friday evening

Dear Marie

Yesterday Guillem made a discovery that could be extraordinary if it is what I think it is, so I will have to stay here and won't be back on Sunday. Can you send the second letter to Carcassonne immediately? Tell the workmen to continue with the stones. Alfred is bringing this with the document and will spend the night if he is too exhausted to carry on to Montazels

In haste

B. Saunière

Letter, page 313

Friends –

It seems that we can indeed say that the first important event once Monsieur Abbé Saunière has become Vicar Capitular is the inauguration of the restored interior of the parish church in Rennes-le-Château and other celebrations to give an even greater splendour, if it were possible, to that fit for the inauguration of the temple's reforms.

Lluís Carreras

Girona 22nd January 1897

Letter, page 318

3rd May 1896

Tomàs Ros i de Batlle

c/. del Pou Rodó, Girona

Dear friend:

I have the pleasure of informing you that Mr Dalmau will attend our dinner on the 16th of the agreed month.

I have also asked the son of Mr Prats i Bosch, a scholar and great performer of religious music, organist at the church of Saint Luke and expert in medieval occult sciences to attend our dinner, as well as the French priest Abbé Saunière, who is especially interested in sacred texts in

French and Occitan since Monsieur Abbé's language is French.

I am also happy to write that the Bishop of Girona is very interested and has yet to officially confirm his attendance at our dinner: it is likely he will attend.

Hoping to meet again on the night you already know, your friend with Christ says his goodbye.

Celestí Pujol i Pera

PATRICE CHAPLIN, novelist, writer and playwright is the author of twenty-six books. Her memoir *Albany Park* was compared to the writing of Laurie Lee and Jack Kerouac; her novel *Siesta* was made into a movie starring Jodie Foster and Isabella Rossellini; her investigation into the circumstances surrounding the death of Jeanne Hébuterne, Modigliani's mistress, was adapted for radio and theatre and performed in several countries.

As a member of the Bohemian scene in the fifties, she spent time with the existentialists in Paris, notably Jean-Paul Sartre and Simone de Beauvoir. Married to Charles Chaplin's son Michael, she lived in Hollywood and worked with various artists including Lauren Bacall, Miles Davis, and Salvador Dalí. She also appeared in a short film by Jean Cocteau. She now lives in London, where she runs a charity.

Quest Books

encourages open-minded inquiry into
world religions, philosophy, science, and the arts
in order to understand the wisdom of the ages,
respect the unity of all life, and help people explore
individual spiritual self-transformation.

Its publications are generously supported by
The Kern Foundation,
a trust committed to Theosophical education.

Quest Books is the imprint of
the Theosophical Publishing House,
a division of the Theosophical Society in America.
For information about programs, literature,
on-line study, membership benefits, and international centers,
see www.theosophical.org
or call 800-669-1571 or (outside the U.S.) 630-668-1571.

To order books or a complete Quest catalog,
call 800-669-9425 or (outside the U.S.) 630-665-0130.

Related Quest Titles

The Fool's Pilgrimage, by Stephan Hoeller

Kabbalah, Your Path to Inner Freedom, by Ann Williams-Heller

The Song of Arthur and *The Song of Taliesin,* by John Matthews

Tarot and the Tree of Life, by Isabel Kliegman

The Templars and the Grail, by Karen Ralls

To order these books or a catalog of complete Quest listings,
call 800-669-9425 or (outside the U.S.) 630-665-0130.

More Praise for Patrice Chaplin's

City of Secrets

"Powerful, romantic fiction in the tradition of Emily Brontë."

—*The Guardian*

"An intriguing story with several levels that indicate a secret history and a mystery."

—Z'ev ben Shimon Halevi, author, *Way of the Kabbalah*

"I fell in love with this wild young English girl, searching for adventure and finding more than she could have imagined. Patrice Chaplin takes us deep into the mystery surrounding the search for the Holy Grail. Amongst the ancient stories of Rennes-le-Château, her real life experiences are more enthralling and chilling than any *Da Vinci Code* story could ever be. It's the best book I've read in two years. I read *City of Secrets* in one night and shall it read again."

—Gayle Hunnicutt, actress